Experience and Knowledge Management in Software Engineering

Kurt Schneider

Experience and Knowledge Management in Software Engineering

 Springer

Prof. Dr. Kurt Schneider
Leibniz Universität Hannover
Fachgebiet Software Engineering
Welfengarten 1
30167 Hannover
Germany
Kurt.Schneider@inf.uni-hannover.de
www.se.uni-hannover.de/fachgebiet/enkschneider

ISBN 978-3-642-10107-6   e-ISBN 978-3-540-95880-2

DOI 10.1007/978-3-540-95880-2

ACM Computing Classification (1998): D.2, K.6, I.2

Cover design: KünkelLopka GmbH

Printed on acid-free paper

9 8 7 6 5 4 3 2 1

springer.com

To my wife,
Barbara

Preface

This is a book for students and practitioners of software engineering. Software engineers carry out knowledge-intensive tasks in software development, project management, or software quality. With this book, they will make better use of their personal knowledge and experience – and also of the knowledge in their groups or companies. In many organizations, there are initiatives to foster knowledge management or experiential learning. Some of them target software departments. Everyone involved in such an initiative will benefit from this book: managers, software engineers, and knowledge managers.

Knowledge engineers may find this book interesting as a view of knowledge management from the perspective of an application domain: software engineering.

At the intersection of software engineering and knowledge management. Software has become the most fascinating discipline in our society. Software controls cars, airplanes, and factories. Travel agencies and the military, banks and games depend on software. And software depends on knowledgeable experts. The ever-increasing demand for software calls for a broader and more explicit application of knowledge and experience. Software engineering is now a knowledge discipline, combining knowledge from computer science, engineering, and the application domains a particular software project is working for. Many individuals working in the software area increase their market value by improving use of knowledge and experience. However, companies should no longer rely on their employees' individual commitment to learning. Many software companies have identified knowledge as a catalyst for success. Knowledge management deals with the creation, management, and dissemination of knowledge in general.

Knowledge management has roots in philosophy, epistemology, and in several other disciplines – and it extends to formal languages and computer support. To make effective use of the techniques and tools, many software engineers believe they need a good overview of related concepts without having to dig into too many details. This book is an attempt to select key issues on several levels and provide an overview of the intersection of software engineering and knowledge management.

There are clear advantages in focusing on this audience. The familiarity of software engineers with computers and programming languages provides a better starting point for knowledge and experience management. Therefore, examples are almost exclusively taken from the software realm. Software engineering imposes a view on knowledge management that differs from the perspective of business or sociology. This book wants to support software engineers better by adopting their perspective.

Taking experience seriously. This book puts an exceptional emphasis on experience. Experience is indispensable around software. However, this general assertion is rarely followed by any concrete consequence. When it comes to planning and optimization, experience is treated as "soft stuff" that resides inside individuals and is not accessible to a team or a company. This attitude gives away many opportunities for improvement. Of course, experience is a delicate material, and it takes dedicated techniques to handle it well. They are similar but not identical to the approaches used in knowledge management. Some techniques are explained in this book.

Neither knowledge nor experience can be collected, stored, and shipped like material goods. Knowledge and experience are effective only in the brain and consciousness of people. Knowledge and experience management can establish links and support learning on individual and organizational levels. Knowledge has been called a company asset. However, this is only part of the truth: software engineers and other knowledgeable *people* should be regarded the assets, as they will make knowledge effective. This insight leads to various consequences: Semiformal and formal descriptions can be well-suited although they are difficult to support by a computer. In certain situations, more formal notations and ontologies are applicable. It is the challenge and art of good knowledge and experience management to identify the best techniques in a given situation and to support smooth transitions between them.

Textbook and resource for self-directed learning. This book can be used as a classic textbook. It is organized in self-contained chapters. Nevertheless, it will be best to read all chapters in sequence. Readers less interested in the formalisms of Web-based languages and ontologies may want to skip the corresponding chapter. They will still be able to follow subsequent chapters on experience and application scenarios.

The book contains several problems as exercises for each chapter. They repeat some of the material presented, and they challenge the reader to reflect on some of the issues. There are solutions to all problems at the back of the book.

A reader studying the full material in a rigorous way, solving the problems and following the interactive examples, will gain the most in-depth insights.

Just for curiosity. Others might read the book with a different goal in mind. Knowledge managers can learn more about software engineering as a particular application domain by looking through a software engineer's eyes. Software experts with a genuine interest in improving their professional working style may pick the chapters and sections they are most interested in. They will be able to gain an overview of an emerging field. Assumptions and challenges are presented as well as opportunities and working lightweight techniques. A selection of application scenarios puts the techniques in context.

Benefits for Readers

This book contains problem sections and solutions. Various learning objectives are pursued. When readers follow the text and solve the problems, they will increase their capabilities and opportunities within a software organization.

Learning objectives of this book. Readers will gain a good overview of knowledge management aspects. As a result, they will be able to make judgments and well-informed decisions.

In particular:

- They will understand which kind of knowledge is important in software engineering, and why knowledge needs to be managed.
- They will know the terminology used in experience and knowledge management.
- They will understand the difference between knowledge and experience in the context of software engineering.
- They will be able to evaluate and discuss a given knowledge management initiative planned in a company.
- They will be able to suggest improvements on knowledge management initiatives.
- They will understand and distinguish management and developer perspectives on knowledge and experience management – and their potential conflicts.
- They will understand why information needs to be structured and reorganized ("engineered") for reuse in software projects.
- They will be aware of the fact that knowledge and experience is deeply related with people – it is not just dead material.

Readers will also be enabled to contribute to improvement initiatives actively:

- Readers will know different techniques and tools for structuring knowledge in software engineering.
- They will understand the meaning and potential of patterns for reuse.
- They will know how to start effective experience exchange in a team or business unit.
- Readers will know and understand recurring problems and misunderstandings that challenge the reuse of experiences and knowledge – and options to overcome them.
- They will know the visions of experience factory, organizational memory, and Web 2.0 approaches like Wikis or blogs, which have been drivers for the development of novel experience and knowledge management techniques.
- They can avoid common pitfalls associated with the introduction of new experience management tools.
- They will be able to recall practical examples of introducing and applying experience and knowledge management in companies for discussions and planning.

Concrete impact on software engineering work. According to Eraut and Hirsh [37], there are a number of concrete benefits associated with improved learning abilities.

Applying knowledge management and experiences to software engineering can have the following impacts:

- Carrying out software engineering activities faster.
- Improving the quality of the process.
- Improving communications around complex software engineering tasks.
- Becoming more independent and needing less supervision, which is important for new employees.
- Helping others learn to preform knowledge-intensive tasks, thus freeing resources for development activities.
- Combining tasks more effectively.
- Recognizing possible problems faster.
- Expanding the range of project situations in which one can perform competently.
- Increasing ability to handle difficult tasks and taking on tasks of greater complexity.
- Dealing with more difficult or more important cases, clients, customers, suppliers, or colleagues.

This list of value-adding abilities shows the potential of focusing on experience and knowledge management – as a learning approach for software engineers.

Hannover, Germany   Kurt Schneider

Acknowledgments

I am a software engineer – and I worked at the intersection of software engineering, experience, and knowledge management for several years. After holding a postdoctoral position at the University of Colorado at Boulder, I had just joined DaimlerChrysler Research and Technology, when one direction of our research turned toward systematic learning from experience. Prof. Victor R. Basili from the University of Maryland at College Park was a promoter and coach for all of our work on experience and experiments in software engineering for years. I owe him many insights and good ideas that made it into this book and also a lot of fun during all our meetings.

Prof. Dieter Rombach, the Director of the Institute for Empirical and Experimental Software Engineering (Fraunhofer IESE) in Kaiserslautern, Germany, was an equally important partner in several collaborative projects. Together with Vic Basili, Dieter Rombach formed the Software Experience Center (SEC) initiative. Five world-class companies met on a regular basis to exchange experience on software engineering issues: ABB, Boeing, DaimlerChrysler, Motorola, and Nokia.

For DaimlerChrysler, the membership in the SEC consortium was an important step. Bärbel Hörger, the head of Software Process Design at DaimlerChrysler Research and Technology, recognized this early and supported SEC. She initiated an internal SEC project within DaimlerChrysler. I had the honor to lead Daimler-Chrysler's part of SEC and work with a large number of dedicated, committed, and inspiring colleagues: Frank Sazama, Frank Houdek, and Heike Frank added a lot of ideas and insights about experience factory and use of knowledge. Stefanie Lindstaedt was a driving force and the leader of the Coronet collaborative learning project, associated with SEC. Dieter Landes, Ton Vullinghs, and J. Kontio provided knowledge and experience on software risk management from several large projects. Jan von Hunnius, Thilo Schwinn, and Thomas Beil made SEC work by putting techniques on the intersection of software engineering and experience management to work. Many people participated in building experience bases, collections of experience, and knowledge, which we then refined and improved step by step. SEC was not always an easy project. We learned many lessons the hard way – but I always enjoyed working with the great people at SEC. Hopefully, this book can give others an easier start to reach an equally rewarding experience *faster*.

When I joined Universität Hannover in 2003, I brought many of the concepts to the university environment. An experience circle with companies was formed; techniques were applied in more than 50 student projects over the first 4 years. We built new and better repository construction kits – and we made new mistakes. By that time, I had already learned to appreciate an uncovered problem as an opportunity for learning and improvement. Dieter Rombach initiated the effort that led to this book. In that process, Eric Ras from Fraunhofer IESE has provided numerous good ideas and corrections. Frank Bomarius read an earlier version very carefully and provided insightful remarks. Sebastian Meyer from Leibniz Universität Hannover has provided many detailed comments to improve the book. My colleague, Prof. Nicola Henze, pointed me to some interesting ontologies on the Web.

Stefanie Lindstaedt, who is now a department head at the Know-Center in Graz, Austria, reminded me of the importance of workplace learning issues. We were both inspired by Prof. Gerhard Fischer from the University of Colorado at Boulder.

Thank you very much!

Contents

Chapter 1
Motivation and Terminology

1.1 Objectives of this Chapter

After reading this chapter, you should be able to:

- Define the basic concepts in knowledge and experience management.
- Distinguish between data, information, knowledge, and experience by defining the terms and by providing short examples.
- Understand why experience and knowledge need to be stored and how they are supposed to be used and reused.
- Give an overview of the entire field of knowledge management, its relationship to experience exploitation, and point out the most difficult tasks in that field.
- Explain why ability, motivation, and opportunity to learn are required for effective knowledge work.

In future chapters, we will use the following overview like a map. It will provide orientation and help to embed future chapters into a bigger picture. We will take a deeper look at all interesting areas, in particular at the more difficult ones. The basic terminology presented in this chapter will be used throughout the book and will be extended where appropriate.

Recommended Reading for Chap. 1

- Nonaka, I. and T. Hirotaka, *The Knowledge-Creating Company*. 17 ed. 1995, Oxford: Oxford University Press
- Senge, P., *The Fifth Discipline – The Art & Practice of the Learning Organization*. 1990, London: Random House
- Polanyi, M., *The Tacit Dimension*. 1966, Garden City, NY: Doubleday

1.2 A Guided Tour of Experience and Knowledge Management

Building and maintaining software is a knowledge-intense endeavor. Software engineers, developers, project leaders, and managers need to know a lot about computer technology, problem domains, and software engineering methods. As the field progresses, all of them need to constantly learn more and new facts and techniques

K. Schneider, *Experience and Knowledge Management in Software Engineering*,
DOI 10.1007/978-3-540-95880-2_1, © Springer-Verlag Berlin Heidelberg 2009

and acquire additional capabilities. Because software is developed in teams, relevant knowledge and skills include social and organizational skills, too.

Before we look at a number of examples that illustrate the importance of knowledge in software engineering, this chapter will take a closer look at the situation described above. What do we mean by **knowledge** – and what aspect will be emphasized in this book? Why should one bother to *manage knowledge* – something that typically resides in the brains of people? And what are the opportunities envisioned by proponents of knowledge management?

Experience is treated as a special kind of knowledge during most of this introduction. In later chapters, the distinctive nature of experience will be highlighted and discussed, but in this overview, we will emphasize commonalities.

Mnemonic 1.1 (Experience)

Experience is treated as a special kind of knowledge.

In this chapter, we travel to the vista points of knowledge and experience management. There will be several short stops along the route; we will try to cover a large area in a few pages. Additional trips will be needed to explore fascinating aspects one by one. Do not worry if you cannot see all the details now – just try to get the bigger picture. Welcome to the tour!

1.2.1 Knowledge Helps an Organization to Act and React Better

The principal motivation for knowledge management is simple: A smarter company reacts better to the demands of customers and markets [77]. When a customer requests a software solution, or a change to a product, a smarter company will be able to provide it faster and at better quality. This is the first, fundamental conviction of knowledge management. Managing knowledge is a means and not an end in software engineering.

Mnemonic 1.2 (Knowledge impact)

Knowledge helps a software organization to react faster and better.

However, this conviction needs to be analyzed further: What exactly is a smarter company? What kind of knowledge does this claim refer to, and how does knowledge lead to better reactions of the entire company? A "better" reaction may refer to a more accurate or more precise response, leading to better software quality. In the end, higher customer satisfaction can be achieved.

The field of **organizational learning** addresses the issue of organizations (such as software companies or business units) that learn and become smarter [32, 99]. An organization can learn in different ways:

- Most importantly, individual members of the organization learn. By their acting on behalf of the company, they make the organization act smarter.
- Pieces of knowledge are collected in a common repository. It can be used by company members or by software that interprets the contents and reacts accordingly.

- Infrastructure within the organization is provided. This allows existing sources and users of knowledge to interact more effectively. Existing knowledge can be brought to bear. Infrastructure includes technical connections and tools, as well as established procedures and processes.

In the third item above, a more intelligent behavior of an organization is not achieved by more knowledge but by better use of existing knowledge. Infrastructure may refer to technical means of exchanging knowledge (access to a repository) and to providing easier access to human knowledge resources as well (yellow pages, knowledge brokers).

Definition 1.1 (Organizational learning)

Organizational learning is an approach that stimulates

1. *learning of individuals;*
2. *organization-wide collection of knowledge;*
3. *cultivation of infrastructure for knowledge exchange.*

Learning occurs on several levels, from individuals over groups to the entire organization. Organizational learning needs to coordinate all levels into a systematic process of acquiring new knowledge and evaluating it. Learning is a complex process; facts are learned in a different way than learning to carry out a complex task or by learning to make decisions under uncertainty (Fig. 1.1).

It is not only the knowledge that makes the difference but also the representation of knowledge and where it resides. To guide human actions, knowledge needs to be *internalized* [77] in human minds. However, not all knowledge is neatly spelled out and documented. Many important pieces of knowledge reside inside people and cannot be "accessed" at will. Even worse, people are not fully aware of everything they know. Polanyi [84] calls this type **"tacit knowledge."** The term alludes to the fact that people use knowledge every day (by acting accordingly), but cannot express it, or might not even identify it as *knowledge*. It will be one of the most interesting aspects in later chapters to envision techniques for *externalizing* [77] tacit

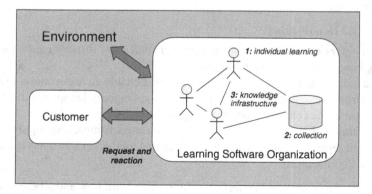

Fig 1.1 Three aspects of organizational learning with the goal of reacting better to changes in the environment or to customer requests

knowledge (i.e., to help its owners expressing it). Explicit information can be stored and disseminated. Dissemination is probably the most visible part of knowledge management – but it is not the most crucial one. Helping software engineers and other project participants to *externalize* their knowledge and others to *internalize* and *use* it is as challenging and as rewarding as the mere process of dissemination. Externalization can imply writing a document or explaining things orally.

Mnemonic 1.3 (Knowledge management)

Knowledge management addresses all of the following:
- *acquiring new knowledge;*
- *transforming it from tacit or implicit into explicit knowledge and back again;*
- *systematically storing, disseminating, and evaluating it;*
- *applying knowledge in new situations.*

Obviously, the notion of learning is part of the bigger picture. Internalizing explicit knowledge into implicit or tacit knowledge is an act of learning. On a higher level, organizational learning occurs in several variants within an organization that takes knowledge management seriously (Fig. 1.2).

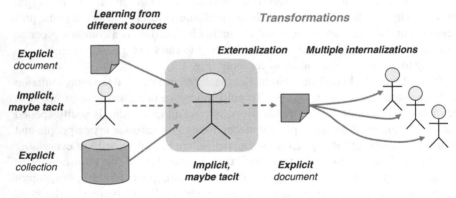

Fig. 1.2 Concepts of externalization and internalization in learning, from the perspective of the person in the center

Definition 1.2 (Know-how)

Know-how refers to procedural knowledge: facts and rules directly guiding action by saying how *to do or achieve something.*

From a more strategic perspective, learning must enable an organization to adapt to new environmental demands and changing goals. Ongoing learning is the necessary response to the constant changes an organization faces every day.

Several authors have investigated these learning aspects more thoroughly [8, 32, 34, 99]. Their refined distinction of different learning modes leads to many questions of practical significance:

- Do we just learn facts and concepts or do we also learn how and where to apply them?

- Do we learn to forget; that is, how do we get rid of outdated and obsolete information and knowledge?
- Does the learning process enable the learners and their organization to put new knowledge into perspective and relate it to existing concepts?
- Do learning and the acquired knowledge stimulate and encourage a better view of the dependencies and dynamic behavior of the organization?

Overall, the question is as follows: How far can a company get with its particular style of learning? We will have to stop and rethink at several points what we really need and want for software engineering.

Kelloway and Barling point out that the mechanisms of learning should not be seen as pure logistics of a material called "knowledge" [62]. Instead, each individual knowledge worker needs to have (1) the ability, (2) the motivation, and (3) the opportunity to engage in knowledge work. As we will see throughout this book, knowledge management initiatives can provide opportunities for learning and experience exchange. Individual software developers can gain or improve their ability for knowledge work by using the techniques described below. The issue of motivation needs to be addressed as well. The culture of a company or a team can be encouraging or discouraging for knowledge management. Working with knowledge requires individual effort of all participants. Software engineers are not buckets an organization can fill with knowledge at will. Opportunity, ability, and motivation for working with knowledge must go hand in hand. Techniques of knowledge representation and sharing must be embedded in a learning-friendly environment. This must be reflected in the design of each knowledge or experience management technique.

1.2.2 Examples of Knowledge Workers in Software Projects

In an ambitious software project, there are many *knowledge workers*, as Drucker calls them [34].

Definition 1.3 (Knowledge worker)

Knowledge workers contribute to company success mainly by gathering, organizing, and applying knowledge. Knowledge can also be created.
   New knowledge is created when a new perspective or a new relationship is established, leading to a conclusion that could not be drawn before. This is a truly "creative act."

Example 1.1 (Knowledge workers)

Most participants in a software project are knowledge workers by this definition. A few examples may serve to illustrate this point:

- Imagine a **project leader** who is a technical expert but knows nothing about his or her new project. How could such a person plan or control the project? There are so many things to *know*: Who is the customer, and what are the key

requirements? There are nonfunctional requirements, and facts about the environment influence planning. There are "soft" aspects to consider: What is this
customer's payment history? Does he have a record of changing requirements
frequently? What do we know about his existing software base that the new system may have to link to? The more a project manager knows, the better plans
can be.

- A designer or **software architect** needs to *know* the requirements, in particular nonfunctional requirements. Those tend to influence the architecture more
  than most functional requirements do: A software system will be structured very
  differently depending on the priorities of speed, robustness, or flexibility. How
  does an architect know what consequences a certain structure will have? A lot of
  experience is required to make appropriate decisions – and experience counts as
  knowledge, as we stated before.
- **Developers** need to *know* programming paradigms, such as object orientation.
  They need to know development tools and techniques. Eclipse is a popular integrated development environment (IDE) in the open source domain. Eclipse is a
  very powerful, extensible tool for developers – but learning to use it is tough.
  Developers need to know a lot before they can write their first programs.
- **Maintenance personnel** often use expert systems or other Web-based tools that
  help them to identify problems. When faced with a broken ticket machine or
  copier, maintenance personnel may feed symptoms into the machine and receive
  potential causes in return. They need to *know* what symptoms to look for. A vast
  amount of *knowledge* is encoded in the support tool.
- In a complex software project, individuals play several roles: project manager,
  quality assurance, developer, architect, tester, and so forth. Each individual needs
  to do his or her job properly, applying the *knowledge* required. However, the
  project will only appear and act "smart" if all participants collaborate effectively. This requires appropriate project structures (like work breakdown structures, teams), knowledge exchange infrastructure – and the attitude of sharing
  knowledge.

This list of short examples sheds some light on the importance and variability of
knowledge present in a software project. Some participants, like the maintenance
technician, need to *know* facts. Developers need to *know* how to handle tools,
designers *know* from experience which program structures worked in the past.
Project managers *know* details, but also relationships about the customer; they *know*
about some vague beliefs and risks when planning the project. The entire project
calls for infrastructure and even "a *knowledge-sharing* attitude."

1.2.2.1 Hypotheses Related to Experiences

Experience was mentioned with regard to the architect scenario above. The term
will be defined in a later chapter. For now, experience can be understood as a piece
of knowledge gained from participating in some activity or event. When we observe
something meaningful, we may learn from it: by drawing a conclusion or by deriving

a hypothesis about the observed event. Why did it happen? How could it have been avoided? What will be the consequence? Those conclusions or hypotheses can be treated like a piece of knowledge: They can be passed on to others or compared with similar experience. Most importantly, experiences can be reused. If a hypothesis is true, the observed event could occur again in a similar situation. This mechanism of transfer is fundamental to understanding the value of experiences.

But what if a hypothesis is not true? Or not true in general? Unlike pieces of "knowledge" from a book, the conclusions drawn from experiences may be flawed. Therefore, experience should be treated with more caution than is accepted knowledge. As Chap. 5 will discuss in detail, the process of acquiring, refining, and reusing experience is a special variant of a general knowledge life cycle. This raises the issue of knowledge acquisition – and the variant of experience elicitation: What are suitable sources? How do we know we can trust them and where we can reapply the hypotheses? These are some of the more difficult questions concerning experiences.

1.2.3 Spreading Knowledge and Experiences

Let us assume that we have acquired or identified several knowledge sources and experiences. To make the organization smarter, many members of the organization should be empowered to use those sources easily. There are several prerequisites for such reuse:

- Experience must be "cleaned" and validated.
- Knowledge must be evaluated and organized (i.e., structured and linked).
- Experience should be transformed into readily usable material. For example, conclusions should be made clear and explicit.
- Related experiences and pieces of knowledge can be combined, reworked ("engineered"), and rephrased. They are turned into **recommendations** rather than observations or experiences. For example, if previous projects experienced a problem using a certain design notation in Unified Modeling Language (UML), the derived " best practice" may recommend using a different diagram or using this diagram in a specific way. New projects can simply follow the advice without the need to derive that conclusion from the experiences again and again.

Knowledge can be created by combining existing knowledge in a new way or by making experiences and conclusions. For example, a software tester may have seen many mistakes before she is able to identify a code pattern that seems to provoke misunderstandings. Creating new knowledge about the pattern builds on a lot of existing knowledge and experience, and it usually entails the use of creative thinking.

Definition 1.4 (Knowledge management)

When experience and knowledge is created, evaluated, maintained, engineered, and disseminated systematically to solve a problem, we call this knowledge management.

Storing knowledge (and experiences) seems to be a crucial point in this management task. For that reason, setting up a database or other knowledge exchange mechanism is important. As we will see, however, this is not the most essential aspect of knowledge management. *Acquiring* material to be put into that storage is equally important. Preparing the material and finding it when needed are other key tasks.

Providing the above prerequisites for knowledge reuse is necessary but not sufficient for successful knowledge management. As was pointed out above, workplace learning is not only an organizational activity but also an individual endeavor. Kelloway and Barling [62] call knowledge workers "investors of knowledge," emphasizing the importance of some "return on investment" for those individuals. Motivation is yet another prerequisite. Many of the discussions below address the issue of encouragement and the need to avoid "demotivation."

1.2.4 What Others Call "Knowledge Management"

Nonaka and Takeuchi propagated the term *knowledge management* in 1995 [77]. Of course, learning occurred in companies long before this term was coined. In software engineering, there is a long tradition of tools offering comparable services, so-called computer-aided software engineering (CASE) tools.

CASE tools typically integrate a graphical editor for a requirement or design notation with a database to store respective models. Often, rules are defined that the CASE tool can apply to its models for checking consistency. During the early 1990 s, when CASE tools were broadly introduced, they were considered *knowledge bases* for the software designers. They offer mechanisms for entering models, combining and engineering them, and analyzing them afterward. When several people use the same model, the tool even supports *sharing* of that knowledge. The repository of a tool preserves all models – unlike developers or designers who may forget (Fig. 1.3).

According to the above-mentioned definition, CASE tools can be considered a contribution to knowledge management in software engineering, but in a very narrow and specific sense. Early CASE tools were strictly oriented toward a structured development method, such as structured analysis and data-flow diagrams [28]. Today, comparable tools offer object-oriented methods and usually UML diagrams. Only a limited piece of information is represented in a CASE tool. Often, the information only refers to the pure functional requirements of the product. Nonfunctional requirements are often missing. Reasons for making design decisions, so-called design rationale, is also often not captured. As a consequence, it may or may not be justified to call the stored texts or annotations a piece in the puzzle of knowledge management. However, typical knowledge management approaches go beyond such a narrow technical focus.

In the 1990 s, *knowledge management* gained high attention, and not only in software engineering. Most companies claimed to do it and were proud of it. Like all fashions, knowledge management transcended its peak at some point in time. Since then, several knowledge management initiatives were renamed but are still important to their host companies. New trends and new buzzwords have arrived.

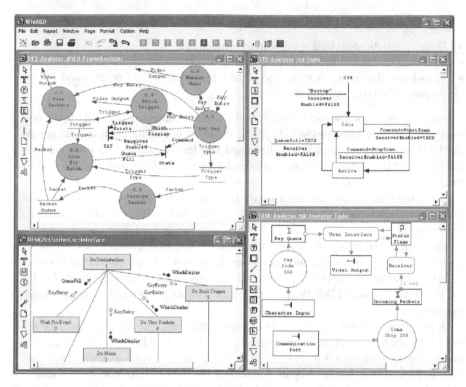

Fig. 1.3 A screen of a CASE tool showing several structured analysis and design models (WinA&D from Excel Software, http://www.excelsoftware.com/sasdtopic.html, printed with permission from Excel Software, 19 Misty Mesa Court, Placitas, NM 87043 USA)

Some people have invested effort and energy into knowledge management for a long time. They may ask for new visions and prefer to do similar things under different headlines. This is very reasonable, but for clarity, this book sticks with the original label: knowledge management.

1.3 Data, Information, Knowledge – and Beyond

The term *knowledge* has not yet been defined sufficiently in this book. In fact, defining this essential concept is surprisingly difficult. Knowledge is an old term that has been used by philosophers, sociologists, educators, and so on for centuries. A general definition that covers all disciplines is beyond our focus: We are interested in a working definition for software engineering.

In this section, the meaning of knowledge will be discussed. Terms like data and information are tightly connected to knowledge. However, we go beyond those terms and look at experience and skills to complete the spectrum.

There is a basic distinction between data, information, and knowledge:

- *Data*: Symbols organized according to syntactic rules.
- *Information*: Data with meaning according to a given interpretation.
- *Knowledge*: Information related to other knowledge in the human mind for the purpose of solving problems.

For example, a software designer draws a **class diagram** in UML for a new subsystem of a software product (Fig. 1.4). *Symbols* in that diagram are defined by the UML notation: rectangles with lines and text labels, arrows and lines between the boxes. UML implies *syntactic rules* for drawing class diagrams. The rules allow lines and arrows between rectangles but no dangling lines. The diagram needs to conform to UML syntax rules. Before we have assigned a meaning to the symbols, the diagram is still *data*. Someone unfamiliar with UML will not be able to interpret the diagram.

However, UML also provides an interpretation: A box indicates a class, showing the class name, its attributes, and operations. Class symbols are connected via associations (denoted by lines) and so on. UML 2.0 semantics is formally defined in the language specification [78]. When data comes with an interpretation, it constitutes *information*.

A programmer who sees the class diagram perceives it as information. According to the above definition, it turns into knowledge only when human beings, like programmers, understand it and integrate it into the network of knowledge they bear in mind. For example, they may associate the class "Simulator" with a similar class they know. As a consequence, they may solve the implementation problem by reusing that other class. A programmer may also remember that there is a tool to generate code from UML class diagrams. Combining the information depicted in Fig. 1.4 and the knowledge about that tool provides more support for problem solving.

However, there is a startling consequence: When we strictly follow the informal definition above, the model in Fig. 1.4 turns into knowledge when a designer understands it. Not so with the generator tool: Because there is no human mind involved, the definition of knowledge does not apply. When the tool generates code, the model remains information rather than turning into knowledge. Although the

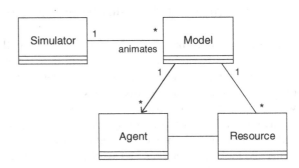

Fig. 1.4 Simple UML class diagram as a "well-formed composition of UML elements"

generated code may solve the implementation problem just as well as does the code manually written by a programmer, information in a machine does not qualify as knowledge.

Because we will use the terms *data*, *information*, and *knowledge* frequently, they deserve more thorough attention. We follow Stapel's excellent summary [105].

Definition 1.5 (Data)

Data *are facts that can be distinguished. They may be composed into well-formed models or terms.*

The presence of a rectangle in a diagram can be distinguished from an oval in that diagram. A character in a requirements text can be distinguished from a different character or from a blank. A number on one page can be distinguished from a number printed two pages later.

Floridi [44] distinguishes four types of data:

- **Primary data** is what we usually mean by data: the content of documents or databases, or messages transferred over a network, or sensor readings.
- **Metadata** refers to primary data by describing its format, version, status, and so forth. Metadata is data about data.
- **Operative data** is a subtype of metadata describing how data is to be used.
- **Derivative data** is derived from the three above-mentioned data types. It can be used to sort, organize, or search for patterns in the above-mentioned types of data.

All four types of data occur in software engineering and need to be distinguished on the conceptual level. Metadata is of particular importance. It specifies the meaning of models. Models are ubiquitous in computer science, and so are metamodels with their associated metadata. Extracting an explicit metamodel can substantially foster automatic and semiautomatic dissemination and use of information. When several people agree on a common metamodel, they can share information more efficiently and with fewer misunderstandings.

Definition 1.6 (Information)

Information *is well-formed data with a meaning.*

Data must follow syntactical rules. Information goes beyond that by adding meaning. There is a reference to the "well-formedness" of the combined data elements because meaning cannot be assigned to terms that violate syntax rules.

Different data can mean the same thing, as illustrated in Fig. 1.5. Vice versa, the same data can mean different things – if it is interpreted in a different way. Because information consists of data and assigned meaning, different data can never be the same information (but can mean the same thing).

In Fig. 1.5, the meaning of a class diagram can also be described in well-formed sentences. Spoken language also qualifies. Audio data are the sounds produced in a language, combined into (grammatically) well-formed and *meaningful* sentences.

Some authors, like the above-mentioned philosopher Floridi [43], further require the information to be "true." This concept is interesting and might provide assistance for distinguishing "true" information from "doubtful" experiences. However, it turns

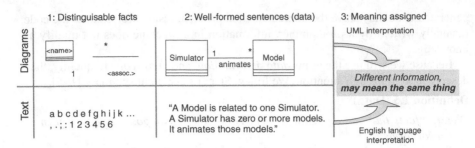

Fig. 1.5 Different data (as text or diagrams) can mean the same thing

out to be counterproductive in software engineering, as the following example will illustrate:

Example 1.2 (Requirements text)

A requirements engineer has interviewed a customer representative and has written down requirements: The primary data consist of strings of characters. This text is written in English words, following the English grammar. It is (rather) well-formed, so others can interpret the data and assign meaning to it. Let us assume that the representative requested a "1-second response time" to a certain hardware signal. In the context of the respective operation, this request obviously has a meaning. Thus, it constitutes information. However, it may be *wrong*: The representative may have *guessed* the required response time. One-second response time may be insufficient. In Floridi's opinion, that requirement could not be called *information*.

Let us extend the exercise in terminology: What if there was some metadata coming with the requirement data? It could say: "This is what Mr. X, the representative, said" – which is well-formed, meaningful, and true *information*, whereas the requirement itself is not true (or not yet true, or no longer true – requirements do change!). As you can see, the appealing notion of *information that is true by definition* is misleading, at least in a requirements engineering environment. It is not a property of the information alone whether it is true or not. Trueness is rather a *function of information plus context over time*. There may be philosophical arguments to defend Floridi's definition. However, from a software engineering point of view, it is simply not helpful. In software engineering, we have to deal with wrong or unsure information, too.

The above example shows how the terminology works when exposed to real-world scenarios. It has practical implications and is not "pure theory"! Information has more facets than that of the short definition above. Referring to the above-mentioned remark, knowledge resides only in people. Information mediates between the lower layer of data (which has no meaning) and the higher level of human understanding and problem solving (more knowledge, additional capabilities). In that model, knowledge can never be transferred directly, "from brain to brain." Each and every transfer operation needs to descend to the information layer

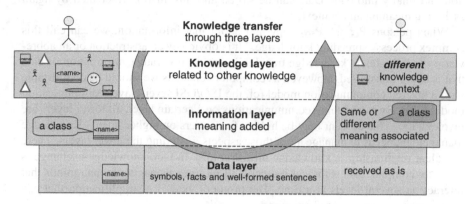

Fig. 1.6   A layered model of knowledge transfer

and finally to the data layer. As Fig. 1.6 illustrates, data reside in a layer of documents, electrical signals, and the like. There are obvious transfer options for those representations. Whenever data are interpreted, a meaning is assigned to the data. Hopefully, sender and receiver share a common interpretation! This is one reason for agreeing to standards or for using the UML: They provide clearly (pre-) defined meaning to well-formed terms or models. Information can be stored and transferred (via data). The layer above interpretation and meaning provides integration with other knowledge in a human brain. One might argue whether machines can count as knowledgeable: Can a generator build and receive knowledge? We want to leave this discussion to others. However, distinguishing between transferable data, partly interpretable information, and nontransferable knowledge helps to clarify knowledge management aspects.

This layered model can be applied to many situations. For example, when we learn by observing a knowledgeable person performing knowledge work, information and knowledge may never be expressed in any explicit form. Nevertheless, even implicit information conveyed by observation relies on the data provided by seeing and hearing. If the knowledgeable person also provides explanations, this data turns into information. Without those explanations, observers can only guess the meaning of the observed data – and why things are done that way.

Sunassee and Sewry [108] define knowledge as:

Definition 1.7 (Knowledge)

"[. . .] knowledge is the human expertise stored in a person's mind, gained through experience and interaction with the person's environment."

This definition provides a link to interaction and experience, and it emphasizes: *Knowledge resides in the mind*. When knowledge management refers to the organizational dimension of learning, knowledge must be spread. In the sense of Fig. 1.6, this can only mean converting the knowledge of person A into information and finally into data. Data can be stored and information re-created by again assigning meaning and context.

When persons P_1, ..., P_{500} copy and adopt that information, we can call this complex process "spreading knowledge." It is obviously an abstraction or an abbreviation to talk about "knowledge transfer," because it is rather information or data that is being transferred. However, as computer scientists we should be comfortable with a layered communication model (cf. the ISO/OSI seven- layer communication model [25]). By establishing communications on a certain layer, all lower layers are invoked, too. This descent may be hidden from users on higher layers. Knowledge management needs to manage all of those aspects, including the lower layers. There is a clear relationship to knowledge infrastructure. In fact, knowledge exchange is far more complex than technical protocols. It requires managing human minds that interact on several levels at a time. The protocol view is a simplification that can help to understand certain phenomena.

Experience is another key term. It has a lot in common with knowledge. In fact, Definition 1.7 of experience-induced knowledge and the following interpretation of experience are almost identical:

Mnemonic 1.4 (Experience requires involvement)

Experience is the type of knowledge a person acquires by being involved.

In this book, experience is used in a slightly more specific meaning: "*An* experience" (singular) refers to the conclusions drawn from being involved in an activity or an event. "Several experiences" (plural) refer to a chunk of those conclusions, gained in one or more activities or events. The following definition [93] emphasizes the emotional dimension of an experience as much as the cognitive dimension:

Definition 1.8 (Experience)

An experience is defined as a three-tuple consisting of

- *an observation;*
- *an emotion (with respect to the observed event);*
- *a conclusion or hypothesis (derived from the observed event and emotion) .*

If someone is involved in an activity – or a project, or an accident – that person makes "**observations**." Unlike learning from a book, the involvement and personal relationship stimulate emotional responses to what has been observed: When you participate in a software test, and 44 critical errors are detected 1 day before delivery, emotional responses are drastic. They may reach from frustration to panic, and they make the experience a memorable piece of knowledge. Emotions can also be positive: Passing a review with no major findings will be remembered as a joyful success, not just a fact.

Because knowledge (including experience) was defined as being applied to problem solving, an experience needs a component to support problem solving. In the above definition, the observation is transformed into a hypothesis (Why did it happen? What could we have done?) or a conclusion (What is the general pattern? What should be done?). In the testing example, one hypothesis may be "Late

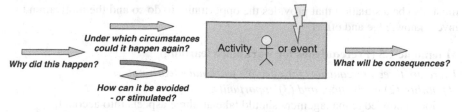

Fig. 1.7 Hypotheses and conclusions around an experience

testing can lead to bad mistakes" or a conclusion may be "Plan to finish testing 4 days before delivery so that you can remove errors in time." This is the rationale part of the experience; emotions are an integral part of the initiating observation (Fig. 1.7).

According to Sunnassee's above-mentioned definition of knowledge, *all* knowledge is created through interaction and experience. This would make experience the one and only mechanism for acquiring knowledge, a conviction shared by positivism [85]. Whoever participates in a formal study program assumes there are other sources: reading a book, solving an exercise. However, book exercises facilitate only small-scale experiences; because of their artificial nature and short-term relevance for a learner, they hardly induce realistic emotions. To conclude, we will treat experiences as a subset and as a special type of knowledge. Experience is acquired by having been involved, and it consists of more than the conclusion: There is always an authentic observation and an emotional "color." This shapes an experience:

- Real involvement and an authentic observation make an experience credible. As a witness one knows: It really happened.
- Intense emotions help one to remember the experience. They are a good motivation for either repeating or avoiding what happened.
- With a rational conclusion, an experience can be used for further problem-solving. This part tells us what to do after the two upper aspects have convinced us why to do it.

Shannon wrote about information: *"It is hardly to be expected that a single concept of information would satisfactorily account for the numerous possible applications of this general field"* [100]. The same is true for the term *experience*. We are satisfied with a definition that helps us to be more successful in software projects.

Skill is another term in the vicinity of information, knowledge, and learning. When challenging tasks need to be completed and problems must be solved, software project participants should have appropriate skills. How do these relate to knowledge and experience?

Definition 1.9 (Skill)

A skill is the talent or ability to perform a task.

According to Kelloway and Barling [62], a skill addresses one of the three prerequisites for effective knowledge work: the ability to do it. To apply a skill, there must also be a situation that provides the opportunity to do so and the motivation to invest knowledge and effort.

Mnemonic 1.5 (Prerequisites for workplace learning)
There are three prerequisites for effective workplace learning:
(1) ability, (2) motivation, and (3) opportunity.
Good knowledge management should take all three aspects into account.

Vice versa, even highly motivated software engineers in urgent demand can organize knowledge support and exchange if they lack the related skills. Knowledge management is not just about good intentions; it also requires able and skilled proponents.

Software engineers are knowledge workers [34]. Performing their usual tasks requires knowledge and experience. Each new piece of knowledge is related to previous experiences and other knowledge. To complete a task, explicit information needs to be internalized; experience and knowledge (e.g., from books) need to be combined.

When developers write a database application, they need knowledge about the particular database system (e.g., MySQL or Access). Having experience is advantageous: Certain malfunctions or awkward features will be foreseen and can be avoided. Those who have encountered problems with an indexing feature, for example, will be able to foresee or avoid that problem in the future. A skilled worker must have knowledge and experience. Personality and noncognitive abilities may also be needed (e.g., for manual labor).

Knowledge management is concerned with acquiring, engineering, and disseminating knowledge for the purpose of solving problems, as we defined above. The discussion about implicit and explicit knowledge has also raised a challenge: How to internalize information in order to turn it into knowledge? Acquiring knowledge must reach beyond individuals and their own commitments. According to the concept of learning organizations, knowledge collections and infrastructure need to be added. Knowledge management should not only make knowledge "available" but also actively advertise and disseminate (i.e., "push") it [120].

The discussion about the three-layered knowledge transfer model is the basis for storing, transferring, and exchanging knowledge. Again, we want to make a few basic distinctions to introduce essential terms and concepts. Details will be discussed later.

There are different channels for transferring knowledge and experience. Strictly following the terminology introduced above, each of the following modes can occur:

From person to person: This is called **socialization** [77]. Unlike the process discussed above, it is possible to transfer tacit knowledge without ever externalizing it consciously. The classic example is an apprenticeship. In that situation, the apprentice observes the master. The master performs a task but usually does not explain it step by step. In a software engineering situation, an apprentice may learn from a project manager by simply "shadowing" her: Like a shadow, the apprentice follows the master. In software architecture, or in interface design, an apprenticeship may be advantageous:

- All those tasks require a substantial amount of knowledge and experience.
- None of those experts has time or is inclined to externalize their knowledge in writing.

Rather surprisingly, apprenticeships are rare in software engineering. Nevertheless, you should be aware of this option.

Stimulating experiences: It has been suggested to expose novice software engineers to certain situations in which they will most probably have foreseeable experiences. There is no direct transfer of experience or information, but an indirect one.

There are different alternative implementations:

- Recommend a **training course**: Send somebody to a course that has helped others to get better.
- **Trainee or internship**: Let somebody observe what is going on in projects without taking full responsibility.
- **Pair programming**: Agile approaches [15, 16] require developers to work in pairs. They interact intensely because they share one computer. A main intention of this concept is to stimulate exchange of experience and immediate feedback in the workplace.
- **Pilot project**: Allow someone to make typical mistakes in a project situation to gain emotional feedback, too.
- **Simulated project**: Expose them to a simulated project with the same intention, but at a lower cost: No real project suffers or is treated as learning object [89].

Using a knowledge base: On the lowest level, we need only a data storage device. As Fig. 1.6 shows, data with interpretation can be considered information. The information can turn into knowledge in someone's mind. With Fig. 1.6 in mind, such a database can be called a "knowledge base" for short. There are many hardware and software platforms available. In principle, a paper-based knowledge base might be sufficient. A group of software engineers may share a folder containing frequently asked questions (FAQs) on their product or even a few experiences with a tool they all use. (Example experience: "Never store in RTF format: There is a bug in the loader; I lost all my formats in the spec file.")

If a paper folder works, an electronic folder might work even better. All software engineers can access an electronic folder from their desktops without walking to the shelf. While one of them reads an experience, others might proceed in parallel. An electronic folder can even be shared over the Internet, which supports larger, distributed teams, and it can be searched much faster and at any time from any place.

Of course, computer science offers more convenient features for a shared collection of data when it can be interpreted as information: A whole range of opportunities opens up for indexing, sorting, searching, and connecting pieces of *information*. Databases are the most popular tool for handling large collections of well-structured pieces of information. Knowledge items or single experiences that are stored as database entries can be easily treated as separate, meaningful units. Depending on the database capabilities, managing those pieces of information is quite easy and convenient. Using database operations and some additional software leads to specialized tools for filtering, comparing, and automatically interpreting pieces of knowledge [5].

This mode of transfer looks very promising. However, it is only applicable to explicit knowledge stored in the rigid structure of the electronic repository. Knowledge passed by socialization is not covered. Nor does a repository reach the large amount of implicit knowledge that is neither explicit nor passed on through socialization. It simply remains inside an expert's mind.

In this introductory chapter, a pointer to some additional mechanisms should be sufficient. Even at this early point, it should be obvious that a technical component like a database is adequate for data and information management. As such, it is a prerequisite for knowledge management, too. But there are many other aspects to consider. Installing a database is only one aspect of knowledge management in software engineering.

Tasks for knowledge management include the following :

- Knowledge owners need to be identified. How do we know who really has something to share – even if those people are not even aware of (the value of) their knowledge [84]?
- Knowledge owners need to be encouraged or convinced or forced to share their knowledge in any of the modes presented above. Why would anybody want to invest effort into making someone else smarter? This is a key question, and we will have to take it very seriously!
- The conversion processes from and to explicit forms need to be facilitated and supported. All participants should face a low threshold for transfer. If effort and annoyance exceed a limit, transfer will not occur. This limit is often rather low.
- Matchmaking plays a crucial role. How can a potential user of a piece of knowledge learn about its existence? There must be a match between knowledge pieces that are needed and those that are available. Humans are good at making those matches. Advanced technical bases may support matchmaking.
- Managing the meaning of information. It is not sufficient to transfer the "raw" data; there must also be metadata about the meaning of the raw data. But this does not solve the problem: How do we know what the metadata means? Sending meta-metadata along will not do the job. We need some quality assurance with regard to the successful transfer of knowledge.
- Managing and supporting the intensity and style of consuming the information. Experiences are more than facts or rules. They contain an observation, an emotion, and a conclusion or hypothesis. If knowledge management wants to provide full-fledged experiences, the emotional aspect needs to be captured, managed, and delivered, too.
- Organizing multipliers. Transferring knowledge from point to point is important. Often, spreading one piece of information to many receivers is required. The same piece is exploited and reused several times, multiplying the benefit and

validating the information as a side effect. This is a specific form of making many matches.

- Oblivion is a somewhat related concept: Sometimes, old knowledge gets outdated or turns out to be inapplicable in a new context and must not be used any longer. Oblivion will be implemented through heuristic selection and deletion of contents or by marking contents as "deprecated" before they are ultimately removed. This issue is very important to keep experience repositories manageable and usable. Users confronted with outdated or wrong information will very quickly lose trust in the knowledge base. At the same time, it is conceptually difficult to identify "outdated information."

Fig. 1.8 summarizes the different tasks of knowledge management.

Challenges arise at conversion points. They occur whenever explicit information needs to be internalized or vice versa. In addition, the database and other data stores need an administrator. Furthermore, not all software engineers should be confronted with all details of knowledge transfer. This situation calls for roles. When the repository and the activities around the repository grow, it is advantageous to assign specialists to some of the tasks.

It is important to remind everyone involved in knowledge management activities: Knowledge management is not the main purpose of a software organization! Knowledge management and organizational learning are important *supportive activities* to the development, operation, and maintenance of software. To support software engineers' knowledge, activities should be integrated seamlessly into normal devel-

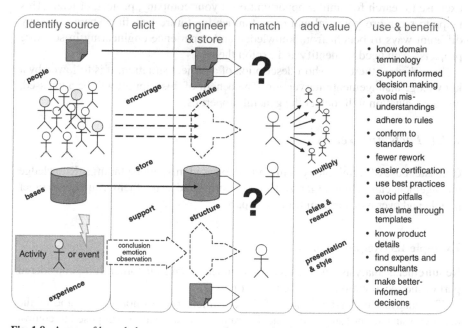

Fig. 1.8 A map of knowledge management tasks supporting knowledge and experience

opment tasks – and they must avoid any unnecessary effort or overhead. Ideally, knowledge management aspects should not be defined in a purely top-down manner but allow for decentralized integration and tuning.

1.4 Application of Knowledge Management in Software Engineering

In the above sections, terminology and basic tasks of knowledge management were outlined. Fig. 1.8 can be used as a map of the main concepts in knowledge management. We will now see how knowledge management can support software engineers in their daily work.

As the terminology sections have shown, knowledge management is concerned with the acquisition, engineering, and dissemination of knowledge for the purpose of solving problems in an organization. In some cases, this goal can be reached by finding a simple fact that is missing from a solution. In other cases, more complex and interrelated pieces of knowledge will be required. It is important to validate knowledge before it is reused. Validation will compare knowledge from different sources, for example. We will now look at the different kinds of knowledge that can be provided by knowledge management.

Examples are ordered from easiest to most challenging in terms of knowledge management. In most cases, this also corresponds with the amount of benefit generated. Each example represents an entire class of similar applications. It is a good exercise to search for similar opportunities in your company, project, or team. This helps to see more potential and opportunities for future benefits. There are many different ways to benefit from knowledge and experience engineering in software projects – you need to identify and exploit them.

In each case, there is a short description of a project situation. It is followed by a knowledge management intervention. The benefit of this support will be addressed, and an evaluation will look at the general properties.

1.4.1 Facts and Terms

Consistent use of terminology is important to avoid misunderstandings. Knowledge management can help to organize facts and terms and make them available to other people and over a distance of time and space.

Example 1.3 (Requirements)

Requirements analysts have received a document from a customer. It is "considered part of the specification," as the customer puts it.

The analysts understand most of the document but do not know some of the acronyms and are not sure about one diagram. Their software is supposed to control a chemical device. Despite its many details, the document fails to explain some of the chemical terms and processes. Analysts and developers are hesitant to ask the customer. They would have done that in an interview situation. With just a document in their hands, they prefer to find out by themselves: They do not want to raise doubts about their competence in the domain. This hesitation may delay the project or even lead to misinterpretations and defects.

First solution: A searchable dictionary can solve most of this problem. Using Google, software engineers will be able to understand most of the acronyms and terms.

Benefits: There is no need to bother a customer with questions software engineers can easily answer themselves.

Follow-up problem: Software development often takes place within very specific application domains. Not all domain-specific terms and acronyms will be known to the software engineers, nor will all of them be accessible via the Internet. And, there may be homonymous acronyms that in turn require further clarification.

Improved solution: A learning company might decide to build up a domain-specific glossary as a knowledge asset. An extended glossary will go beyond terms and contain more complex pieces of knowledge.

Evaluation: Implementations can range from a paper folder to a dedicated database with a Web front-end. Dedicated repositories should not make an attempt to replicate external sources. They will contain specific material only and may refer to other external sources, such as the Internet. A good structure will help, and a search engine should complement it. The benefit is manifold: Engineers will not spend as much time searching for domain information. The contents of the internal repository are more credible than those from external sources, such as anonymous and volatile Internet sources. Being able to get the information fast will lower the threshold to check when in doubt. Without that opportunity, engineers are tempted to guess what the customer wants – which is a costly trap especially when applied in requirements engineering. Wrong guessing leads to severe problems later on. Repositories can be built and run with existing technology. Seeding (i.e., initially loading) and updating repositories are crucial aspects and will be discussed in later chapters.

It should be noted that even a simple mechanism like a domain glossary consumes a fair amount of effort. A high-tech solution may be debatable. Small and medium-size companies will often take the risk of relying on the Internet instead – or just ask the customer. No matter what size a project, it is advisable to build a domain glossary. Asking the customer for a term *once* may be acceptable; having three people ask for the same term several times is annoying and unprofessional. Ignoring customer terminology is even worse. Striving for easier and faster access to recurring key terminology is always worth the effort in the long run.

1.4.2 Rules and Standards

Software engineering is a term that alludes to the traditions and achievements of engineering in other domains. Among the strengths associated with engineering is a commitment to reuse. This includes reuse of terms, established procedures, and standardized criteria. Norms and standards represent an agreed-upon body of knowledge to be shared by all serious software professionals. Knowledge management can contribute to using those standards more systematically. First of all, software engineers must be made aware of existing and relevant standards.

Example 1.4 (Software standards)

Examples of relevant standards include IEEE 610.10-1990 (software engineering terminology), ISO 8402 (software quality assurance and management), ISO 9126 (quality and usability criteria), and ISO 61 508 (security of electrical systems). Whereas a domain-specific term may be unknown to a novice project participant, *software engineering* terminology should be used properly in all domains. A customer can expect professional developers and their managers to interpret standardized terms accordingly. Some standards refer to terminology, whereas others also refer to procedures and rules. In ISO 61 508, for example, a security impact classification is given according to which programmable systems are classified by applying a set of specified rules. This standard recommends (or requires) certain procedures and techniques to ensure adequate levels of security in the system under development. Although standards are mentioned in most software engineering classes and books, they are not easy to obtain. They cannot be downloaded free of charge but must be ordered and cost more than $100 each. Just having a look is not so easy.

Knowledge management: A few hundred dollars will not be a problem for a professional software organization. Essential standards need to be bought and provided to the developers. Again, a paper-based solution in the company library is the easiest solution, and it may be a good one. Electronic access is not always permitted because of copyright and fees.

Benefit: Lowering the threshold for actually referring to a standard will avoid unnecessary uncertainty. Therefore, a professional development organization should keep relevant standards ready for reference. This way, developers can refer to standards whenever appropriate. If they do not have access to a standard, they can only guess whether it might be relevant. When the standards are provided, there is no need for guessing.

Follow-up problem: Many standards are long and boring to read. It is not obvious what they mean in terms of a concrete organization.

Improved solution: A more ambitious knowledge management approach will try to interpret a relevant standard once and then spread the interpretation. There can be concrete implementation hints, experiences from those who have tried it, and even tools or templates to get started faster.

Evaluation: Standards are similar to terminology, but they can be either domain-specific or generic to software engineering. In both cases, a professional organization and its members should have fast and easy access. Putting them on a shelf may meet that requirement – provided there is an effective mechanism for relating those who need a standard to that standard document. Such a look-up service can be integrated with the fact retrieval mentioned above. All add-on functionality that exploits the analysis and experience of one project to help many others is welcome. As we will see, however, this vision is difficult to implement.

1.4.3 Procedures and Templates

Many software engineering tasks are complex or difficult. Several roles and people need to interact in a synchronized way. It should not be necessary for each and every employee to reinvent the best way of performing those tasks. Instead, procedures and templates can offer guidance. They should be based on previous experience and best practices.

Example 1.5 (Risk management)

A senior software project leader wants to start systematic risk management on her project. She has participated in earlier projects and knows the power of risk management to avoid critical problems. However, she does not remember the details of doing it. Risk management is a basic technique most advanced projects should apply. In a business unit, similar risks will occur (e.g., with management, or with similar subcontractors, or with a similar environment). Therefore, there should be support for those procedures. Without systematic knowledge management, the project leader will probably ask colleagues who have done it in the past. If she is lucky, she might pick someone who has done it recently, remembers all the tips and tricks, and is willing to provide material for reuse. If she is less lucky, she might run into someone who tried it 3 years ago, did not manage to set it up properly, and gave up. Hopefully, this person will be too busy to share those experiences or provide unproved or flawed materials.

Knowledge management: A network of project leaders can support the exchange of information. An index by topic can help to find knowledgeable people faster. Knowledge management can do much more: Procedures and templates (e.g., typical risks, risk indicators, and mitigation procedures) can be collected and disseminated. There can be a tool or a database, or a Web site for accessing crucial process support.

Evaluation: A reliable and credible source for procedures that have already been tailored to the environment encourages others to reuse the knowledge. This saves time and money for reusing the tailored procedures.

We found the management of procedures and templates rewarding in several areas [92]. Procedures like reviews, risk management, or some requirements engineering activities are rewarding for a knowledge management initiative in software engineering [91]. We used experience bases to support both acquisition and dissemination of knowledge. Unlike the fine granularity in the terms and standards examples, a package for a procedure (like risk management) is larger, contains a variety of related templates and tools, and sometimes comes with a set of related experiences. Therefore, a full-fledged experience base faces more management challenges than does a simple dictionary of domain terms.

1.4.4 Engineering and Production Data

Large companies often develop software as just one component of a bigger system, which may be an administrative system or an embedded software product. In both cases, software engineers need access to data produced during the engineering or production of other components. Software may control mechanical parts, so developers need to take physical properties into account. Other software may interface with a legacy system – developers will need to know many details about version and interface formats, and so on.

Knowledge management: Knowledge management should provide easy access to all the construction data available. No single developer will know it all, so there needs to be a tool to make it available upon request. It will need to handle IDs, part numbers, and construction drawings. Computer-aided design (CAD) tools hold a lot of the information needed. CASE tools are an equivalent means for software parts. Indeed, the family of electronic data management (EDM) systems was introduced to deal with the large variety and overwhelming number of details involved in engineering projects.

Evaluation: Getting access to the company's own engineering data is mandatory. For knowledge management in software engineering, however, EDM tools are not sufficient. For instance, managing the different versions and configurations of software modules often exceeds their capabilities. Software developers need to know the exact configuration when they make a change or when they fix a bug in a delivered release. The biggest benefits can be achieved when an EDM product can be combined with a tool to manage software versions and configurations, like the open-source tool Subversion [111].

1.4.5 Competencies and People

Sometimes, a software project needs advice or instant help by an expert. It will not always be possible to breed or transfer competencies within a short period of time. Instead, it may be easier and more appropriate to ask an expert directly. For that, it is necessary to identify experts quickly.

Example 1.6 (Database expertise)

A project needs to connect to a new database. No one on the team has implemented such a database connection before. Learning from scratch takes weeks. The customer might get impatient, and implementations may be error-prone. One could hire an external consultant or try to find someone internally to help out.

Knowledge management: In a large company, someone might have performed this task before. Knowledge management needs to support the matching of those who need a competence for a limited amount of time with those who could offer it. Approaches like yellow pages, or marketplaces of skills, or expert networks can help to make the match. Those mechanisms may be strictly internal, or may also contain links to external consultants who have delivered good services in the past. Each large company has a list of established subcontractor relationships. It is a challenge to set up such a matchmaker, and even more so to keep it up to date. Many yellow pages soon get out of date and are no longer useful. However, in this section we will not worry about this aspect.

1.4.6 Skills and Relationships

Building up a skill takes time and cannot be achieved within a few hours or days. Many skills are acquired during formal education or in training programs. Skill management is a difficult task usually supported by human resources departments. Knowledge management can hardly play this role. It can support certain aspects. In software engineering, there are some technical skills that are more suitable for being managed.

Example 1.7 (Java skills)

A team needs to implement a user interface in Java. They have a background in C and C#, including the libraries used in those environments. Because Java is gaining importance, the manager decides to assign two developers to Java interfaces from now on. He does not want to rely on external consultants for this key skill.

Knowledge management: There is no magic in knowledge management. Building up a skill, like using object-oriented constructs in Java as opposed to C#, cannot be done just by reading a few tutorials. However, there are two things knowledge management can do: In the long run, a learning company should organize and manage individual learning of its members. If several people in different projects need to learn Java, there could be an in-house course, with follow-up experience exchange circles over several months. Although the individual's actual learning is mainly beyond knowledge management, organizing courses and feedback is a meaningful task. When a task is dominated by a complex structure of dependencies, formal knowledge management tools could help to reason in that jungle of dependencies. For example, no single project may have reported: "We need someone to learn Java in order to migrate some of our C# interfaces to that language." However, if a formal structure of knowledge exists, which contains all projects with their programming languages, and if there is a developer profile, then a reasoning mechanism may identify: "...those projects that use Java AND that use C# AND where THERE IS NO developer whose profile CONTAINS Java." What looks like an awkward database search query in this example can become quite an elegant usage of pieces of knowledge when seen in context.

Knowledge management can manage people and long-term learning. If there is formally structured and encoded information, a powerful search mechanism can help to see relationships and find people in a similar situation.

1.4.7 Opinions and Decisions

Long-term opinions and resulting decisions cannot be influenced by short-term interventions. Knowledge management can mainly provide support on underlying layers. In the end, an opinion can change. Decision-support systems try to provide leverage in concrete cases.

Example 1.8 (Adopting UML)

A project manager is about to start a new project. State charts are a common tool in the company, but many developers are not yet familiar with UML diagrams. In conferences and journals, UML is clearly state-of-practice, so this could be an opportunity to get started. However, the project must not suffer. What are the risks and chances and what needs to be considered when shifting to UML?

Knowledge management: Decisions are made under uncertainty. This is true almost by definition, as no decision is needed when the next step can simply be "derived." Rational decisions will take data and information into account and will also consider the opinions of other knowledgeable people. If not all reasons and rationale can be externalized and explicitly stated, a decision maker can still try to find similar situations in the past and study their outcome. Case-based reasoning [61] is one technique that helps to identify similar situations (or "cases").

Evaluation: A lot of additional information comes with each case, providing a decision maker with data, information, and opinions. There are some other techniques that try to support complex decisions by means of simulation, modeling, or formal reasoning. This problem is far more severe than finding a definition for a term. Knowledge management contributions to solving the decision-making problem require sophisticated approaches. They may not work in each and every case, but in some niches, they may provide very powerful support.

1.5 Facilitating Workplace Learning

The above examples refer to different contents of knowledge in software engineering. However, software engineers will also **learn how to learn** in the workplace. This cross-sectional ability can improve the effectiveness of learning new facts, new skill, and so forth. Learning is not usually listed as a key competence of software engineers. Much like other knowledge workers, software engineers are left to their own devices when it comes to learning.

Strengthening this ability of software engineers will indirectly strengthen a whole range of process-related and product-related software aspects. Researchers [62] claim the effectiveness of knowledge work in a workplace environment depends on three related prerequisites: ability, motivation, and opportunity (see Mnemonic 1.5). Software engineers can increase their learning abilities by learning about techniques of knowledge and experience management, for example by reading this book.

They will be able to build up some intrinsic motivation or gain motivation from the benefits of mastering more demanding tasks.

Beyond those individual contributions, learning in a workplace environment is framed and determined by the company or organization. Learning and acquiring new knowledge should be encouraged and supported by necessary external mechanisms. In a way, external motivation should be added to intrinsic motivation. Along the same line, knowledge workers need opportunities to exercise and apply their learning abilities and also their increased knowledge and experience. There is a lot of business administration and management literature on motivation. Many of the discussions in experience and knowledge management will be influenced by considerations of perceived benefit, motivation, and the need for creating opportunities for effective learning in the workplace.

Knowing more about the mechanisms of learning and experience-based improvement can by itself increase motivation. All together, working toward a learning-friendly company culture reinforces the prerequisites for more learning. In the ideal case, the success of learning will enable more learning in the workplace.

In the following chapters, we will look behind the scenes of approaches that were mentioned in the examples.

1.6 Problems for Chapter 1

Problem 1.6.1: Data, information, and knowledge

A customer calls the requirements engineer and tells her about a feature they forgot to put into the specification. Where are data, information, and knowledge in this example?

Problem 1.6.2: Missing the expert

Explain what could happen if a customer cannot reach the requirements engineer but reaches a salesperson instead. Assume the requirements engineer knows the project very well.

Problem 1.6.3: Exact meaning

Your company has a cooperation project with an offshore development organization. You are not sure whether they use the same version of UML as you do. How do you make sure you transfer not just data but also the information implied in your UML 2.0 diagrams? Discuss your attempt using the terminology introduced in Chap. 1.

Problem 1.6.4: Experience in a review

During a review of a design document, the team finds out that there was a misunderstanding among customer representatives: They did not really need a distributed system. As a consequence, most of the design effort invested was wasted. Two of the authors participate in the review; one will be told about it later. What will be the experiences of the authors and reviewers? Describe their observations, their emotions, and possible conclusions they may draw. Emphasize differences between different authors and between authors and reviewers.

Problem 1.6.5: Experience capture form

Sketch a one-page form for capturing experiences when they occur. Explain your design and discuss how you will be able to effectively and efficiently collect what you need for your form and how you will use the collected information later. Did your first sketch cover all relevant information for successful reuse?

Chapter 2
Fundamental Concepts of Knowledge Management

Chapter 1 provided an overview of the basic terms and goals of experience and knowledge management. Tacit, implicit, and explicit knowledge were distinguished. The basic concepts of data, information, and knowledge were introduced and discussed. A layered model for knowledge transfer was built upon those terms. In the end, the benefit of a number of knowledge management interventions in software engineering situations was evaluated. In Chap. 2, we will look a little deeper into the theoretical foundations of knowledge management. This will provide the background for the remaining chapters.

2.1 Objectives of this Chapter

After reading this chapter, you should be able to:

- Explain iterative models of learning.
- Sketch a typical knowledge management life-cycle and point out its challenges.
- Explain the relationships of individual, group, and organizational levels in learning and knowledge sharing.
- Identify software engineering situations where knowledge management can make a contribution and explain how value can be added in those situations.
- Recall the structure and outline of the Software Engineering Body of Knowledge (SWEBOK) [56].

This chapter refers to the overview given in Chap. 1. It details some of the core concepts, such as learning, organizational levels, and adequate application scenarios. Underlying theories of the above-mentioned issues are fundamental to knowledge engineering in general. The SWEBOK catalogue of software engineering knowledge [56] is a foundation for identifying learning topics in software engineering.

Recommended Reading for Chap. 2

- Nonaka, I. and T. Hirotaka, *The Knowledge-Creating Company*. 17 ed. 1995, Oxford: Oxford University Press

K. Schneider, *Experience and Knowledge Management in Software Engineering*,
DOI 10.1007/978-3-540-95880-2_2, © Springer-Verlag Berlin Heidelberg 2009

- Argyris, C. and D. Schön, *Organizational Learning: A Theory of Action Perspective*. 1978, Reading, MA: Addison-Wesley
- Argyris, C. and D. Schön, *Organizational Learning II: Theory, Method and Practice*. 1996, Reading, MA: Addison-Wesley
- Schön, D.A., *The Reflective Practitioner: How Professionals Think in Action*. 1983, New York: Basic Books
- Johnson-Laird, P.N., *Mental Models*. 1983, Cambridge: Cambridge University Press
- Fischer, G., *Turning breakdowns into opportunities for creativity*. Knowledge-Based Systems, 1994. 7(4): pp. 221–232.

2.2 Learning Modes and the Knowledge Life-Cycle

Learning and knowledge are two central concepts of knowledge management. There are a number of very well known and influential theories on learning and knowledge. We will first look at Argyris' and Schön's seminal work on loops in learning [7, 8]. It explains the iterative character of learning, which is also inherent in knowledge management. Schön puts an emphasis on reflection. His work on reflection-in-action [98] has a major impact on practical approaches to learning in a working environment. The work by Nonaka and Takeuchi [77] reacts to Argyris and Schön and to many other sources. It is well known for its view on the tacit-explicit dichotomy in knowledge modes. Implications of those concepts lead to a generic knowledge life-cycle. It can serve as a reference model for more software-specific and tailored variants of knowledge management processes.

Some further related work will be put into perspective:

- We will take a glance at the logical patterns of deduction, induction, and abduction that are the theoretical foundation of reasoning with experience and knowledge.
- Mental models are not only a theoretical concept but also a background and driver of some practical techniques described in later chapters.
- Learning is foremost an individual activity. Organizational learning has several aspects that transcend individual learning, but it will only work with employees who are willing and able to contribute to learning at the workplace.
- A look at Popper's famous philosophical work on theories and their merits will close this section. His argumentation is of general value for everyone working with knowledge, theories, and experiences of unknown credibility.

2.2.1 Loops in Learning: Argyris and Schön

There are numerous theories on learning in general. Everyone studying knowledge management or learning issues needs to know the core of Argyris' and Schön's concepts of single-loop and double-loop learning. In general, they see learning as a cyclic process.

Definition 2.1 (Governing variables)

There are governing variables that determine the goals and constraints of acting in a certain situation.

An "**action strategy**" is derived from those governing variables. It leads to intended or real *activity*. When those actions or activities are carried out, certain "consequences" follow. Learning occurs by comparing consequences of actions with the desired consequences of the *action strategy*, which are dictated by the governing variables. If there is a deviation between planned and perceived consequences, the action strategy will be modified. The intention is to better meet goals and governing variables and, thus, to reduce the deviation of actual from desired consequences.

It is important to note that this loop does not necessarily need to be carried out in reality. Both actions and consequences may also occur in the minds of knowledge workers, or in a simulation model, to name just two alternative options. Therefore, a learner does not need to make all kinds of mistakes: It is sufficient to imagine making them. Real or imagined feedback on the outcome will lead to an improved action strategy. Governing variables stay unchanged and provide the criteria by which "improvement" is being evaluated. Learning is considered a cyclic process of reducing deviations in consequences. Argyris and Schön call this process "single-loop learning," as there is a single feedback loop of (real, simulated, or imagined) consequences back to the actions that caused them (Fig. 2.1).

Fig. 2.1   Single-loop learning

Example 2.1 (Single-loop learning in software engineering)

In software engineering, single-loop learning can occur, for example, when a developer writes a program in a language she is not very familiar with. Whenever there is a compiler error, or when tests uncover unexpected behavior, the developer will modify her programming actions to reach her goal of producing a program for a given set of requirements. Constraints include the syntax and semantics of the language, and the requirements for the program constitute the goals.

Feedback is an essential ingredient of learning according to that theory. There is no improved behavior without feedback on (potential or real) consequences of possible actions.

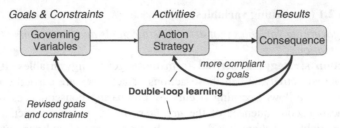

Fig. 2.2 Double-loop learning

Argyris and Schön argue that there is a second mode of learning that transcends single-loop learning. As Fig. 2.2 illustrates, the above loop is maintained but enclosed in a second, outer loop that affects the governing variables. A deviation is again identified by using the governing variables to compare consequences. However, unlike single-loop learning, the outer loop may modify the governing variables: Reflecting on the background and reasons of a deviation may lead to *changing constraints and goals* as well. In single-loop learning, a specific problem is solved by adapting the action strategy. In double-loop learning, a set of governing variables (goals and constraints) is questioned, which may impact many future problems. Knowledge is acquired on that higher level. Both action strategy and governing variables may be adjusted in order to satisfy (adjusted) goals and constraints better.

Example 2.2 (Programmer)

The programmer in the above example conceives a module. If its foreseeable behavior differs from the specified (required) behavior, the programmer either can change the module (single-loop learning) or may challenge the requirements and try to extend the constraints. Maybe there was a misunderstanding? If customers agree to change the requirements, the new requirements may be fulfilled without changing the module. This is an example of double-loop learning. Corrected requirements or improved requirements engineering procedures will help to avoid similar problems in the future.

How can people carry out action strategies without acting? The concept of **mental models** helps to better understand what this means. Johnson-Laird [60] defines mental models: "... humans create working models of the world by making and manipulating analogies in their minds." In their recommendations for double-loop learning, Argyris and Schön refer to mental models. Mental models convey the schemata and frameworks for anticipating the outcome of actions. Therefore, Argyris and Schön use *maps* (their word for mental models) to find common ground with decision makers and knowledge workers.

Just for exercise, we can interpret Fig. 1.8 as such a map: It provides a simplified overview of a complex piece of reality, namely knowledge management. By using that map as *governing variable*, one may develop an *action strategy* for setting up a knowledge management initiative. For example, the map in Fig. 1.8 uses dashed lines to indicate direct communication during experience elicitation. It thus encourages us to consider interviews, meetings, or other forms of direct communication rather than document templates. Single-loop learning within the limits of that mental model might imply asking programmers to call in instead of writing. In double-loop learning, the assumption of the mental model is challenged: Maybe, under certain circumstances, a phone call is less appropriate than a written note. This will change the map and the governing variable it represents, adding a solid line for written experience reports. By taking that possibility seriously, the initiative may *encourage written complaints* as yet another form of urgent, emotionally intense kind of experience. This transcends the initial goal and modifies the mental model we started with. In both cases, the deviation between assumed and real outcome has been reduced. Either the outcome or the assumptions has been adjusted.

Mental models provide guidance for our actions and plans. Maps like Fig. 1.8 can be seeds for mental models. By conveying a lot of information, a single map can guide single-loop learning and become an initial reference for double-loop learning, too.

2.2.2 A Knowledge Management Life-Cycle

We have already encountered a central topic of Nonaka's and Takeuchi's theory of knowledge creation [77] in Chap. 1: the dichotomy of tacit and explicit knowledge. In their theory, they considered the work by Argyris and Schön but extended it to a three-dimensional life cycle of knowledge management.

The first dimension of knowledge creation is the tacit–explicit dimension. In Fig. 2.3, those two modes are shown twice: The matrix describes the four possible **conversions** of the two modes of tacit and explicit knowledge. When tacit knowledge is converted into explicit knowledge, this is called *externalization*, as we saw in

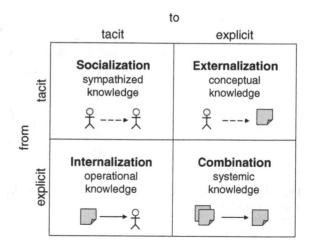

Fig. 2.3 Conversions between tacit and explicit knowledge

Chap. 1. Vice versa, *internalization* stands for converting explicit into implicit and finally maybe tacit knowledge. Simple examples are reading (internalization) and writing (externalization). Usually, internalizing a skill will take more time and more effort than will internalizing a simple procedure. Operational knowledge is typically being internalized: A person reads a recipe and tries to gain cooking knowledge. Often, conceptual knowledge is externalized: From all the tacit knowledge in someone's head, only the concepts (abstractions and simplifications) get documented.

There are two more conversions: We have briefly touched on *socialization* in Chap. 1, indicating the transfer of knowledge from one person directly to another. In socialization, there is no explicit intermediate externalization and internalization as we defined it. However, the consequences of one person acting or speaking (externalization) are observed or heard by the learner (internalization). This is often a very intense but not highly efficient mode of transfer. Making knowledge explicit helps making the transfer of knowledge faster, more reliable, and accessible to a larger group of learners.

Example 2.3 (Combination)

When explicit knowledge is converted into other explicit knowledge, this is called *combination*. For example, a middle manager may combine a company policy with a concrete project budget to instantiate a concrete quality assurance plan for that project. If the contribution of that manager is small compared with the knowledge within those documents, this move is called combination. (Otherwise, we would consider it an invention of "new" knowledge.)

Nonaka and Takeuchi imply an iterative learning process by drawing a spiral in Fig. 2.4. Time progresses along the spiral, and the amount of knowledge learned grows with the diameter of the spiral. It starts with socialization: Someone acquires knowledge by directly observing or talking to someone else. This constitutes a dialogue. After some time, there is a need to write down some of the learned knowledge. By externalizing the key concepts, the documented knowledge will

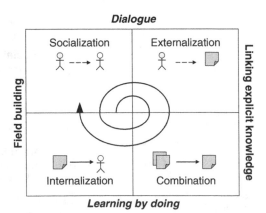

Fig. 2.4 Learning process as a spiral over knowledge conversions

be linked to preexisting explicit knowledge. This is when externalization shifts to combination.

The situation changes again when the knowledge is applied. It turns into operational knowledge, which can be used in actual work. This conversion starts out as learning by applying knowledge in a practical situation (learning by doing). After some experience and exercise, the operational knowledge is internalized better. Gradually, a field of knowledge is built up. The iteration is about to start again. Because of the extended knowledge, the diameter of the spiral grows.

Nonaka and Takeuchi point out several subtle properties of their model:

– They see knowledge as "action, belief, and commitment to an end" [77]. They emphasize the personal relationship over a perspective of knowledge as passive "material." For that reason, knowledge management is not just a matter of logistics but a challenge for learning and creating new knowledge. The opening spiral alludes to creating new knowledge, too.
– Along the same lines, knowledge is created inside an organization and delivered to the outside – not just absorbed and digested outside-in.
– Double-loop learning requires "questioning and rebuilding existing perspectives, interpretation frameworks, or decision premises" [8]. Nonaka and Takeuchi are concerned with managing such a learning process. Who could trigger it, and who could direct it in the sense of managing it? They suggest there needs to be a continuous, ongoing process of learning that includes the rearranging of mental models. Therefore, there is only one spiral that refers to both kinds of learning loops.

The spiral in Fig. 2.4 iterates over the conversion modes. It grows into a knowledge management life-cycle when additional dimensions are added. In Fig. 2.5, not only the tacit/explicit and conversion dimensions are used; this model also refers to the sources and sinks of knowledge. The spiral in the middle of Fig. 2.5 corresponds

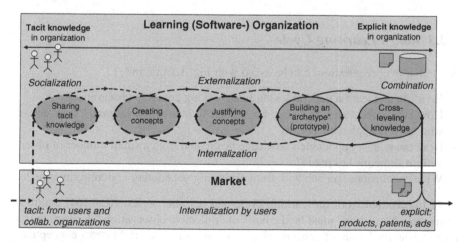

Fig. 2.5 Life cycle of knowledge management according to Nonaka and Takeuchi [77]

with the spiral in Fig. 2.4 when it is stretched along the five stages of maturing knowledge. It is embedded within a larger learning spiral that includes the market. Maturing knowledge is externalized and used in the market as explicit knowledge (patents, products, or services). It is internalized by users. They feed it back as suggestions, complaints, or requirements. Together with supporting knowledge from collaborating organizations, this feedback drives the inner knowledge spiral. Do not confuse the outer spiral with the outer loop of double-loop learning: There are two different user groups intertwined in feedback loops of different speed and granularity. All of them constantly improve both *solutions and mental models*. Dashed lines indicate the flow of tacit and implicit knowledge, and solid lines indicate more explicit knowledge. The small symbols highlight the main media used at both ends of the spectrum. They are people on the tacit end and documents or data stores on the explicit end.

A learning software organization must organize externalization and internalization of knowledge; it also needs to provide opportunities for direct learning via socialization. Life-cycle models like Fig. 2.5 show the conceptual or cognitive phases for sharing knowledge in a company. We are obviously living in a "knowledge society" that depends on learning on all levels. However, Eraut and Hirsh claim:

> Although organisational learning sounds like something the organisation controls, it has become increasingly clear that organisations only truly learn when they give much of that power back to individuals and self-selected groups. [37]

While it is important to keep this warning in mind, we may still look at knowledge logistics and cognitive mechanisms for creating and distributing knowledge. Promoting individuals to responsible drivers of their own learning processes is definitely important for successful learning – and also for organizational learning. In the end, both individual learning commitment and knowledge logistics need to come together.

2.2.3 Kolb's Learning Cycle

A number of core questions can be asked with Fig. 1.8 in mind:

- How can one learn a general lesson from making concrete observations?
- How can conceptual knowledge be applied to a situation at hand? How do we whether it is applicable or not?
- How can widely applicable knowledge be created from a small number of observations someone has made?
- What conclusions can we draw from observing yet another concrete situation?

In his seminal work on learning cycle and learning styles, Kolb [64] claims a "concrete observation" must be the basis of "reflective observation." Reflection is a prerequisite for "abstract conceptualization," as Kolb puts it: Abstract conceptualization is the process of drawing a conclusion from a single or a few observations.

Fig. 2.6 Kolb's learning cycle [64], simplified by Davies [27]

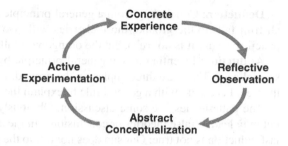

That conclusion will be more general (hence, more "abstract") than the initial observation(s). More abstract and more general conclusions apply to more situations. They can be reused better (Fig. 2.6).

In our terminology, an *experience* includes Kolb's

- "Concrete experience," which corresponds with "observation" in our terms.
- *Results* of "reflective observation" and "abstract conceptualization." The latter results are called *hypothesis* or *conclusion* in our terminology.

Kolb points out that derived conclusions must be used and challenged actively. This will help to validate them – and stimulate making new experiences. Our definition of *experience* includes an emotional aspect. It is missing in Kolb's model. Our definition stresses the difference between an "emotionally neutral" piece of knowledge and an "emotionally loaded" experience. In compliance with Kolb's learning cycle [64], learning from concrete observations and experiences can abstract to conclusions. When such a conclusion is validated and deprived of its emotional aspect, it may gradually turn into knowledge.

2.2.4 Classical Modes of Reasoning

All theories presented above see knowledge from an action-oriented point of view. Creating knowledge and improving knowledge by iterative learning are closer to psychology than to formal logic. A few short remarks should be sufficient to cover the *logical aspects* of learning and reasoning. They are rooted in **epistemology**, the science of learning and understanding.

Definition 2.2 (Reasoning patterns)
From a logical perspective, reasoning in knowledge engineering follows certain patterns: induction, deduction, and abduction. These concepts provide a guiding structure for all abstractions or applications of knowledge.

Induction: Concluding from one or more specific cases to a general principle. Example: An apple falls to the ground. So does a pear. Induction: All fruits fall to the ground. Further induction: All dead material falls to the ground. Yet another induction: Everything falls to the ground.

Deduction: Concluding from a general principle to a specific case. Example: If all fruit falls to the ground, those cherries will also fall. I cannot know about this pencil (because it is no fruit), but the orange will fall.

Abduction: Inventing a new general principle by deriving a hypothesis from a special case. There are three apples on the ground. I hypothesize that they fell from the tree. I come up with a general rule to explain the one case I have seen (Fig. 2.7).

The patterns deserve some discussion. Obviously, induction is very powerful – but may lead to false theories or conclusions. In the above-mentioned examples, the last induction is not true: Our sun does not fall to the ground of the earth. As we will see, however, practical knowledge management cannot succeed without induction: Inducing new principles is a characteristic of double-loop learning.

The difficulties in the examples above were not due to subjective or psychological aspects. They are purely logical. Of course, induction is applicable to physical and social phenomena alike – but it assumes a *logical* perspective on both. Statements about personal taste, such as "I like chocolate, so does my friend," can be combined by induction to derive "everyone likes chocolate." This induction obviously went too far: There are many people who do not like chocolate. Induction is a logical operator, not a consensus-building activity.

Mnemonic 2.1 (Deduction)

Deduction, if applied according to the rules, never yields wrong results. It is rather too cautious.

In our example, pencils are not fruit and are, therefore, not covered by our knowledge of falling fruit. We may not deduce a pencil will fall. The rules only allow deducing cases that are covered by the general principle. Here lies a challenge for deduction in practice: What exactly is covered by the general principle? Do only apples fall – or also pears, and maybe pencils? This question is easy to answer in formal environments but sometimes very difficult in practice.

Whereas induction and deduction go back to Greek philosophers, abduction was mainly promoted in the 19th century by Charles Sanders Peirce, a proponent of semiotics [52]. Semiotics is the discipline of signs, symbols, and their meaning. Pierce argued for a process of understanding that started with abduction (*I have an idea and generalize it to a principle*), deduction (*if the general principle is true, it*

	Induction	Deduction	Abduction
Given		$\forall\, f\, \varepsilon\, Fruit \Rightarrow f$ falls	
Observed	Apple falls, Pear falls	There is an Orange (ε Fruit)	Apples on the ground
Derived	$\forall\, f\, \varepsilon\, Fruit \Rightarrow f$ falls. *may be more general:* $\forall\, f\, \varepsilon\, Object \Rightarrow f$ falls	Orange will fall. *I know nothing about pencils.*	Apples fell from the tree and in general: $\forall\, f\, \varepsilon\, Fruit \Rightarrow f$ falls

Fig. 2.7 Comparison of induction, deduction, and abduction

applies to these specific cases), and induction (*because the principle was valid with those examples, I assume my principle is correct*).

2.2.5 Reflective Practitioners and Breakdowns: Donald Schön

Donald Schön studied the conditions under which practitioners could create knowledge. In particular, his work on "reflection-in-action" is influential for making knowledge engineering work in practice.

In his book *The Reflective Practitioner* [98], Donald Schön investigated how working and creating knowledge interact. He observed working practitioners and noticed that they hardly reflected on what they were doing *while* they were doing it. While they carried out complex and difficult tasks, they were operating "in tacit mode." Being absorbed by their demanding tasks, they invested all their attention into solving their problem. Afterward, they could not explain what they had done either, because they did not remember in sufficient detail.

Schön found:

Mnemonic 2.2 (Reflection in action)
Interrupting knowledge workers in their task helps them to reflect.

Donald Schön called this a "breakdown" that can lead to reflection and – finally – better understanding. Gerhard Fischer [40, 41] has integrated the concept of breakdowns into the construction of critiquing systems: When a practitioner uses a computer system for a design task, certain situations trigger a critiquing message warning the practitioner. For example, a software design may contain too-deep inheritance of Java classes. A design tool may notice that and remind the architect of the respective design recommendation. This constitutes a breakdown, allowing the practitioner to "wake up" and reflect on the tacit knowledge he has just applied or failed to apply. When you need to externalize tacit knowledge, planning for appropriate breakdowns can help.

2.2.6 Popper: When Should We Trust a Theory?

We have seen the theory of single- and double-loop learning by Argyris and Schön. Schön has suggested eliciting tacit knowledge by generating breakdowns. His theory assumes people will be able to reflect better when they are interrupted. Nonaka and Takeuchi have proposed a sophisticated theory of knowledge creation. In the above section on formal reasoning patterns, we saw a sequence of abduction–induction–deduction, which can produce a theory and test it. Theories abound, plus hypotheses from all experiences! It is obviously important to find out when to trust a theory and when not.

Philosopher Sir Karl Popper is famous for his work on theories [85]. He suggests a good theory must be *falsifiable*: It should be easy to demonstrate that it is false – *if* it is false.

Definition 2.3 (Falsifiable theory)

A theory is falsifiable if it allows making predictions. In addition, it must be easy to recognize when a prediction is violated.

Example 2.4 (Falsification)

For example, a tourist may come up with the theory "it never rains in Southern California." One single day of rain will falsify that theory, which makes it a good theory. As long as it never rains, the theory gains in credibility – but it can never be proved. Even after 100 sunny years, there might be rain eventually. According to Popper [85], this is true for all theories: As long as they are not falsified (despite their falsifiability), theories gain in credibility. As soon as there is one counterexample, the theory is obviously false. This reasoning is very close to the abduction–induction–deduction pattern.

Practical knowledge management relies on experiences and induction for improvement. How can we know that resulting "best practices" are actually better than the original ones? Following Popper, hypotheses gained from experiences (or from other sources) should imply predictions. As long as they hold, this is strong support for the hypotheses. If, however, only a single prediction fails, the hypotheses cannot be true in general. It needs to be either refined or refuted.

Mnemonic 2.3 (Pragmatic use of theories)

In practice, however, one will even stick to theories and hypotheses that have been falsified – as long as no better alternative is available.

2.3 Knowledge in People, Teams, and Organizations

Knowledge management exceeds individual learning. Organizational learning was briefly introduced as a term, and the concept was put into context in Chap. 1. In this section, we will see how the theories by Argyris and Schön and by Nonaka and Takeuchi explain organizational learning *beyond individuals*.

Senge [99] adds a perspective rooted in system theory. The organization is seen as a complex system with many interactions and interdependencies. Other researchers have emphasized the importance of learning for competent behavior. Wenger describes "communities of practice," and Simon [102] focuses on decision-making by managers. Those well-known approaches were selected to represent the foundations of using and managing knowledge in an organization.

2.3.1 The Scope Dimension in Knowledge Creation

Nonaka and Takeuchi extend their above-mentioned theory on learning into an organizational setting. The dichotomy of tacit and explicit knowledge is the starting point. It represents the dimension of epistemology in their model (Fig. 2.8). Epistemology is the science of knowledge and belief. Tacit and explicit are two different epistemological modes of knowledge. As we have seen above, learning occurs as an

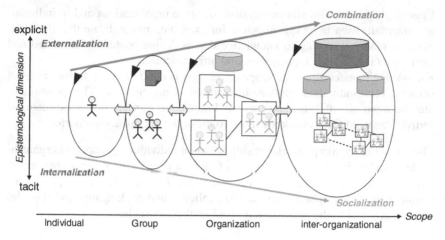

Fig. 2.8 Additional scope dimension of the spiral learning curve with conversions, adapted from Nonaka [77]

iterative process over those modes. The spiral in Fig. 2.4 showed a cycle of conversions between those modes: There is a continuous back and forth between tacit and explicit knowledge.

We will now look at the scope that can be reached through iterative conversions. In a way, the spiral will be stretched over yet another dimension, namely the spectrum of individual versus organizational scope. An individual goes through conversions of tacit and explicit knowledge. By being a member of a team or work group, individual learning feeds into group learning. It cycles through tacit and explicit phases again. A similar iteration occurs on the organizational and even interorganizational levels. There are many intertwined iterations over the epistemological dimension. They can be read from both sides of the scope: Individuals share their knowledge and experience through socialization and combination. At the same time, the cycle of larger units keeps the iterations of smaller units turning.

When looking at Fig. 2.8 from the right-hand side, this scope dimension is invisible. From that perspective, we would only see an oscillation between tacit and explicit knowledge. Fig. 2.5 detailed activities and conversions during this oscillation, thus providing a second dimension. The scope dimension in Fig. 2.8 introduces a third dimension: in Ref. 77 it is called "ontological dimension," but in the context of our current topic, *scope* is a better term.

There are some core messages conveyed by Fig. 2.8:

- The iteration links individuals, groups, and organizations. For example, a sequence of externalizing and then internalizing knowledge is a way to transfer previously tacit knowledge from one person to another, or even to an entire group. Conversions drive the spiral and at the same time allow others to participate and benefit.

- Epistemological modes and conversions occur in organizations and in individuals. Internalization in an organization, for example, may indicate that the organization reacts according to knowledge that is deeply rooted (internalized and tacit) in its individuals, repositories, and infrastructure.
- Knowledge transfer along the scope dimension is not a one-way traffic. Fig. 2.8 shows several individuals and one instance of an organization. The spiral mediates between all of them, and there is knowledge transfer in both directions: Individuals need to receive knowledge to make the organization smarter.

There is a highly complex relationship between individual, group, and organizational knowledge. From a practical point of view, it is most important to remember (1) that it is an iterative process and (2) that it transfers knowledge not just in one direction. Knowledge cycles from tacit to explicit – and back again. And it cycles from the individual to the organization – and back to individuals.

2.3.2 Group Interactions and Shared Maps

Argyris and Schön discuss organizational aspects of learning with respect to their notions of single-loop and double-loop learning modes. For the purpose of knowledge management in software engineering, we will focus on the interrelations between the two learning modes:

As Smith [103] points out, Argyris and Schön consider many organizational learning activities as "Model I" or single-loop learning. However, pure single-loop learning improves behavior only as long as goals and constraints are correct and adjusted to organizational needs. Leaving them unadjusted for a longer time may lead to less advantageous results: Behavior keeps being "optimized" with respect to an outdated measure, which diminishes success.

The inherent **warning** in this argument is as follows: If we support and enforce single-loop learning abilities too much and make it too efficient, its positive outcome will degrade and even turn against the organization. Our goals should not remain static but follow external pressures and demands. Organizations tend to regulate learning (e.g., in knowledge management initiatives) and promote single-loop learning (Fig. 2.9).

Overly efficient single-loop learning may be counterproductive, as the third sketch illustrates: It still hits the old target; but in the meantime, the target has shifted. Double-loop learning helps to adjust goals and targets. It combines elements to better hit a target – and others that help adjusting goals and targets.

Example 2.5 (Adapting or adjusting)

If a software company considers top quality its highest priority, steering projects closer to that goal will be an improvement – for a while. It can be achieved through single-loop learning. But the company needs to notice and to adjust when customers request fast and agile projects more and more often. Sticking to the traditional

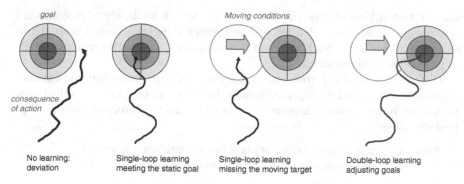

Fig. 2.9 Impact of single- and double-loop learning, with static and moving goals

top-quality goal will prevent people and their projects from learning how to develop in a more agile way.

Mnemonic 2.4 (Adjusting goals)

Outdated goals and "governing variables" prevent learning from adjusting. Shifting goals are more likely to be missed when goals of learning are not adjusted.

Individual software engineers may change their goals and constraints more readily when they are not guided by a company policy ("governing variables"). There is an obvious need for a compromise between guidance toward efficient single-loop learning and opportunity for higher-order double-loop learning.

Productive and nondegrading organizational learning, according to Argyris and Schön, requires double-loop-learning ("Model II"). This setting is characterized by a number of factors – and those need to be promoted by knowledge management, too:

- *People construct maps together.* A map is a mental model that facilitates shared understanding. A map is a schema or model on the "governing variable" level. By revising maps, goals and procedural rules are adapted. When a problem is encountered, there needs to be not only the efficient single-loop option of fixing it but also the double-loop option of rethinking and reframing. Fig. 1.8 can be considered a map in that sense.
- Shared maps constitute shared understanding. Although shared maps will be constantly revised and updated, the process and interaction of constructing a common view is at the core of organizational learning on a double-loop level.
- Not only must a learning organization permit shared construction of maps; there also must be active interventions to encourage group interactions and updating of knowledge repositories. Smith [103] writes:

  For organizational learning to occur, "learning agents," discoveries, inventions, and evaluations must be embedded in organizational memory. [7]

Although Argyris and Schön consider double-loop learning a necessity, they concede it is difficult to reach on an organizational level. Eraut and Hirsh [37] claim that a different kind of expert is needed on the higher levels where problems are increasingly vague and ill-defined, and an expert's experience mainly helps her to *assess* situations better. Such an expert may not even have superior reasoning skills or problem-*solving* capacities.

Different levels of expertise and experience require different learning environments, incentives, and different techniques. Dreyfus and Dreyfus [33] (cited after [37]) identify five levels of learning that can be related to degrees of (double-loop) goal reflection:

1. Rigid adherence to taught rules or plans (as in single-loop learning).
2. Situational perception still limited, but improved awareness for situation.
3. Standardized and routine procedures at reduced cognitive load.
4. Setting of priorities: Perceives deviations from the normal pattern.
5. Intuitive grasp of situations based on deep tacit understanding.

It is an achievement to learn and follow rules, as on level 1. Single-loop learning is an essential ingredient of a learning organization. It leads to more efficient work at the middle levels. Routine procedures and processes have driven software process improvement over more than a decade with maturity models the like Capability Maturity Model (CMM) [83], its Integrated new version CMMI [29], or the SPICE standard with European roots (ISO 15 504). However, at some point and for some tasks, software engineers need to transcend efficient adherence to given plans. Recognizing patterns is more flexible and calls for more experience. As experience grows, it will become more and more tacit. Gifted software engineers can reach a level of understanding they are not able to explain. It is based on numerous observations and cases and patterns they have seen in their career.

A learning organization does not have to focus on the highest levels of learning only. There are numerous software engineering tasks that call for defined procedures that are communicated and taught well within a business unit. Supporting this level is an honorable and demanding endeavor. Of course, knowledge management should encourage software engineers to assess situations more effectively and, thus, choose the appropriate processes more deliberately.

On the highest level of intuitive and tacit understanding, a knowledge management initiative can still provide information access and infrastructure. At the same time, highly experienced employees will often be knowledge providers rather than knowledge receivers. They turn into the knowledge and experience bottleneck in an organization. Knowledge management can offer them a welcome multiplication and dissemination mechanism to spread what they know to more junior colleagues – at a lower personal effort.

2.3.3 Other Related Theories and Approaches

Nonaka and Takeuchi emphasize different aspects than do Argyris and Schön, but the core of their theories are compatible, at least at the level we need to see in this book. However, there are a few other well-known approaches that influence practical experience and knowledge management in software engineering. They provide

additional pieces for the puzzle that underlies knowledge management initiatives
and learning from experience. For that reason, some additional ideas are presented
below. We will meet them again in later chapters.

Senge [99] is one of the pioneers of system thinking in organizational learning.
He was a student of Chris Argyris, and his bestselling book, *The Fifth Discipline*,
shows some common ground with his former teacher. For example, mental models
are considered one of the five disciplines Senge describes. The five disciplines are
considered prerequisites for organizational learning:

1. *Personal mastery*: An organization learns through its members, and those "parts"
   of the organization need to develop knowledge, skills, and mastery.
2. *Mental models*: The way we see the world and how it works. Like the above-
   mentioned maps, mental models are deeply held beliefs, often tacit and sometimes shared.
3. *Shared vision*: An organization can act smarter than each of its parts if it is guided
   by a common goal.
4. *Team learning*: An organization needs to streamline and bundle the activities and
   knowledge of its parts.
5. *System thinking*: An organization is a complex and interrelated system of parts
   and dependencies. More important than optimizing a part is improving the structure of the system.

Senge's main contribution to knowledge management is his strong emphasis
on **system thinking**, the "fifth discipline" in the above list. This distinguishes his
approach from all others discussed in this section. All authors (including Senge)
stress the importance of individual learning for organizational learning. Senge, however, emphasizes the structures of the system, whereas all others underline the social
and process-related aspects of organizational learning.

Argyris and Schön talk about loops in learning. Their above-mentioned theory
on building organizational maps in double-loop learning is obviously dominated
by interaction. Nonaka and Takeuchi depict the process as a (spiral) line. By spi-
raling through epistemological (tacit vs. explicit) modes and different holders of
the knowledge, they describe continuous exchange and interaction. In addition,
they highlight knowledge *creation,* which occurs during that process. Nonaka and
Takeuchi criticize Senge for focusing too much on individual learning. They advo-
cate creation and development of knowledge as another important source of organizational learning. Our Definition 1.1 (organizational learning) includes collective
repositories and a infrastructure as well. The infrastructure includes tools, collaboration opportunities, and processes that guide systematic work in the workplace.

Wenger [119] studied communities of practice as a key part of a learning organization. **Communities of practice (CoPs)** are groups of knowledge workers who
share experiences and knowledge in a common field of practice. A CoP is usually
a self-organizing group of people that cuts across organizational structures. Unlike
a team or organizational unit, members of a CoP do not need to work on the same
project or even in the same team. They are volunteer members of the CoP, motivated
by their own perceived benefit. Mechanisms of sharing experiences and knowledge within a CoP follow the above-mentioned theories. By not being hierarchically

organized, and by reaching into different parts of an organization, a CoP can facilitate organization-wide learning and spreading of knowledge. Some companies have explicitly founded and encouraged communities of practice as a major component of their knowledge management initiatives, such as Siemens [26]. In many other companies, aspects of cross-cutting volunteer groups are used in different variants. Communities of practice emphasize interactions of individuals.

Dodgson summarizes the structural *and* behavioral aspects of learning organizations [32]: "Learning organizations purposefully construct structures and strategies as to enhance and maximize organizational learning." Obviously, both aspects are needed.

2.4 Software Engineering Knowledge

The foundations of knowledge engineering discussed so far are not specific to software engineering. Because this book is about experience and knowledge management in software engineering, this specific knowledge area is sketched below. This helps students to understand the bigger picture of the examples and discussions throughout the book. Practitioners are reminded of some knowledge-related aspects they will probably know from their own experience. In the remainder of this book, the discussion builds on this selection of software engineering knowledge aspects.

2.4.1 Software Engineering from a Knowledge Perspective

We have seen theories about learning and how knowledge transfer works according to selected famous theories. But what kind of knowledge is worth being managed in software engineering? This depends on what we mean by "software engineering." This term is widely used to refer to any activities related to building software. This intuitive characterization is sufficient for many practical purposes. It can be helpful to define the term more precisely to understand better where knowledge is needed within software engineering.

2.4.1.1 Defining Software Engineering

In 1968, the term *software engineering* was coined. It expressed the desire to turn software development into an engineering discipline, just like electrical or mechanical engineering. Engineers obviously follow a systematic and disciplined process to achieve their results. In computer science, many developers saw themselves rather as artists than as engineers. They emphasized the creative aspect of building software, whereas the engineering perspective emphasized predictability of duration and cost, reuse, and quality-oriented behavior. Software engineering encompasses both aspects. There are many activities that require creativity, knowledge, and experience. At the same time, many critical tasks can be carried out with a systematic and disciplined approach, thus harvesting the benefits of engineering wherever possible.

According to IEEE Standard 610.12 – 1990, software engineering and software are well-defined terms:

Definition 2.4 (Software Engineering; SE)

1. *The application of a systematic, disciplined, quantifiable approach to the development, operation, and maintenance of software; that is, the application of engineering to software.*
2. *The study of approaches as in (1).*

This definition includes operation and maintenance along with development of software. The scientific approach to study and improve those aspects is also included under the term "software engineering." Many people associate software with program code. However, it does not cover the entire meaning of the term, according to IEEE Standard 610.12 – 1990:

Definition 2.5 (Software; SW)

Computer programs, procedures, and possibly associated documentation and data pertaining to the operation of a computer system.

Documentation, data, and procedures required to install, configure, and operate a computer program are part of software, too. From a knowledge perspective, a substantial amount of technical and application knowledge is represented in manuals, technical documentation, and configuration parameters. All of those are part of software, and software engineering is concerned with acquiring that knowledge and guiding it into program and associated material. Because software engineering targets a systematic and disciplined approach for development, the required knowledge must not be taken as a given – in many projects, most of the application domain knowledge must be acquired or built during the project. Practitioners know that disciplines such as management, psychology, and all the application domains of the software products affect the development of software. There is much more knowledge to handle in software engineering than one may think at first glance.

It is advantageous to share a common understanding of fundamental knowledge challenges relevant to "typical software engineering tasks." We cannot provide a complete or very detailed enumeration of those tasks and challenges here. Instead, pointing to some examples of knowledge-intensive tasks is supposed to create a common basis for both experienced practitioners and students of software engineering.

Tasks will be briefly introduced. This introduction stresses the mission and purpose of tasks, and it highlights their relationships with each other. In particular, related knowledge is emphasized. This short overview provides motivation for considering this task as a rewarding application area of knowledge management. In the next section, those tasks are summarized within the Software Engineering Body of Knowledge (SWEBOK). SWEBOK presents the essence of knowledge-related software engineering tasks. It can serve as a reference model. All examples in this book are largely self-explanatory. However, most of them refer to situations covered in the following summary. They highlight selected aspects of the bigger picture of software engineering.

2.4.1.2 Core Activities: Requirements, Design, and Software Construction

Software engineering is mostly associated with programming. Writing code in a programming language is a core task. In addition, manuals and technical documentation must be written. According to Definition 2.5, "associated data and documentation" are part of software. Knowing syntax and semantics of a programming language is only a small fraction of the knowledge required in software construction. The ability to transform a given algorithm to a computer program is a skill often acquired during computer science education. An industrial environment requires programmers to adhere to standards and guidelines. Standards come from external sources and regulate the use of techniques that have proven useful. Guidelines and conventions, such as the Sun code conventions (http://java.sun.com/docs/codeconv/), are internal regulations. Coding conventions tell programmers how to comment and format code, how to name variables and identifiers, and how to structure programs in packages, classes, and methods. Developers need to know what relevant standards, guidelines, and conventions are and what they require. More than that, developers need to know how to apply guidelines in their workplace. Some standards must be followed strictly, whereas internal recommendations can be ignored if there are good reasons to do so. Distinguishing good from bad reasons is often tacit knowledge.

Requirements engineering: A piece of code is useful only with respect to a customer or user. If the code does not meet the requirements and expectations of the customer, it is useless. Because there may be different user groups, there will be different sets of requirements and expectations. Knowledgeable developers need to know a lot about all of them. Even well-commented and technically well-structured code cannot compensate for missing or misunderstood requirements. Therefore, requirements analysts need to understand the real requirements before they can be fulfilled. This is an important task and a major effort. It requires knowledge and insight into the application domain; the ability to communicate with domain experts; and technical skills to map requirements to possible solutions. Without the last ability, unrealistic requirements are uncovered too late in the process.

Requirements engineering refers to all activities related to requirements as outlined in Fig. 2.10: elicitation of requirements in interviews, workshops, and workplace observations. Facilitating negotiation between so-called stakeholders is also part of the job. A stakeholder is any person or group that is potentially affected by the software. By this definition, not only users but also managers, administrators, and even workers who may lose their jobs due to the new software must be considered stakeholders. Obviously, a subset of all those stakeholders must be identified and involved in the process. This requires interviews and workshops to be prepared, moderated, and analyzed. Software engineers need to master moderator tasks. There are informal and formal techniques to elicit, visualize, and validate requirements in those situations. When requirements surface, they need to be interpreted (to avoid

Fig. 2.10 Analysis and management activities in requirements engineering

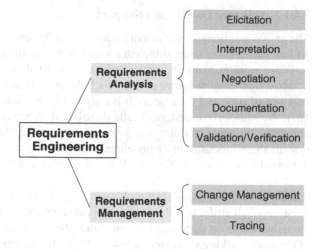

misunderstandings and inconsistent use of terminology) and documented in a specification, set of use cases, or other forms. Of course, final specifications should be checked by the stakeholders to remove errors. During a project, requirements often change and need to be traced into design decisions. Requirements engineering is a subdiscipline of software engineering.

The gap between requirements engineering and software construction is bridged by software design. Rough decisions and structures are defined in the software architecture. This structure is then refined and filled during detailed design. As a result, specified requirements should be met by the constructed software, including associated documents. Functional requirements describe the features and functions of the program, whereas nonfunctional requirements refer to speed, volume of data processed, and other aspects. Architectural considerations need to take nonfunctional requirements into account: A suitable structure, use of frameworks, and distribution of components is often a prerequisite to reaching desired performance, maintainability, and flexibility.

Software engineers need technical **knowledge** in all areas affected by requirements, design, and software construction. In addition, they need experience in order to choose alternatives, prioritize and select stakeholders, and make informed decisions. For many of those decisions, there is no single optimal solution that could be taken from a textbook. Instead, experience and tacit knowledge must guide developers as decision makers. Software engineers make many decisions under uncertainty. Having access to more knowledge sources and experiences can increase confidence in their decisions.

2.4.1.3 Software Quality and Support

The above-mentioned basic activities are obviously not as basic as they first seemed. At first glance, they seem sufficient for developing software. However, high-quality software requires many supportive tasks to be carried out.

Most nontrivial software projects include more than one developer and several versions of code and documents. It is easy to lose track in that situation, in particular, if the workforce is geographically distributed. When contributions are integrated manually, the same modules may be modified by more than one person, leaving the system in an inconsistent or undefined state. Configuration management tools are the usual way of solving this problem. They offer a repository of artifacts, such as code modules of different size, and document chapters. A system is composed of a defined set of artifacts. The tool ensures conflicts will be detected and updated versions of all artifacts will be composed into a product release. Configuration management works in distributed settings and allows different variants of flexibility: "Optimistic locking strategies" allow multiple developers to access the same document d, as in Fig. 2.11. Developers add new documents and commit them. Others check out and may modify documents in parallel. Then, the first developer commits the changed version back to the system. If there are conflicting changes, they are detected when the second author tries to return his work. In that case, he needs to update his working copy, fix inconsistencies, and recommit. "Pessimistic locking" avoids this effect by locking all artifacts when someone checks them out for changing them. As a result, the above-mentioned conflicts cannot occur. At the same time, potential parallelism of work is rather limited.

Global software projects impose additional challenges, resulting from different time zones to cultural differences.

Nonfunctional requirements often refer to quality aspects like performance, maintainability, robustness, and so on. Assuring, maintaining, and managing software quality is yet another demanding (and knowledge-demanding) task within software engineering. Quality engineers or quality agents are a subset of software

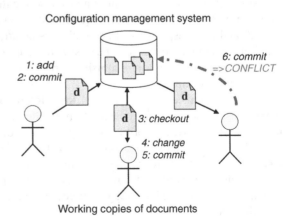

Fig. 2.11 Principle of optimistic locking in configuration management systems

engineers. Their tasks include checking code for errors. However, good quality must start much earlier in the development of software. Almost like a shadow project, software quality must be planned and pursued along the entire duration of the software project. Producing good quality requires formal and informal verification of development results. It should also include validation of requirements: Does the product reflect the customer requirements correctly? Did the requirements change since they were elicited?

Testing is a well-known subtask of quality assurance. In testing, a piece of code is executed with the goal of finding errors [75]. Of course, the final goal is to remove those errors and improve functional correctness and quality of the code. However, testing is almost a discipline in itself. If we want to uncover errors that produce wrong results or reactions, we need to know what the correct results are. Only if a test engineer (yet another software engineer!) prepares for testing, she creates a long list of test cases. A test case consists of the stimulus and the desired reaction or result. If we use many tests, we need many results. Unfortunately, desired results can only come from the customer or the specification. Who else could know what the customer desires? There are only very, very few cases in which desired results can be derived automatically from another formal source. In most cases, creating test cases includes a substantial amount of manual work (Fig. 2.12).

Knowledge helps to reduce effort in testing. There are several strategies to optimize the set of test cases. Ideally, a small set of test cases will find many errors. According to one test strategy, testers use only the specification to create "black-box test cases." Because the specification is considered a valid representation of the customer's desires, covering each requirement in the specification by at least one test case is a good heuristic. In "glass-box testing," testers look *into* the piece of code under test. They see more or less complex structures and data types. In glass-box testing, testers try to stimulate complex parts more frequently. They argue that errors are more likely to occur there. Knowledgeable testers use more sophisticated strategies and tools to determine the "coverage" of their test cases. When both all requirements and all structures in the code are stimulated ("covered") by test cases, testers can be quite confident to do a good job. However, complete testing of all possible executions of a program is infeasible in the general case, so testers have to resort to a strategy that has worked in the past. They know from experience that this strategy finds many defects. Software quality in general is an area that requires experience and a sense of economical pragmatism. For example, it may be desirable to review

ID	Set up	Parameters	Correct result
1	Set to 10:00 a.m.	1:45	11:45 a.m.
2	Set to 11:00 a.m.	2:15	1:15 p.m.
...			

Fig. 2.12 Two example test cases for a method that adds times and durations. Many more test cases are needed in a realistic testing environment

all documents produced. This implies a group of reviewers should read, comment, and discuss their findings. Reviews have been found to be very effective; up to 60% of all errors can be detected [38, 48]. At the same time, reviews are rather slow and take a lot of effort. Finding an adequate compromise requires knowledge of different variants of reviews and inspections with their properties [101]. More than that, quality agents need experience in planning and carrying out reviews effectively in their environment.

Management: Software engineers elicit requirements; they develop architectures and design code. Software engineers take care of software quality; they review documents and test code, among many other activities.

After a successful job as a programmer, a software engineer may be promoted to project leader. Managing projects is an important activity for software engineers – and it depends on knowledge and engineering. A project manager has many tasks. Project planning is the responsibility of a project manager. Planning depends on a good understanding of the required deliverables and a realistic estimation of effort and time to complete those deliverables. A knowledgeable project leader does not just "guess" effort and time. There are techniques to come up with sound estimations. They assume the project leader can assess and classify the project. Despite the formulas and techniques, most software estimations contain a good part of gut feeling and experience. Project managers provide work-breakdown structures, provide PERT charts, and milestone plans [53]. They control progress and consider error and quality measurements. And they present their projects to higher management and the customer. Of course, software engineers acting as project managers are also responsible for their fellow software engineers working in the project.

Software engineering is supposed to adopt a systematic and disciplined way of building software. In such an approach, successes should be repeatable. A learning organization will try to eliminate errors in their activities and improve their processes by building on proven practices. A process *prescribes* sequences and alternatives of activities to be carried out. Many processes also define roles and responsibilities. Deliverables are specified with respect to their roles in a process. Project managers have to instantiate and follow a project. On the one hand, a defined process will help the project manager and all participants to comply with good practices. On the other hand, an overly demanding process can put the project at risk. There are many examples of projects that made wrong decisions: Some neglect the process and deviated from plans and deliverables. They may finish in time but compromise quality and process conformance. Others strictly follow the process but are not able to complete the project in time. A project manager needs substantial experience and background to make a responsible decision for a good compromise. Processes incorporate past knowledge, but because technology and project pressures change constantly, there must be constant adaptation and tailoring.

Software projects involve risks. An interesting project cannot be sure to achieve all of its goals. Many things can go wrong: The customer may change her mind, making a lot of work obsolete. Developers may leave the company, removing essential knowledge from the team, which can delay progress. Or a subcontractor may not deliver in time, which can affect the project's own schedule. A risk is defined as a potential problem that may occur but is not certain to occur. If it will certainly occur, we just call it a "problem," not a risk. A professional software process supports managers by risk management. **Risk management** is a technique for systematic handling of risks. Using checklists and iterative risk management procedures, risk managers identify risks through interaction with project participants. A risk is classified according to its probability and the potential damage it causes. The team will then develop mitigation plans for each of the top risks. Members of the team or the project leader are assigned mitigation tasks. In the above-mentioned example, a customer changed her mind about a requirement. A possible mitigation would be a contract that defines a price for each change request. A different mitigation can be an iterative process, which repeats requirements and construction in order to identify and fulfill changing requirements (Fig. 2.13).

Knowledge of many kinds is needed to lead a software project well. Of course, a project leader needs to know as much as possible about the problem to solve. A good estimation requires a realistic evaluation of environmental parameters. A good estimation is the prerequisite of a realistic project plan. All information available about the customer and his goals should be taken into account to reduce uncertainty and risk. Risk checklists from previous projects can provide a good start. Warnings and recommendations from the experience of other projects is an invaluable source for good decisions and compromises.

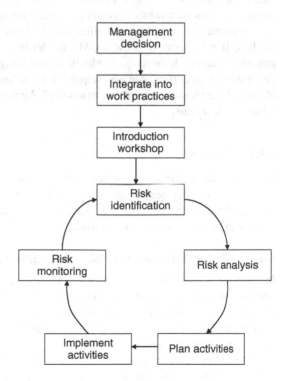

Fig. 2.13 Typical risk management process with set-up activities and iterative part

2.4.1.4 Domain Knowledge and Other Knowledge Areas

Software supports customers in carrying out their tasks. If you want to build good software, you need to know the customers and their tasks. For example, embedded software will run within a system or device constructed by electrical engineers. When requirements analysts talk to electrical engineers, they will face a specific attitude and language. When they talk to medical doctors about that same device, their perspectives and terminology will be very different.

Knowing the application domain with its traditions, terminology, and particularities is essential for success. Some domains, like safety-critical systems, have their own standards and rules. They are common to everyone working in the domain. Software engineers changing their working domain run the risk of not knowing some of the relevant standards. Ignoring them is a major risk, as it will lead to unusable software.

There are many other areas in software engineering with a huge number of additional knowledge areas. Agile methods, for example, offer a new approach to fast and flexible software projects [15, 16]. They apply incremental and iterative processes that involve the customer on a regular basis. Agile methods sound good in textbooks, but they require a lot of discipline and experience. Boehm and Turner [21], for example, claim that only those software engineers should work on agile projects who have proved their ability to work successfully in a traditional project.

Generating code is another technology that attracts a lot of attention [72]. The idea is old, but there are new contributions every now and then. In principle, code generation tries to produce more code faster than any programmer can write. The goal is to multiply development efficiency. Code is generated from macros or from models. If it is easier to draw a UML model than to write the code it represents, generating this code from the model is an appealing idea. However, using the code generators in an appropriate way requires a lot of knowledge. Should a certain piece of code be generated or written manually? Again, experience is needed to make informed decisions.

2.4.1.5 Summary

Obviously, basic textbook knowledge is rarely the problem in software engineering. Developers, quality personnel, and project leaders need good qualifications and a lot of technical expertise. In particular, decisions under uncertainty on several levels call for experience and specific knowledge.

Mnemonic 2.5 (Informed decisions under uncertainty)

In software engineering, experience and knowledge is needed to make compromises and decisions under uncertainty. There is no way of knowing the optimal decision. Context specifics and experiences must be taken into account.

The research of Orasanu and Connolly [81] into decision-making in practice showed that real-life settings include many of the following characteristics that are also typical of software engineering work. The following list applies their findings to the above-mentioned situation in software projects:

- Problems are ill-structured: It is difficult to see all relationships and dependencies of requirements, constraints, and stakeholders.
- Information is incomplete, ambiguous, or changing: Requirements change in all major software projects. Requirements tend to change because many stakeholders did not have sufficient expertise, imagination, or simply time to produce a concise and consistent set of requirements. Change is a symptom of growing understanding, which is one reason why agile software methods "embrace change" [15].
- Many participants contribute to the decisions, and goals are shifting, ill-defined, or competing: Stakeholders of a complex software project may include users, managers, and those workers who will lose their jobs when the software is installed. Usability goals compete with cost constraints and vague goals of saving jobs.
- Typically, time constraints exist and stakes are high, which makes decisions difficult and urgent at the same time. Limited information and knowledge access delimits well-informed decision making.
- The decision maker must balance personal choice with organizational norms and goals [81]. Software quality standards may be high – according to the company process model. An experienced quality engineer may know where corners can be cut e.g., in the case of a budget cut. Such a situation is often not explained in process manuals.

This short section on software engineering tasks and challenges has outlined the wide range of knowledge and experience needed in practice. It evades all phases and activities of a software project, and it ranges from simple factual information (on context, domain, requirement constraints, etc.) to delicate experiences and tacit assessment capabilities for decision making.

2.4.2 The Software Engineering Body of Knowledge

As the previous section shows, the range of knowledge in software engineering is huge. There is no exhaustive list of knowledge areas or knowledge transfer mechanisms. However, there is a reference classification of software engineering knowledge, the Software Engineering Body of Knowledge (SWEBOK) [56]. **SWEBOK** in itself can be regarded as a knowledge transfer mechanism: Every practitioner and software engineering scientist may have certain requirements in mind: What does a qualified software engineer need to know? SWEBOK is more than an intersection and less than a union of all those expectations. For our purpose of experience and knowledge management in software engineering, SWEBOK can serve different purposes:

- *Classification*: As we will see in Chap. 3, a stable, agreed-upon classification of terms is important for managing knowledge. Because of its broad approach, SWEBOK offers a category for most pieces of knowledge one can imagine in software engineering.

- *Checklist for personal development*: An individual software engineer may use SWEBOK as a reference to identify weak spots in his or her competencies. Individual learning can aim at closing any gaps. However, it is overly ambitious to aim for full coverage: Without practical project experience, many lessons can be learned only superficially. When working in a company, however, there is no need for a wish list like SWEBOK to identify room for improvement. Several deficits will become apparent in daily work. But there will be little time and opportunity to study what is missing.
- *Matching problems with existing knowledge*: This leads to the home ground of knowledge management: What can we do in a concrete, specific situation to act competently, although some knowledge is missing? SWEBOK can be used as a classification and index. When someone has a problem or demand, a common vocabulary will help to make the match with experiences and knowledge available in the organization.

Definition 1.4 (knowledge management) refers to the purpose of "solving a problem" as opposed to "completing computer science education." In general, knowledge management should be directed by actual or foreseeable demands, not personal interests in fictitious applications. Learning on demand is preferential in a company setting. This is where knowledge management takes place.

When we now look at SWEBOK, we do that with the above-mentioned considerations in mind: We are not trying to describe the perfect software engineer, but we see whether SWEBOK can help in classifying and indexing pieces of knowledge. At the same time, we treat SWEBOK as an attempt to structure a complex field of knowledge. This is a good exercise for Chap. 3, where structuring domain vocabulary is the focus.

Fig. 2.14 shows the outline of SWEBOK [56]. There are 10 main knowledge areas defined in SWEBOK. They are depicted as horizontal bars with attached subtopics. Each bar shows the knowledge area according to SWEBOK on the right. Related areas are labeled in SWEBOK as an additional knowledge area number 11. SWEBOK is represented by a rectangle that covers most of these knowledge area bars.

There is one more box in Fig. 2.14: it represents the growing number of related aspects and knowledge areas. They are considered outside software engineering (hence outside the SWEBOK rectangle) but are highly relevant for a knowledge management initiative in software engineering. Knowledge areas are grouped in Fig. 2.14 for the sake of this overview. Those groups called "core activities," "quality and support," and "management" were introduced in the previous section. They show where those discussions feed into SWEBOK.

There are recurring patterns of subtopics in the knowledge areas: Concepts or Basic Concepts introduce the knowledge area and its terminology. There are Key Issues to detail certain aspects. In some fields, there is an established set of activities, such as in Software Requirements: the labels are almost identical to the ones used in Fig. 2.10 and in many other sources on requirements engineering. Other labels reflect the challenge of finding useful abstractions, for example "Techniques

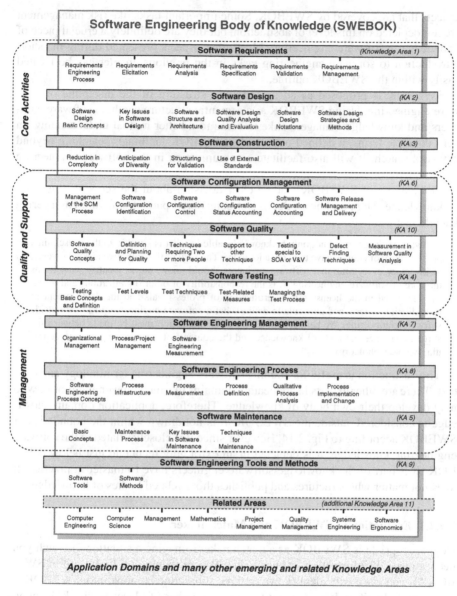

Fig. 2.14 SWEBOK structure as a classification scheme for matchmaking [56]

requiring two or more people" within Software Quality. It is difficult to summarize and classify all the knowledge relevant for an emerging and quickly growing field like software engineering. Not all new trends can be covered by SWEBOK, but a big portion of the core of software engineering is captured and organized. Fig. 2.14 could be further detailed to show the concrete types of tools, methods, and test aspects that are covered by SWEBOK. Some important tasks like risk management are not depicted on this level of abstraction, but they are definitely a crucial piece of knowledge in software engineering. Most other aspects presented during the short introduction to software engineering tasks in the previous chapter can be located easily within the SWEBOK outline.

SWEBOK is proposed as an agreed-upon structure of the discipline of software engineering. Using SWEBOK as a semantic structure can help software engineers and knowledge managers alike to come to a better mutual understanding. In very concrete terms, a defined outline like SWEBOK facilitates searching beyond keyword search. It will also facilitate communication in the software engineering community.

The authors of SWEBOK made a clear decision about the scope of this body of knowledge. Domain knowledge is not considered part of software engineering knowledge:

> Software engineers must not only be knowledgeable in what is specific to their discipline, but they also, of course, have to know a lot more. The goal of this initiative is not, however, to inventory everything that software engineers should know, but to identify what forms the core of software engineering. It is the responsibility of other organizations and initiatives involved in the licensing and certification of professionals and the development of accreditation criteria and curricula to define what a software engineer must know outside software engineering. We believe that a very clear distinction must be made between the software engineering body of knowledge and the contents of software engineering curricula. (www.swebok.org)

This distinction is useful for framing software engineering terminology and context. There are other experts in application domains like medicine or automotive who may develop their own body of knowledge. Therefore, application domain knowledge is considered outside the SWEBOK. It is not drawn within the boundaries of SWEBOK according to Fig. 2.14. However since it is closely related to the software engineering knowledge, it is depicted in an extra gray rectangle just below SWEBOK. It is part of the knowledge software engineers have to master in practice. It does not matter who structures and publishes those related bodies of knowledge.

2.4.2.1 Evaluation of SWEBOK as a Matchmaker

How appropriate is SWEBOK as a matchmaker? Imagine a situation in which you need a piece of information or knowledge: Where would you look it up in SWEBOK? If you can easily identify two or three subsections to look into, SWEBOK is a powerful classifier. It guides you to a small number of places to check. If, however, no label really fits or if too many categories might be relevant, SWEBOK is less adequate.

But even if you are sure where to look: Will relevant material really be there?

From the knowledge authors' point of view, the situation looks different: Without knowing future demands and problems that could possibly be addressed by a piece of knowledge they want to store, authors are asked to categorize it. This is more difficult than one might think. Any real problem or solution will touch on more than one category. Should an experience be classified by problem area, or by solution, or by some blend of both? How should we consider context? It is often a hard piece of work to imagine what future users might want to know. *Engineering* knowledge and experiences is concerned with that question, among others. Engineering includes structuring, indexing, and comparing with other knowledge. Chapter 3 is devoted to engineering knowledge for reuse.

SWEBOK refers mainly to "hard software knowledge": technical skills, not soft skills. Many problems in software projects go back to personal conflicts, misunderstandings, and poor social skills. When we look at software engineering knowledge from that angle, we definitely need to add corresponding categories of knowledge.

The discussion about SWEBOK as a matchmaker shows:

- It is not easy to develop a good classification scheme for experiences and knowledge. An index looks different from the authors' and the users' points of view. Effective matching requires engineering of knowledge.
- Matching keywords will rarely do: Each piece or demand might need several keywords or categories to describe it.
- SWEBOK has many merits that we did not even mention here. We are only interested in knowledge management for the software engineering area. Other goals and contributions have been omitted.

For the remainder of this book, we treat SWEBOK as a good overview of knowledge areas within software engineering. We are aware that it is not the one and only possible classification scheme for software engineering. As we will see later, part of a classification should grow out of the problems and applications – not be imposed top-down. In essence, there is no static borderline around software engineering knowledge relevant for knowledge management.

2.5 Appropriate Knowledge Management for Software Engineering

Before Chap. 3 starts the discussion of techniques, we should mention the diversity in knowledge management research. There is not just one orientation but a whole variety of research directions.

In a workshop on learning software organizations and requirements engineering (LSO+RE 2006), the editorial discusses what makes software engineering special as a domain for knowledge management [20].

Software process improvement intersects with learning organizations. Both fields aim at improving efficiency; both fields apply iterative approaches to feedback and learning. The concept of "Experience Factory" [11] is the first well-known systematic approach to organizational learning in the software engineering field [11, 31]. It will be discussed in detail in Chap. 4.

What sets a learning *software* organization apart from other learning organizations? Software development is a very knowledge-intensive form of work. Software organizations are also more mature in the usage of information technology. In fact, the input and outcome of software engineering is information. As a consequence, we might expect software organizations to make better use of available tools.

Table 2.1 Schools of knowledge management, according to Earl [35]

School		Attribute: Focus	Aim	Unit	Philosophy
Technocratic	Systems	Technology	Knowledge bases	Domain	Codification
	Cartographic	Maps	Knowledge directories	Enterprise	Connectivity
	Engineering	Processes	Knowledge flows	Activity	Capability
Economic	Commercial	Income	Knowledge assets	Know-how	Commercialization
Behavioral	Organizations	Networks	Knowledge pooling	Communities	Collaboration
	Spatial	Space	Knowledge exchange	Place	Connectivity
	Strategic	Mindset	Knowledge capabilities	Business	Consciousness

Earl [35] has developed a framework to categorize studies on knowledge management according to different research directions, which he calls "schools," as shown in Table 2.1. The "technocratic" approach to knowledge management focuses on systems, cartography (maps), and engineering of knowledge, whereas the "economic" school looks at the commercial value of knowledge. "Behavioral" approaches focus on organizational, spatial, and strategic aspects of knowledge management.

As Table 2.1 shows, each direction focuses on different aspects that are rooted in a specific philosophy and attitude toward knowledge management. There is a typical aim and associated focus and a certain kind of unit that will often pursue the respective kind of knowledge management aspect.

Example 2.6 (Systems school)

For example, a philosophy of codification ("knowledge needs to be coded explicitly") may aim at building knowledge bases. For those repositories, technology is an obvious focus. Often, an entire domain of knowledge is addressed. For example, building a knowledge base for estimating software project duration and cost may be pursued by setting up a data exchange system for the estimation community. CeBASE is a software engineering initiative for developing experience bases in a community [76].

Example 2.7 (Organizational school)

Someone convinced of the power of collaboration (as a philosophy) may aim at pooling knowledge, including tacit knowledge. For a community, building a network may be the focus. For example, a department head may decide to institutionalize the exchange of software quality experts (a community) by inviting them to regular meetings. Networking can also be supported by yellow pages or other systems, but such a technocratic approach would rather point to a cartographic view. Usually, an initiative reflects a certain mixture of different influences.

We will use Table 2.1 as another map for orientation. Real companies will need to exploit several knowledge management aspects together. In the following chapters, techniques can be mapped to aspects to find similarities. Maps or mental models

Fig. 2.15 Philosophy and kind of unit point to appropriate support for matchmaking

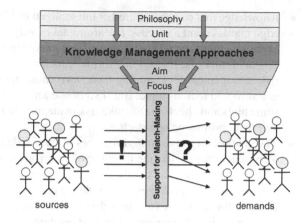

help people (and organizations!) to develop shared understanding. As a reference for problems, existing experiences, and ongoing research, they can be catalysts. Whereas SWEBOK was a rather linear reference for software engineering knowledge, the schema provided by Earl's table provides categories for knowledge management approaches. As Fig. 2.15 illustrates, knowledge management approaches can be characterized by the philosophy they represent and by their respective unit. Those search criteria lead to an approach, which implies an aim and a focus to pursue. The selection will be an approach that complies with the philosophy and kind of unit. All selected approaches support making the match between those in demand of knowledge and those people who have that kind of knowledge – tacitly or explicitly.

There are some general lessons learned associated with picking knowledge management approaches. They can be used as general guidelines for designing appropriate knowledge management initiatives:

- Managing knowledge is more successful if there is already something to manage. Starting without sources and without existing knowledge is difficult. Imagine you need some information on a software tool. If software engineers find an empty knowledge base, and no links to experts, this would not help a lot. Therefore, knowledge management in software engineering must provide an initial content for a base before it is delivered to its users. This is called a "seed."
- Capturing knowledge without concrete demands is difficult, too. The purpose of knowledge management is not to store and encode knowledge, but to deliver it to those who need it. Knowledge acquisition needs to be aware of what is needed. Imagine someone who has been working with a tool for a while. How should this person know whether it is worth the time to put something into the knowledge base about that tool? And what kind of information would be most appropriate?
- There is good potential for reuse if many knowledge workers need the same kind of knowledge frequently. Imagine the company using a software tool only for certain tasks (e.g., risk management). Risk management should be carried out by each project, but only as a background activity. As a consequence, knowledge about the tool is needed on a regular basis, but not frequently enough for everyone to know it by heart.

- Knowledge that can be acquired or internalized fast is more likely to make knowledge management a success. If learning takes very long or requires a teacher and exercises, that type of knowledge is less adequate for knowledge management. It should rather be learned in a formal education program. In the example of the risk management tool, gaining basic awareness about risks in software projects is a slow and tedious topic. But if someone knows those basics already and finds some hints and checklists to make risk management more effective, this is a faster and more promising approach.
- The **granularity** of meaningful pieces of knowledge should be small to medium. Very small chunks, like the meaning of an acronym, can be handled with nonspecific search engines and hardly justify expensive knowledge initiatives. However, very voluminous packages of knowledge take too much time and are difficult to evaluate for relevancy (see item above). Medium granularity provides substantial support but is still economical to read, evaluate, and internalize when needed.
- **Tacit knowledge** is important and must not be excluded. Restricting an initiative to explicit knowledge cuts out the source of most interesting experiences and may restrict it to single-loop learning [7, 8].
- However, relying on tacit knowledge alone is often too time-consuming and takes too much effort. Knowledge management techniques can unfold their capabilities best when there is also a reasonable portion of explicit knowledge to spread.

Ideally, knowledge workers already know a lot about the software engineering domain they are working in. Knowledge management can build on this prior knowledge and enable knowledge workers to exchange details, facts, new rules, and hints. New knowledge combines with existing knowledge, as Definition 1.7 (knowledge) implies. Tacit and explicit sources and mechanisms for making matches can be exploited. In short, knowledge management is most promising in software engineering when all parts of Fig. 1.8 are activated.

For example, software engineers in an automotive company know how to build brake system software. They benefit from a knowledge management approach that does not need to convey all their basic knowledge but supports them with details of brake hardware, new safety regulations, and experiences from their fellow software engineers. It should also support them in feeding back what they have learned individually. There are both experience exchange opportunities and mechanisms for capturing and externalizing tacit knowledge. Newly created knowledge will be engineered and matched to future demands. An appropriate approach can be ambitious. It should be neither oversized nor too modest. Appropriate approaches meet the above-mentioned success criteria.

Example 2.8 (Supporting managers)

Supporting software managers is a promising field within software engineering. Managers need data and information to plan a project. They need progress information to control it. And they need support from simulations (based on "explicit mental simulation models") and experiences for predicting and estimating project parameters. There are many chunks of medium-sized information. Several pieces of knowledge will be communicated from person to person because no one writes down all his gut feelings. Managers will still make their decisions by themselves: Simon [102] showed that managers do not act fully rationally; the bounded rationality they apply is informed by adequate knowledge management, but there is no need to oversize heuristic support. The decision *will and should* be made by the managers, not by a resolution mechanism.

2.6   Types of Tools Supporting Knowledge Management

Earl's classification of knowledge management schools illustrates the broad variety of approaches, goals, and mechanisms for supporting knowledge management. Some are tightly associated with a certain kind of tool like knowledge directories or bases. Some specific tools will be mentioned in the respective chapters below (e.g., for ontologies and mind maps).

Many aspects of knowledge management may be carried out manually, but a larger number of knowledge workers usually require tools, too. For that reason, tools are fundamental parts of knowledge management. Even without going into detail about any particular tool, there are two types of tools that are associated with their respective type of knowledge management approach.

Our map of knowledge management (Fig. 1.8, repeated below as Fig. 2.16) shows many tasks in perspective, starting with the identification of appropriate sources of

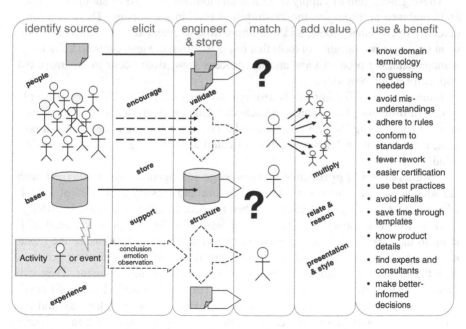

Fig. 2.16 Map (repeat of Fig. 1.8) to show product- and process-centered aspects

knowledge. Eliciting tacit and explicit knowledge leads to structuring, engineering, and storing knowledge. To add value, a match must be made between available material (sources) and knowledge workers who need this material.

If a single tool had to support all those aspects, it would need to be highly specific and very versatile. Because all companies are different, tailoring would be important. That makes a tool very expensive. In practice, relying on existing components will be less expensive *and* more powerful. If a new tool is introduced, learning cost often exceeds tool license fees. In addition, the psychological barrier can be a problem. Knowledge workers must have good reasons to adopt yet another tool. They will not do it when they *perceive or believe* the new tool only replicates functionality of well-known tools they already know. Therefore, providing adequate information on new benefits must be part of the introduction.

Example 2.9 (Supporting communication)

Imagine communication about knowledge: Would you rather use your familiar e-mail tool, or would you prefer to learn using a dedicated tool with similar features? How would you like checking for messages in two tools? Since knowledge management is itself a discipline *supporting* software engineering, it should not erect unnecessary hurdles for mastering new tools. Instead, a knowledge management initiative should identify and bundle existing tools and relevant features and help to use them for exploiting knowledge resources better. Specific tools will mostly be limited to highly specific tasks (e.g., for automated reasoning).

These general remarks apply to almost all environments: Tools should be picked and combined according to the existing tool base in a company. There is a huge diversity of customary tools, and it is impossible to even list them all. Instead, we want to look at two families of tools that relate to different viewpoints on knowledge management: the product view and the process view. Both occur in our map, but both call for different tools.

Mentzas et al. [73] compare the two approaches nicely. The difference is deeply routed in different philosophies and schools: One of them views knowledge as a product (or a "thing" to be moved around). The other considers knowledge a process; as in Definition 1.7, knowledge is treated as something residing in people's minds.

Product-centric approaches to knowledge management are concerned with knowledge logistics: how to package and store and classify a "piece" of knowledge in order to find and "deliver" it when needed. In this world view, knowledge workers live in a supermarket of more or less "tasty" servings of knowledge. It is up to the supermarket management to organize the offers and ensure the freshness of the products. Knowledge workers are responsible for selecting products with the support of the structures and pointers created by management. They will swallow and digest those pieces at their own pace. When new chunks of knowledge come in from "somewhere," they are checked, repackaged, labeled, and put on the shelves. Artificial intelligence has pursued a similar approach in computer science. Approaches from that direction are often technocratic (cf. Earl [35]) and product-centric. Powerful mechanisms are available in this field. Search and information retrieval tools help to match demands and offers. Using metadata helps to go far beyond keyword search. Pieces of knowledge are stored in expert systems and knowledge-based systems. Reasoning mechanisms use ontologies and Semantic Web technology for automated classification, comparison, and mining of information relevant to a task at hand [73]. Selected approaches are explained in more detail in Chap. 3.

Process-centric approaches to knowledge management are centered on the learning of individuals and teams. Because knowledge resides in people, networking is a social, psychological, and cognitive necessity. Empowering people to carry out learning loops and reflection is the focus. In this world view, knowledge workers live in a community of chefs in a gourmet restaurant. Ingredients for their great meals need to be fresh, and that is a concern. However, much more important is the tacit experience that their colleagues have acquired when working in various great restaurants before.

Example 2.10 (Socialization)

Kitchen apprentices watch the master chefs and copy what they see: Socialization is taken very seriously. New knowledge about recipes and refinements is created by bringing experts together in an empowering environment. Knowledge consumers out in the restaurant enjoy the sophisticated solution and benefit, too. A gourmet restaurant does not scale up to feed as many people as a supermarket.

Yellow pages help to establish and maintain networks. Technologies for exchanging information in a group, such as groupware, and computer-supported cooperative work will support group learning: They facilitate remote or multimodal meetings. People modify the same document while they talk or chat over the Internet.

Obviously, a product-centric view alone will miss a large portion of knowledge creation and engineering potential. On the other hand, a purely process-centric approach might not be sufficient to feed a large company. It will usually be a wise decision to go for a balance between both views. There is no principal competition between those world views – but proponents typically come from different research and work backgrounds. This might lead to a (tacit) controversy. You should rather pick the best of both worlds: Why not have great knowledge masters refine knowledge and disseminate it with product-centric logistics and formalisms?

2.7 Problems for Chapter 2

Problem 2.7.1: Single- and double-loop learning

What is the difference between single-loop and double-loop learning? Explain both modes and give a short example from software engineering for each of the two.

Problem 2.7.2: Framework XY learning scenario

A software company has used a certain framework XY for building business applications. Problems using that framework are reported to a hotline. The hotline releases a new version of its newsletter "XY Procedures." New projects are supposed to follow those procedures. This is supposed to spread learning through all projects. What kind of learning is this? How could this type of learning turn out to be counterproductive? Refer to the XY example. What concrete activities could help to prevent that negative effect?

Problem 2.7.3: Formal reasoning patterns

You are working as a test engineer. Over the years, you have noticed that many tests fail due to the incomplete initialization of variables. Describe the three formal reasoning patterns (abduction, deduction, induction) and label the following statements with the corresponding reasoning pattern name:

- *"...there are often errors in initialization."*
- *"Initialization looks so trivial, so many people are not very careful about it."*
- *"Programmers make more and more mistakes."*
- *"Setting a counter to 0 or 1 is often forgotten."*
- *"Flawed initialization is easy to find by testing; that is why we find so much, because we test more systematically."*
- *"Programs have errors."*

Problem 2.7.4: Schools and approaches of knowledge management

A company wants to encourage the exchange of knowledge among its software engineers. For each of the following suggestions, identify the respective school according to Earl and approach (product- or process-centric) it belongs to:

- *"We develop a knowledge database and send an e-mail to all software engineers asking them to enter their knowledge."*
- *"Let's put an info terminal in the main lobby; every time you enter the building, you will see a new 'knowledge item of the day.'"*
- *"We could use a Wiki Web to record everything we think others might need."*
- *"Okay, but there needs to be a moderator; plus, we should have monthly meetings of the Wiki User Group."*
- *"Let's put up a coffee machine and two sofas."*
- *"There are powerful networks now, so we can even send movies. Everybody gets a camera on their desk, and when they want or have something interesting, they record a movie."*
- *"Great idea! We hire a person who can index all incoming movies according to their SWEBOK category, and a few other attributes. We build a resolution machine that helps to match new entries with stored ones."*

Problem 2.7.5: Knowledge management life-cycle

Draw Nonaka and Takeuchi's knowledge management life-cycle. Explain it by applying the concepts to the example of a group of software project leaders who meet in a community of practice (CoP) to learn about cost estimation.

Chapter 3
Structuring Knowledge for Reuse

3.1 Objectives of this Chapter

After reading this chapter, you should be able to:

- Explain why structuring and engineering knowledge is important for reuse.
- Read and draw mind maps for vague information.
- Define what a glossary is, give examples for using it in software engineering, and explain how it structures knowledge.
- Explain the relationship between glossaries and domain models.
- Name and briefly describe well-known informal and semiformal approaches in the area of structuring knowledge for reuse.
- Formulate knowledge as patterns and explain why patterns are important for representing knowledge.

Many informal and semiformal structuring techniques address elicitation of knowledge and the process of making it reusable. They are concerned with the human and cognitive abilities of humans.

Recommended Reading for Chap. 3

- Cockburn, A., *Writing Effective Use Cases*. 14th printing. 2005, Reading, MA: Addison-Wesley
- Gamma, E., et al., *Design Patterns – Elements of Reusable Object-Oriented Software*. 1995, Reading, MA: Addison-Wesley
- Larman, C., *Applying UML and Patterns: An Introduction to Object-Oriented Analysis and Design and the Unified Process*. 2nd ed. 2002, Upper Saddle River, NJ: Prentice Hall

K. Schneider, *Experience and Knowledge Management in Software Engineering*,
DOI 10.1007/978-3-540-95880-2_3, © Springer-Verlag Berlin Heidelberg 2009

3.2 The Vision of a Shared Language

The map in Fig. 1.8 showed various interfaces between sources of knowledge and those in demand of knowledge for carrying out a certain task. Creating and transferring knowledge is at the core of knowledge engineering. For explicit knowledge, certain tasks are crucial:

- Logistics of knowledge: how to transfer and route knowledge through a network of people, computers, and repositories. This is mainly a technical task.
- Encoding existing knowledge and experience in a form suitable for storing, transferring, and engineering.
- Engineering knowledge, which means to compare, evaluate, and combine it. Knowledge also needs rephrasing, restructuring, and representing in a way appropriate for *users*.

Note the emphasis on structuring and presenting knowledge for the user! Structure and representation of knowledge do not need to be optimized for the author, but for the intended readers. This claim holds not only on technical levels but also for content and representation. Matching existing material to new demands is a difficult task. To be successful, one must establish a connection on all three levels: technical, contents, and presentation. Those three levels resemble the three levels of Fig. 3.1: Language and technical connections establish data transfer. Contents and structures use the data connection, but effective information transfer also requires mechanisms for agreeing on contents. An author has managed his part of the knowledge transfer successfully only when the transferred information is presented in a way that allows users to associate their own knowledge and context with it. In Fig. 3.1, the correspondence on each level is emphasized.

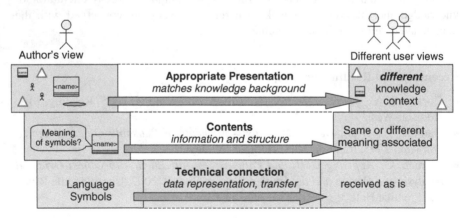

Fig. 3.1 Effective knowledge transfer requires appropriate connections on three levels

Example 3.1 (Challenges for effective knowledge transfer)

There are several reasons why such a connection is difficult to establish and to use effectively:

- Some of the "existing" knowledge is tacit and can only be accessed by talking to its owners. For example, a project manager carried out many project estimations but never cared to describe how he performs them.
- The terminology used by the participants is inconsistent. There is often a mutual misunderstanding when requirements analysts talk to developers: Analysts try to use customer terminology, whereas developers prefer to think in terms of solutions. Even the terms they use are different.
- Customer vocabulary is often highly specific to their respective domain. It takes analysts a long time to learn it and to use it correctly. Problems and constraints of a domain need to be expressed in the right vocabulary in order to fully understand them. Using the right vocabulary is also a prerequisite for customers to validate captured requirements. Fischer [42] calls this relationship the "symmetry of ignorance" between those who do not know possible solutions and those who do not really understand the problem.
- Different sources of knowledge use inconsistent terminology, which makes it hard to compare, evaluate, and combine their contributions.
- Users in demand of knowledge use inconsistent terminology: When they make a query or ask for support, their requests cannot be mapped to existing terminology.
- Users in demand of knowledge ask on the wrong level of abstraction. Instead of stating their "problem," they ask on the solution level, because they are already locked into some solution path.
- A user often needs more than one piece of information or knowledge. It is not sufficient for the knowledge management initiative to deliver one piece per query. Instead, several pieces must be combined in a new way. Different contexts and different problems may be able to reuse knowledge, but rarely just as is.
- Knowledge engineers sometimes prefer a format or presentation that knowledge workers are not interested in. A formula may have a lot of appeal for knowledge engineers, but software engineers working with natural language requirements might not like it (Fig. 3.2).

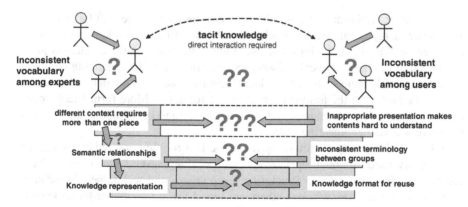

Fig. 3.2 Overview of challenges in the three-level communication for knowledge transfer

A language common to all stakeholders could help to overcome several of these hurdles. However, developing a common language is a nontrivial problem. Chapter 4 will comment on some endeavors undertaken to establish common languages with a precisely defined vocabulary and logically sound connectors for forming unambiguous sentences, such as `and`, `or`, `xor`. In software engineering, such a vision is still out of reach and may always be.

When we intend to define a **common language**, we need to consider three aspects:

- Syntax: symbols and well-formed terms compiled from those symbols.
- Semantics: the meaning of well-formed sentences and terms.
- Pragmatics: the way of using the language properly, "as intended."

Those three aspects are well-known from programming languages. They must also be considered when defining a language for human use. Not all aspects must be fully or formally defined – but if they are not, there is room for interpretation and misunderstanding.

Please keep in mind our goal: We want to cope with the above-mentioned challenges of sharing and transferring knowledge. We propose languages to express knowledge in an appropriate way. Some situations call for sophisticated formalisms, whereas others are better served by rather informal techniques.

Mnemonic 3.1 (Elegance and usefulness)
From a software engineering perspective, we should not fall in love with an elegant formalism but keep the initial goal in mind. Professional software engineers need to balance effort for structuring with improved ability to carry out their knowledge-intensive software engineering tasks.

3.3 Overview and Comparison of Structuring Approaches

In this chapter, different ways of building a common reference will be discussed. A number of representative approaches will be described and related to software engineering. We will start with simple and rather informal techniques, such as glossaries and mind maps. Typical software engineering methods of defining common reference models include use cases, domain models, and metamodels. They cover the middle ground in the following spectrum of formality. More formal techniques based on ontologies or Semantic Web are only starting to be applied to knowledge-intensive software engineering tasks.

Table 3.1 shows a **spectrum of approaches**. It is roughly ordered by the degree of formality used, although approaches diverge along several dimensions. There are more or less fine-grained structuring mechanisms and techniques. Some support human interaction, whereas others are tuned toward computer-based knowledge engineering. About half of the approaches are specific to software engineering, whereas the others are generally applicable.

Table 3.1   Spectrum of selected approaches for semiformal knowledge structuring

Application domain	Input	Approach	Output
General	• Tacit knowledge • Individuals in a group • Method and tool	**Mind maps**	• Simple map • Hierarchical, links • Vague terms • Shared map
Software engineering (in particular: requirements)	• Tacit or explicit • Ready for interpretation • Method and templates	**Use cases**	• Information organized by use case slots (aspects) • Solicited aspects • Specific format • Terms may be inconsistent
General	• Recurring terms and acronyms • Distributed definitions • No tools	**Glossary**	• Directory of terms • Some cross-references • Reference for spelling, synonyms, and homonyms
Software engineering	• UML notation and tools • Information gained through other activities • Many tools and approaches	**Domain model** (specific class model)	• Precise terms (names) • Some aspects of meaning defined (details) • May describe status as-is or as-required
General	• Structured view of the knowledge domain	**Ontologies**	• Defined schema of elements • Inference or reasoning capabilities • Search and combination • Ability to create instances from ontology classes

Because there is no one single, agreed-upon formalism for representing knowledge, professional software engineers need to know several options. When they face a concrete problem in a project or software organization, they should be able to choose from a collection of alternatives. This chapter is supposed to present an overview of rather diverse options. They may all be relevant to daily software engineering work.

Using Table 3.1: When choosing an approach for a software engineering task, one should consider goals and constraints:

– Will the output match the demanded format and contents for the task at hand? There is no need to speculate about advanced properties of a given formalism if it cannot possibly provide the required outputs.
– Will participants be able and willing to provide all required inputs?
– Will participants be able to handle the approach in terms of formalism, previous knowledge (concerning software engineering concepts), and representation of the output?

- Is it economically feasible to teach those participants who do not know the formalism yet or does the approach work even when the technique is not fully mastered?
- What degree of formalism and granularity, hence effort, is required to identify and present a desired subset of existing knowledge? Is that effort in balance with expected gains?

Example 3.2 (Use case terms)

Use cases do not offer mechanisms for consistent terminology. But use cases are fairly well accepted by customers and software engineers as a common language. Although the inputs should be easy to provide, use cases must not be considered a potential approach for deriving consistent vocabulary.

Example 3.3 (UML domain model)

A UML domain model may serve that purpose but will not be appropriate in many other situations: If intended participants do not know UML, many of the well-known advantages of UML do not count.

Example 3.4 (Generating code)

Along the same line, generating code from metamodels may be a valuable approach in many environments – but only if there are skilled people to provide models in short time. A sophisticated technique like code generation may require a long learning process. This can be a psychological and economical reason for avoiding such a technique, although it could be useful in the long run.

3.4 Structuring Vague Information: Mind Maps

In many software engineering activities, the expertise and knowledge of several experts need to be combined. Examples include early requirements phases, project planning, or software process improvement. Sometimes, creativity techniques will be applied to elicit vague and tacit knowledge from stakeholders or engineers. From the viewpoint of structuring knowledge, there are a number of techniques to support stakeholders in externalizing and structuring unrelated pieces of knowledge.

Example 3.5 (Brainstorming and mind maps)

Imagine a team developing administrative shrink-wrap software for personal tax declarations. Some of the features in their next release have been defined through earlier announcement or triggered by customer requests. However, the team wants to add a few unique selling points to the software. For that purpose, the project leader schedules a meeting with marketing, developers, and a quality specialist. After the introduction, there is a brainstorming session. Brainstorming is a general creativity technique with defined rules:

- There is a clear topic, announced by the moderator.
- Participants are invited to associate freely and contribute whatever they want. There is no criticizing or discussion during the brainstorming session.

- The session is up to 20 minutes long.
- Participants are encouraged to refer to earlier contributions, so that combined associations transcend individual ideas.

The team ends up with a blackboard full of words and short phrases (Fig. 3.3). There are several suggestions for new features, but also the name of a low-cost supermarket (PennyWise) as a role model for marketing the software successfully. Someone suggested starting a PR campaign. From the feature of "automated tax calculation," someone was inspired to add "one-click tax wizard." This idea caused a lot of laughter and sparked several new ideas – although no developer could imagine exactly what a "one-click tax wizard" would do or how it could be implemented.

Brainstorming is a good way to open the mind for unexpected relationships and associations. In our terminology, brainstorming can be a first step toward externalization or map-building. However, brainstorming results usually require interpretation, structuring, and critical reflection. Whereas criticism and discussion are not allowed during the brainstorming session itself, there is even more demand afterward. In the above example, the one-click tax wizard may be unrealistic, but it can be a vision for packaging a set of new features. Some surfaced ideas might be interesting but too expensive to implement.

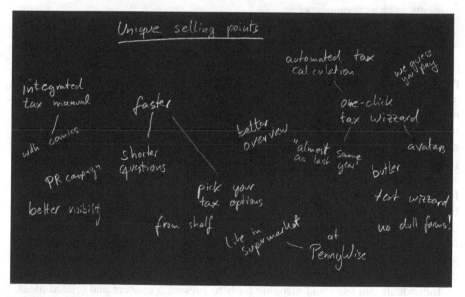

Fig. 3.3 Blackboard with brainstorming results about "unique selling points" for tax software

Therefore, there needs to be a structuring step in which the brainstorming results are reviewed, explained, and sorted out. Mind maps are close to vague and tacit knowledge. Although they have even been used to take notes during brainstorming, brainstorming purists will not use mind maps for brainstorming: Mind maps impose structures on the contributions, which they consider too much undesired guidance.

There are numerous other occasions during a software engineering project when a group of people needs to organize and structure their ideas about a certain topic. Initially, there were several similar approaches that are now often summarized as "mind maps."

Common principles **of mind mapping** are as follows:

- Words or short sentences are written on a commonly visible surface (blackboard, whiteboard, or computer projection). Participants build on the contributions of one another and develop a common understanding of their topic.
- Unlike pure brainstorming, terms and ideas are related through lines or arrows, indicating relationships. This structure provides additional information on top of otherwise unrelated chunks of ideas.
- A central concept is often put in the center of a mind map, with related concepts placed around it. All concepts shown are directly or indirectly connected to the central concept.
- Hierarchical refinement is the major mechanism for relating concepts in a mind map. The central concept is refined by all labels or terms directly connected to it by lines. Each of them can be further refined, thus spanning a conceptual hierarchy of terms or concepts.
- In most variants of mind maps, there are additional mechanisms for cross-cutting relationships on top of refinement. There may be different markers or attachments, such as documents.

Conceptually, mind maps can be drawn manually on a whiteboard (Fig. 3.4).

There are now several **tools for creating and managing mind maps** on a computer. Some tools are available as open source [104], whereas others are commercial products, like MindManager [74]. Fig. 3.5 shows a mind map drawn with MindManager. The central concept (Unique Selling Points in version 7.0) is depicted as the box in the middle of the diagram. Next-level refinements are indicated by direct lines to the central concept. Many refining terms or ideas are refined again. This hierarchical structure is at the core of a mind map. A flag indicates a certain status of a planned item or a concept; in Fig. 3.5, a green flag and priority one (circle) indicates a preference to implement this feature. More concise questions also have a "starter flag" but are not as urgent: priority is set to three. A free comment indicates that this branch was not considered very innovative. Curved lines around the "spider" of hierarchically refined concepts indicate further links: Automated tax declaration is not only a new feature but also a contribution to faster tax declaration. There are several more options, links to calendars, attached files, and symbols to highlight certain aspects.

Individuals can use mind-mapping tools to present a concept and related ideas. Because the mind map does not imply an order of refining items, the structure

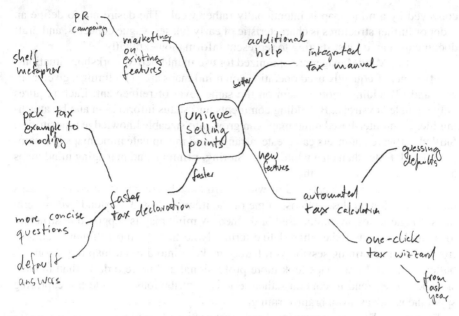

Fig. 3.4   Mind map on a whiteboard

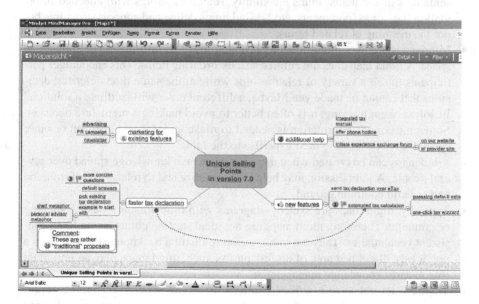

Fig. 3.5   Mind map in the MindManager tool, showing the tax software example

conveyed by a mind map is intentionally rather weak. The desire not to define an order or further structures is characteristic of early phases, vague concepts, and draft documents that are just starting to represent information explicitly.

Tools like MindManager are optimized for use in interactive workshop situations. The two most frequently used operations on mind maps are (1) refining a given concept and (2) adding another item on the same level of refinement. Each requires only a single keystroke. By adding comments and status information and by attaching files, computer-based mind maps can grow into sizeable knowledge repositories. Skilled software engineers can create, arrange, and manipulate mind maps in a computer much faster than on a whiteboard. Storing, printing, and managing mind maps are also much easier when they reside in a computer.

Compared with a blackboard or whiteboard sketch, computer-based mind maps tend to have longer descriptions. Some of the items in Fig. 3.5 extend over several lines. Single terms are rarely used or defined. A mind map is supposed to structure ideas and concepts rather than define terms. Note that the most "funny" remarks from the brainstorming session will hardly make it into a mind map (e.g., comics, butler, avatars). Mind maps look more professional and more orderly than manual sketches. They tend to contain rather serious contributions – while not capturing spontaneous ideas, as in brainstorming.

Summary: We can summarize the characteristics of mind maps:

- Mind maps are generic tools that can be applied to some software engineering tasks, too. There is no specific support for software engineering.
- Mind maps facilitate creating spider-like diagrams of terms or concepts that are refined by other terms or concepts. Mind maps have no access to the meaning or semantics of the items. Items are simply treated as strings with attached information (i.e., links, comments, etc.). Mind maps define and support structures but not the meaning of related terms.
- Mind maps are two-dimensional representations of an information or knowledge space. A mind map does not enforce strictly ordering items. This encourages participants to see a variety of relationships while at the same time deferring decisions that cannot be made yet. Maybe, a different order will facilitate a solution? In software engineering, it is often better to avoid making a premature decision. Sometimes, more information is needed to make an informed decision or other specialists need to bring their expertise to the table.
- Mind maps can be created when there is vague, tacit knowledge spread over several people. A joint session may help to externalize and to relate that information and to build common ground.
- Typically, mind maps are sketchy diagrams with little attention paid to spelling or grammar. Therefore, mind maps are not ideal starting points for building consistent vocabularies. They are rather meant to distill a backbone structure from a previously ill-defined area of discussion. As such, mind maps play an important role in early knowledge management.
- There are several situations from requirements engineering via planning and process improvement that benefit from mind maps. Whenever several people need to externalize vague ideas, mind maps should be considered.

Obviously, a reference model can benefit from deriving some of the relationships from a mind map. Precise definition of terms and semantics should not be expected from this technique.

3.5 Semiformal Approaches in Software Engineering

Brainstorming notes and mind maps are informal representations of knowledge and ideas. Words and terms are not precisely defined. There may be typos or undefined synonyms. Informal representations arise in human interactions. They are often a first step toward externalization. In mind maps, relationships are typed: There is a defined meaning of a refinement relationship. Markers and links may be typed, too.

In this section, semiformal approaches will be discussed. Like informal representations, use cases and glossaries were used long before knowledge management was an issue in software engineering. They facilitate the transition from vague, individual knowledge in someone's brain to explicit, approachable items of knowledge that can be managed. Semiformal approaches bridge the gap between process- and product-oriented knowledge management.

In a formal representation, semantics are encoded in form. Mathematical formulas are written in a mathematical notation others can read and understand. Therefore, the entire meaning of a formula is expressed in its form. Manipulation of contents can be replaced by ritualized manipulation of formulas. In a semiformal representation, not all aspects are completely encoded in forms. Others are described in free text or diagrams that cannot be automatically analyzed or synthesized. There is a tension between formal and informal parts of semiformal approaches. In practice, semiformal approaches are among the most useful techniques in software engineering.

3.5.1 Use Cases

Use cases were introduced into software engineering practice in the 1990s [4, 68]. A use case represents a set of functional requirements that arise in an interaction between users and a computer system or among cooperating computer systems.

Example 3.6 (Typical use case: Withdrawing money at an ATM)

For example, withdrawing money from a bank account makes a good use case. The account holder is the human user who has a clear goal: to get money from her account. The use case is a structured description of the typical and desired interaction between that user and "the system" (i.e., an ATM plus the system behind the ATM). The interaction may be initiated by the user inserting her banking card into a card reader. The system should respond by asking for the personal identification number (PIN). The user will provide it, which will allow her to make further selections; given the provided PIN is valid. At the end of the main scenario, the user should have reached her goal (i.e., received the money). Errors or exceptions are

treated in a separate category of the use case. The main scenario assumes desirable
process steps without any problems or exceptions.

Note that neither acronym (ATM, PIN) is necessarily defined in the use case.
There is a clear actor for each step. Combined steps (as in 5) must have the same
actor. The focus of a use case is the interaction needed to reach a goal of the primary
actor. In Fig. 3.6, the primary actor seems to be a customer who wants to print the
account balance.

1. Customer inserts ATM card into slot
2. ATM asks for authentication (PIN)
3. Customer enters four-digit PIN
4. ATM shows account balance and offers withdrawal
5. Customer prints the balance and terminates session
6. ATM shows initial greeting screen

Fig. 3.6 Core of a use case: sequence of steps for printing the account balance at an Automatic
Teller Machine (ATM)

There are several variants of use-case formats known in the literature and used
in companies. They all share the principal idea of describing an important scenario
that can occur when a user interacts with the software or the system.

However, use cases are slightly more generic than concrete stories:

- There may be more than one user involved, but a *primary user* is the reference
  defining the goals pursued in the use case.
- A scenario will describe actions but should not go into any details about user
  interface design or interaction with a menu. A use case models the process in
  terms of interaction, not implementation details.
- A scenario is a *typical* procedure, not a concrete example including names, specific input values, or desired output reactions. Use cases are more abstract than
  examples. Each use case represents a whole family of concrete examples.
- Finally, *secondary* scenarios may be included in a use-case description. Exceptions or unusual variants of a procedure can be denoted in a similar style but in
  a separate part of a use case. This separation is meant to keep the main scenario
  simple. Branches and loops are usually prohibited in a scenario; each scenario
  describes exactly the one path considered "typical and desirable."

The simplest form to write a use case consists of a title and a short abstract of
text that tries to capture the above-mentioned information (Fig. 3.7).

This basic format encourages people to express requirements in terms of entire
interactions, not just isolated features: Requirements are less fragmented and add
up to more useful requirements when they are rooted in goal-driven scenarios. Use

Withdrawing money from ATM
"Peter is a customer of A-Bank. He needs money for shopping, so he approaches the ATM. After inserting his ATM card and entering his PIN, Peter types in the amount of money he wishes to withdraw. The machine releases his card and pays the money."

Fig. 3.7 Very short variant of a textual use case ("narrative")

cases at this level are mainly a mental tool to remember value-adding procedures during requirements elicitation.

The requirements engineering literature has embraced use cases as an easy-to-use, semiformal technique for eliciting and documenting functional requirements. For that purpose, more sophisticated templates for use cases have been developed. Cockburn's "fully-dressed" style of use cases is widely used in companies [24]. It offers a table with several slots that must be completed for each use case. The meaning of those slots is described in Fig. 3.8.

Use Case 4	Withdraw money from bank
Environment	Automatic Teller Machine installed in a wall
Level	Essential, main level
Primary Actor	(Bank) Customer
Stakeholders and their interests	**Stakeholders Interests** Customer: wants money fast and safely Bank: wants to reduce manual handling effort and provide safe transaction (no fraud possible) Waiting customer: wants other customers in the queue to leave quickly
Precondition	Customer has valid ATM card. ATM displays welcome screen.
Guarantee	Money is paid to the customer if and only if the amount is deducted from the account balance (transactional behavior)
Success case	Customer receives money, amount is subtracted from the customer's account, ATM shows welcome screen
Trigger	Customer inserts ATM card
Sequence of Steps	**Step Actor Activity** 1 Customer inserts ATM card 2 ATM asks for authentication (PIN) 3 Customer enters four-digit PIN 4 ATM offers choice of services 5 Customer selects withdrawal 6 Customer enters amount 7 ATM pays amount, releases card 8 ATM displays welcome screen
Extensions	1a If ATM card unreadable, THEN eject it and display warning.Back to start. 3a If PIN incorrect, THEN display warning and ask for correct PIN. Try up to three times. If unsuccessful, keep card and terminate. 7a If amount cannot be paid, THEN display message and return to 6
Technology	If there is a finger print reader, Customers may use it for authentication (instead of PIN).

Fig. 3.8 Example template for fully dressed use cases showing the ATM example

3.5.1.1 Use Case Aspects in Detail

The template shown in Fig. 3.8 [24] contains an example use case. Each aspect has a defined meaning but will not be described in a formal language.

- **ID and name**: Each use case needs to be identifiable. A unique ID (mostly a number, 4 in Fig. 3.8) facilitates managing use cases as objects. A use-case name should be an active phrase referring to the goal pursued by the use case. "Withdraw money from bank" indicates the goal not the details of the activity.
- **Primary actor**: There is one person or actor whose goals are pursued by carrying out the use case. Often, a role name (like Customer) will be provided for the primary actor. In more elaborate use-case templates, there are additional fields for specifying goals, benefit, and their measurement.
- **Level of use case**: Three levels of use cases are distinguished. Essential use cases describe activities at the level in which a user typically wants to interact with the system. Overview use cases abstract from that level. "Electronic banking" is more abstract and less active than "withdraw money from bank." Supportive activities refine essential use cases. For example, checking the PIN is not a user goal in itself, but it is required for many essential activities. Supportive activities are below the level typical users think about when they describe value-adding functionality.
- **Stakeholders and interest**: The primary actor always interacts with the system when a use case is executed. Stakeholders are all people, groups, or systems affected by a use case. "Withdraw money from bank" may affect clerks who are in charge of filling up ATM money. They might want to influence the banknotes paid by the ATM. If the ATM is short on one kind of bills, it may compensate by paying in different bills. The bank itself is obviously affected by a system that allows customers to withdraw money. The bank's interest may include saving cashier personnel and making transactions more efficient. Customers are both stakeholders and primary actors. They wish safe and fast transactions when they use the ATM. Customers waiting in line are in particular interested in short waiting times.
- **Trigger**: An event that initiates the use case to be carried out. The trigger will also be the first step in the main scenario.
- **Precondition**: In contrast with a trigger, a precondition is not an event. A precondition is rather a state or condition that needs to hold at the moment when the trigger tries to activate a use case. Only when the precondition is true can the use case be executed. This is a logical statement, not a piece of execution semantics. When software engineers phrase a use case, they can assume that the precondition holds at the starting point. The use case neither needs to check the precondition nor does it have to cope with violated preconditions. By definition, the author of each use case can assume all preconditions will be fulfilled when it gets executed.

- **Success case**: In all cases in which the use case is carried out, its postcondition must hold afterward. The implementation of the use case has to fulfill that assertion.
- **Guarantee**: Extensions (see later) are a mechanism for specifying a problem or exception. This will lead to a branch in execution. However, even when one of the specified exceptions occurs, the *guaranteed* condition will still hold. Guarantees are far less ambitious than success cases. They just describe indispensable assertions the stakeholders insist on. For example, a transfer of funds must be either complete or completely deleted (transactional). If the transaction of sending money to the receiver fails, it must not take it from the sender either.
- **Sequence of steps**: There is a numbered sequence of steps, each of which should be phrased in a short, active sentence. It must be clear who does what in each step. Many notations of use cases allow single steps to be refined into lower-level use cases. Usually, this is denoted by the refining use-case name being underlined in the respective step. This sequence is the typical, desired main scenario of interactions, with no alternatives mentioned.
- **Extensions**: Foreseeable deviations (e.g., exceptions) from the desired sequence of steps are described in the extensions section. Cockburn [24] and other authors [69] emphasize the importance of not using control structures (like if, while, switch) in the main *sequence of steps*. The main scenario follows a single thread. If an exception or variant may occur at a certain step, this variant is described as an extension. Cockburn uses a different numbering scheme for the steps carried out in an extension. A number "3a" refers to an alternative in step 3. For example, the customer might not take her banking card back. The extension should describe all steps to bring the interaction back to the main scenario. In our example, it may be sufficient not to release the money and to display a warning when the banking card is not taken. If there is more than one alternative branch at a certain step, the letters a, b, c are used to indicate this.
- **Technology**: In some cases, different technology available will impact some steps or the entire use case. For example, a fingerprint reader may affect authentication in one or more steps.

The **template** imposes a consistent structure on all use cases. Like a checklist, the list of aspects in the template reminds requirements engineers to ask the right questions about each valuable interaction. This exceeds the simple variant of use cases, which only reminded software engineers to consider value-adding interactions *at all*. Of course, the above template may be adapted and modified by a company or a project. It is important, however, to stick to a common template once it has been tailored. The advantage of creating a common structure for functional requirements is often a higher priority than is making a template a perfect fit for each and every single use case.

We are interested in structuring knowledge in software engineering. With use-case templates, we have reached middle ground:

- There is a template to be consistently used throughout a set of related use cases. All use cases "inherit" the same structure from the template. If filled out correctly, contents in the slots will also follow a similar style.
- On the other side, there is no attempt to strictly regulate terminology in any of the text entries. Stakeholders, for example, are listed. This list may be cross-checked with other use cases or with other documents referring to stakeholders. That cross-check may detect typos or missing entries. However, the intentions of those stakeholders do not follow any prescribed format. There is no easy way to understand or manage knowledge expressed in those little snippets of text.

Because of this dichotomy, it is fair to call use cases "semiformal" representations. By providing a guiding structure, a use case helps requirements engineers to elicit more consistent and more complete requirements. Lack of formalism for wording entries keeps the threshold low for software engineers: Use cases are close enough to normal language.

Only formalized aspects of use cases can be used for computer-based comparison and resolution. There is only little formalized information in a use case, but some authors have tried to push use cases a little further: By defining a few more rules on use cases, tools can interpret more of the knowledge contained in a use case.

Example 3.7 (Formal use cases)

For example, Volhard [112] requests no additional rules to be followed. Volhard requests numbering use-case steps strictly: He interprets those steps as a hint to simulate use-case execution. The process of the interaction is expressed in the order of use-case steps. Steps are numbered by a tool, and extensions (exceptional branches) are also administered automatically. Users will not notice a difference, as steps need to be numbered anyway.

Example 3.8 (Deriving other models from use cases)

Diegel pursues an approach to combine use cases into event-driven process chains (EPCs; a process modeling notation). Several related interactions are first described as use cases. Those use cases are then woven into a single process model by identifying preconditions that match the postconditions of other use cases. [30]. Such an approach could use logic calculus or it can stay at the syntactic level. Diegel argues for simply considering cases in which preconditions and postconditions are exactly alike. More powerful reasoning mechanisms may build on a more general basis if a previous use case fulfills the preconditions for subsequent use cases [71].

Examples 3.7 and 3.8 illustrate different opportunities to interpret more aspects of a use case in a more formal way. There is obviously a trade-off between rich representation and easy handling of use cases.

Use cases are a technique from requirements engineering. Originally, there was no relationship to knowledge management. However, when a substantial amount of knowledge about functional requirements is captured in the form of use cases, we should consider potential links:

- Use cases structure vague and otherwise incomplete information into defined aspects. Other software engineers know where to look and how to read entries. This constitutes a first structuring step.
- More powerful structuring approaches exploit further details:
  - The list of stakeholders can be compared with the actors in the use-case steps. Actors are either the system or one of the stakeholders.
  - Stakeholders can be compared with other use-case stakeholder lists. Identical stakeholder names can be used to derive associations between use cases.
  - Refining use cases must be represented by their full and correct names. This is yet another opportunity for cross-checking a set of use cases.
  - Tools can derive use-case diagrams. A use-case diagram is a UML diagram depicting an overview of a set of related use cases. By referring to use-case names and stakeholders, use-case diagrams can be created automatically.
  - Even conditions (preconditions, postconditions, and guarantees) can be exploited in order to use semantics. Matching conditions can enrich the knowledge base represented by use cases.
  - Specific approaches may request formalizing more aspects; this leads to a trade-off between computer accessibility and ease of use.

- A semiformal notation like a use case allows software engineers and customers to bridge their language gap. There is a template and a set of rules on how to apply that template. This facilitates the elicitation, explication, and initial structuring of requirements. Requirements are an important subset of knowledge in a software project.

Semiformal notations often do not insist on precise definition of terms. Glossaries are a semiformal concept for defining terms. Glossaries support knowledge engineering by complementing the above-mentioned approaches.

3.5.2 Glossaries

Each domain uses its own vocabulary. Because of their different traditions, a technical domain will use different terms than will a hospital or a financial institution. Different terminologies indicate different challenges, tasks, and different perspectives on software.

A software project needs to use terminology consistently and correctly. It should also be aware of rules, relationships, and traditions that dominate its domain. When software engineers write requirements, develop user interfaces, or write programs, they should use terms familiar to the users of their products. Otherwise, delayed communication and misunderstandings will hamper the project.

Definition 3.1 (Glossary)

A glossary is an ordered collection of entries. Each glossary entry consists of the term to be defined and a short definition or explanation of its meaning.

A software engineer often works in different projects or even in different domains at the same time. Most software engineers will work in different environments during their careers. Nobody can possibly know and remember all "reserved words" or specific terms used in all those environments, let alone all conventions and unspoken rules associated with them. Even experts in a domain sometimes confuse terms. Glossaries are a simple mechanism for collecting defined terms and their meanings. A glossary resembles a dictionary for a specific vocabulary.

In principle, all kinds of terms can be defined in a glossary:

- Domain-specific terms like electroencephalogram (hospital), glossary, or hedge fund (financial), as in Fig. 3.9.
- Technical terms for describing potential or suggested solutions (like framework, model-view-controller, design pattern).
- Everyday words that are used in a special meaning within a certain context (like a requirement "oracle" or a "user").
- Acronyms or abbreviations: The meaning of an acronym is the full text it represents.

A glossary entry typically consists of the term itself and a text defining or explaining it. Explanations are usually short (less than half a page) and mostly written in natural language. Formal elements or formal languages are not typically used

EEG: electroencephalogram
x-ray picture of the brain taken by encephalography

Glossary (Wikipedia, May 15, 2007):
A **glossary** is a list of terms in a particular domain of knowledge with the definitions for those terms.
Traditionally, a glossary appears at the end of a book and includes terms within that book which are either newly introduced or at least uncommon.

Hedge fund (Wikipedia, May 15, 2007):
A hedge fund is an investment fund charging a performance fee and typically open to only a limited range of investors. In America, hedge funds are open to accredited investors only. Because of this restriction they are usually exempt from any direct regulation by the →SEC, →NASD and other regulatory bodies.
Though the funds do not necessarily hedge their investments against adverse market moves, the term is used to distinguish them from regulated retail investment funds such as mutual funds and pension funds, and from insurance companies. (...)

Fig. 3.9 Three glossary entries from different knowledge domains

in glossaries. A glossary is intended to be read and understood by humans, not computers.

There are a number of possible extensions to glossary entries, some shown in Fig. 3.9:

- There may be links to similar or related terms. →**SEC** is an example.
- Entries are usually sorted in alphabetical order and may be assigned certain attributes. In Fig. 3.9, terms are sorted, but there are no attributes.
- Relationships between terms can be treated as first-order objects (as entries in their own right) or may be treated as annotations or links to other entries. No relationship is defined in Fig. 3.9.
- There can be comments, annotations, examples, or metadata associated with each glossary entry. References to the source of definitions (Wikipedia) are metadata in Fig. 3.9. Metadata describes the entry as such, not the term defined in the entry.

3.5.2.1 Variants of Glossaries

Glossaries are not restricted to software engineering. Within software engineering, glossaries are used for different purposes, and implementations of different glossaries can vary drastically:

- *Glossary in a project*: Many software projects decide to maintain a glossary of essential terms. This collection will consist of domain terminology, specific project terms, and so forth. A dozen entries in a defined document may be sufficient for a small project in a familiar application domain. Such a glossary requires very little effort to create and to maintain. It may facilitate consistent use of the few terms defined. When software engineers talk to a customer representative, they should use customer terminology and understand tacit associations that come with those terms. A glossary can assist here.
- *Glossary beyond a single project*: A company or business unit that carries out several projects may find it tedious to start a new glossary with each project. For that reason, a larger long-term glossary for a given domain will be a better solution. It is always a good idea to keep a glossary in a separate document. This is good advice for one-pagers, but it is mandatory for a glossary containing hundreds of terms and several pages. This kind of glossary is copied into several project documents instead of being rewritten from scratch. There may be a few project-specific extensions every time it is used. Knowledge management should be concerned with an orderly process of feeding back corrections and additions to the master copy of the glossary. A rich and well-kept glossary is an asset. However, a glossary must not compete with general-purpose collections, such as Wikipedia. There is no benefit in duplicating generic definitions if they do not have specific meaning or relevance for an organization.
- *Glossaries for entire domains*: Large companies or domain interest groups maintain voluminous books of precise definitions. A bank, for example, defined about 8,000 terms of specific banking terminology. Effort invested into creating such

a large collection of definitions pays back only through extensive use. The bank will insist on using that dictionary throughout all software projects, and also in many other business contexts. For example, training of new employees should encourage use of the glossary. Huge glossaries pose new problems: Each project needs only a fraction of the entries, and no single person has a complete overview of what has been defined. Searching becomes more of an issue. If a project runs into a term that might or might not be defined: How should software engineers find out whether that term already exists in the glossary? What if there are similar terms or synonyms? Full-text search is easy, but searching semantically by contents is a more demanding task.

Creating a glossary is only the first step toward knowledge engineering. The power of a glossary unfolds only when there are procedures and support mechanisms for finding terms, using their definitions, and updating the glossary in case of errors or changes. Creating a glossary forces experts to discuss and agree on exact meanings of terms. They may need to make explicit or to negotiate their opinions and views.

Example 3.9 (Using glossary for a software engineering task)

For example, a software engineer writing a specification may encounter a word he does not understand. In that case, looking it up in the glossary is straightforward. However, what if he types a word that is defined – but does not know it is? What can a glossary do to help anyway? Active assistance is a key concept in this area of knowledge management. Existing knowledge should "notice" when it is referenced. An active glossary may compare typed strings with defined terms. But what should be done upon detecting a match? Maybe the software engineer knows about the glossary entry, and a warning is inappropriate. Maybe the software engineer does not *know* this word to be a defined term; indicating that fact may prevent him from a misunderstanding. A subtle way of indicating the match (like underline or different color) will be appropriate. It should not interrupt the writing process.

Depending on the size and purpose of a glossary, technical implementations may take different forms:

- A simple, short list of explanations can be maintained in a document of a few pages. It will simply be attached to all documents referring to it.
- A longer list could be maintained in a spreadsheet or in a file under version control. Several people will access the list for reading and update. The longer a list, the more users should benefit from using it. Therefore, processes and rules of working with the glossary need to be defined explicitly.
- Databases are obvious candidates for implementing larger glossaries. They can be sorted and filtered, and attributes can be used to select subsets of a glossary.
- Glossaries can also be implemented as blackboards or Wiki webs. Those representations can be modified over the intranet and Internet. Stakeholders receive access rights for reading and/or modifying them interactively.

There is a tension between two desirable properties of a larger glossary:

- It should be flexible enough to be modified and updated easily by all affected personnel. This request refers to concepts and technical support.
- At the same time, well-defined and explained terms should be used consistently. Changing definitions in each project is counterproductive. Consistent usage of terms requires long-term stability of key terms.
- Access rights need to balance the requirements of stability and flexibility.

3.5.2.2 Summary: Strengths and Weaknesses of Different Approaches

Mind maps help to brainstorm and find an initial definition of certain structures but do not result in defined terms. Use cases introduce more detailed structures through their templates. Again, correct and consistent usage of terms is not the focus of use cases. As we have seen in the examples above, simple cross-checks can detect typos, defined terms, or synonyms. However, original use cases lack a glossary mechanism. Glossaries complement structuring approaches: A glossary could add knowledge management capabilities to use cases or mind maps. Today, those semiformal approaches are often maintained separately. This is partly due to the fact that the respective tools are not integrated.

Meaningful requirements must build on well-defined terms. Transferring and applying knowledge requires the knowledge to be comprehensible to the receivers. Misunderstandings need to be avoided. Knowledge engineers will try to use both structures and definitions in order to establish a common language. A definition or explanation is a good starting point. It supports human users who read those definitions and who may use them for more consistent documents. Semiformal approaches do not attempt to encode knowledge in formalized statements. With domain models and ontologies, we will take two more steps toward a computer-accessible convention for a language.

3.5.3 Domain Models

Domain models are a specific software engineering tool for describing domains. The main intention of building a domain model is to capture key concepts of a domain and to show how they are related.

Glossary entries treat terms as the basis of a requirement or a document. Along the same lines, domain models treat concepts as the basis of future software engineering models. Domains can be modeled in different notations or languages. Today, **UML domain models** are the most common variant. Therefore, this section refers to UML domain models. Several books on UML cover domain models in depth. Larman [69] provides a good introduction to UML and recommends good practices on how to use it *well*. Following Larman [69] and Fowler [45], we define a domain model.

Definition 3.2 (Domain model)

Visual representation of conceptual classes or real-world objects in a domain of interest.

"Conceptual model" is an older term that has now been replaced by "domain model." Both terms stand for defined vocabulary. Larman calls domain models a "visual dictionary of abstractions." As in a glossary, there is a collection of defined concepts, but those concepts are drawn as rectangles on a two-dimensional surface. The placement of symbols will need to take associations into account, and these will affect the readability of the diagram. For example, crossing lines should be avoided. Domain models combine elements for defining concepts, expressing specific relationships, and adding additional information. However, syntax is only one aspect. Because we are interested in knowledge management implications, we need to consider the pragmatic aspect of notations: how they are supposed to be used in practice.

Syntactically, a domain model is a simplified Entity Relationship or UML class model. Like every model, it represents a part of the real world. We will now look at the symbols used in domain models. We will then discuss the relationship of domain models to other formalisms. Elements and their syntax will be explained using the example in Fig. 3.10. They should look familiar to those who know UML class diagrams.

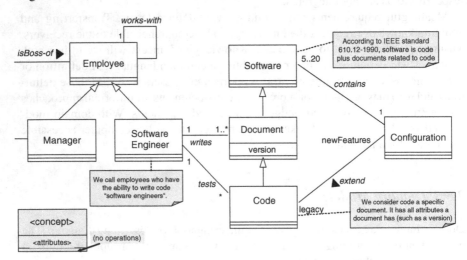

Fig. 3.10 Domain model of a software engineering situation

3.5.3.1 Elements of Domain Models

UML domain models consist of the following elements:

- **Domain concept symbol**: a rectangle containing class name and attribute names (optional). Concept symbols correspond with class symbols in a UML class diagram, but they refer to real-world concepts instead of program components. Unlike class symbols, domain concepts do not show method or operation names.

- **Generalization**: A line with a wide arrowhead. An employee is a generalization of a manager and a software engineer. Generalizations in domain models are less frequently used than inheritance in class models.
- **Association** is depicted by a line between class symbols. An association may link a domain concept with itself, like Employees working with other Employees in Fig. 3.10.
- **Comment symbols** (document symbols with a folded corner) are often attached to a symbol or an association. They contain free text defining or explaining a concept informally. According to Larman [69], they convey the "intention" of the concept. For instance, the comment on Software Engineer states that instances of that concept need to be able to write Code.

As defined in UML [78], there is a rich choice of details and annotations for UML associations. Those refinements can be applied to domain models, too. They include:

- **Role names**: Because associations connect concept symbols, the roles of those concepts with respect to the association can be attached as labels. In Fig. 3.10, labels clarify that newFeatures extend legacyCode.
- **Reading direction**: A black triangle can be added to the association line to indicate reading direction.
- **Multiplicities** are important aspects of associations. They describe how many instances of a concept can be associated with one concept of the other role. Often, only "none, one, or many" are distinguished and denoted as "0, 1, n, or ∗." Ranges of possible values are indicated as:

  - 0...1 zero or one
  - 0...∗ from zero to any number
  - 1...∗ any number, but not zero
  - Other values, for example, 5...20: from 5 to 20 (including both).
  - Concrete values other than 0 and 1 are rarely used in practice.
  - Note: In Fig. 3.10, a Software Engineer writes at least one Document (1...∗), which may be Code (a specific Document, as declared by inheritance) or any other "Document."
  - A Software Engineer tests from zero to any number of Code (Documents) in Fig. 3.10.

From the perspective of a common vocabulary, domain models are similar to glossaries combined with mind maps. Table 3.2 gives a concise overview of several aspects relevant for our knowledge management purposes.

In general, **updating a glossary** entry is an essential operation. Even small glossaries will change, and larger models of any kind will need to be modified. But this is not sufficient. Domain models, for example, are bound to change during the clar-

Table 3.2 Comparing semiformal approaches for structuring information

Notation aspect	Glossary	Mind map	Use case	Domain model
Purpose	Define important terms unambiguously.	Make ideas explicit and start sorting them.	Elicit and present requirements on interactions and related aspects.	State concepts and their main relationships in detail.
Format	Ordered list of entries. An entry is a term together with an explanation or definition.	"Spider diagram" with one concept in the center and related concepts linked by lines.	Template of aspects (described by short texts), describing one interaction with the system.	Defined diagram type, such as UML class diagram, maybe with slight modifications.
Terms defined	Main and only purpose: Define terms for human readers.	Not defined. Typos occur frequently.	Not defined. Only stakeholders' interests are specified.	Concepts defined in relationship to other concepts. Intention can be described informally.
Relationships defined	Usually not defined.	Only generic relationship. Specific relationship types not specified. Additional links possible.	Relationships not explicitly modeled.	Formally modeled. Similar to Entity-Relationship models.
Machine readable?	Full-text search.	Full-text search.	Usually not. Advanced approaches operate on selected aspects (e.g., conditions).	Semantics defined based on UML metamodel. Machine accessible.

ification process. As long as a common model (a shared "mental model" [60]) is missing, domain modeling remains difficult and error-prone. Larman [69] and other authors emphasize the importance of an iterative approach for domain modeling. This goes far beyond "a series of changes": Access rights and version control need to be considered, and changing a defined term may invalidate several documents and pieces of code – those that rely on the outdated definition. Therefore, references to a term need to be updated together with the definition of that term. Is it worthwhile applying a history mechanism or a reference to the source of the definition to a glossary or a use case? In some cases, it definitely is.

Formalizing product knowledge will often not be sufficient. Processes for handling that knowledge will also need to be captured, modeled, and improved. Earl [35] would call these aspects of knowledge management "technocratic," even though processes are concerned. In this and the subsequent chapter, we focus on defining, structuring, and other "technocratic" contributions to knowledge management. They are essential for dealing with large quantities of fine-grained knowledge.

There are many commercial and open-source graphical editors for UML class diagrams. They can be used to create and modify domain models. StarUML [107] is an easy-to-use UML editor that is available for download. Omondo [79] is another open-source UML graphical editor with some advanced capabilities. Omondo is a little awkward to use in real projects, but it allows producing complex domain models.

Domain models are simple enough to be sketched by hand. This is important for discussing them on a blackboard. Simple knowledge presentation formats like mind maps, glossaries, use cases, or domain models support different subtasks in software engineering. Domain terminology and vocabulary can be captured, structured, and modeled.

Emphasis can be put on

- eliciting tacit knowledge (mind maps);
- providing a reference for all future project activities (glossaries);
- helping to organize statements (use cases); or
- modeling a domain as a system of interrelated concepts (domain models).

Establishing a reference for a common language is a never-ending endeavor. Many terms in a project and its environment can be defined or explained. Not only does the intended product of a software project call for definition and structuring; procedures and processes, rules and activities can be defined in order to establish a common language.

3.5.3.2 Misuse Cases for Security, or "What Must Not Happen"

In the realm of security, many software experts have started to define what must *not* happen: Undesirable sequences of events or features that must not be accessible to certain people are modeled explicitly. We can construct effective protection mechanisms only when we have a good understanding of situations to avoid. Misuse or abuse cases apply use-case mechanisms and extended use-case diagrams to describe forbidden activities. Fig. 3.11 is an example inspired by Alexander [3] but set in the realm of software engineering.

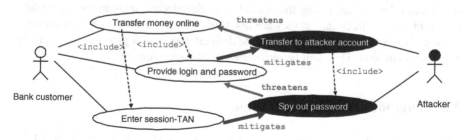

Fig. 3.11 Example of a misuse case. An attacker wants to misuse online transfer features

In the use-case diagram of Fig. 3.11, white ovals stand for use cases, and black ovals indicate misuse cases. They represent interactions that must not occur. Solid lines indicate which stakeholder participates in what use cases. When there is an include relationship, the included use case (or misuse case) is a mandatory part of the including one. Arrows labeled "threatens" and "mitigates" are specific for misuse cases. They describe how "good" use cases and "bad" misuse cases were developed to respond to each other. Mitigations respond to threats, and new threats try to bypass mitigations.

Example 3.10 (Misuse case)

A bank customer has an online account. One of the useful use cases of an online bank account is the transfer of funds. However, there may be "bad" stakeholders involved: The attacker threatens the operation of transferring money online by transferring that money to his own account (see Fig. 3.11). As a reaction to that possibility, online banks have included access control by login and passwords as part of money transfer. If the attacker still wants to misuse the account, he now has to overcome the protection created by the password. Spying out the password is an option. The attacker could mimic the bank interface and try to let the customer enter the password (so-called phishing). The attacker could also try to find the password on the customer computer – many people still store passwords. The attacker could read the keyboard strokes from a distance or try any other way to spy out the password. Fig. 3.11 does not go into any detail about the implementation of spying out passwords. Many online banks respond in a way that mitigates all those threats: They request a six-digit session TAN (transaction access number) that is not reusable. A bank customer receives them via paper mail, which is more difficult to intrude upon.

As this example shows, white and black use cases stimulate each other. There is a competition of threat and mitigation, which is characteristic of security requirements. Knowing what to avoid is an important piece of knowledge in software engineering.

Summary: The semiformal approaches presented in this chapter are easy-to-use techniques, some with dedicated tools. Syntactic consistency is not an issue in glossaries or mind maps, whereas domain models impose a set of UML syntax rules. Many researchers and practitioners have made attempts to extend the power of well-defined languages. Extending capabilities to manipulate knowledge requires additional rules for describing that knowledge. Semiformal techniques are a starting point in that direction, but they are not sufficient. If we want to reason on contents, the semantics of a statement must be defined, too. Ontologies are an important approach to do that. They will be introduced in the next chapter.

3.6 Metamodels and Instantiation

Semiformal structuring mechanisms often define terms on a conceptual level but do not refer to individual instances of those concepts.

Example 3.11 (Instances or classes)

A glossary or a domain model will refer to `"SoftwareEngineer"` or `"CodeModule"` but not to a specific person or a particular module. Even use cases use role names for stakeholders and actors rather than individual names: In a use case, one might find `"student"` or `"tester"` interacting with `"the System"` rather than `"Peter"` or `"Mary"` as actors.

However, there are situations in which both the conceptual and the individual levels are referenced. We need terms to distinguish those levels. And we need languages to describe knowledge on both levels.

As a software engineer, you are familiar with the concept of classes and objects. Classes are mechanisms for creating objects that follow the structure and pattern described in the class description. Objects or instances are the individuals that can be created in an object-oriented language. The behavior of a program is made up of the numerous interactions of instances. The relationship between a class and each of its instances is called "instantiation."

Instantiation is different from **subclassing**:

- A class `Employee` may have both a subclass `Developer` and an instance called *Dieter Schulz*.
- Every instance of `Developer`, like *Jim Jonas,* is a `Developer`.
- Because of the subclass relationship, Jim is also an `Employee` and has all attributes and features of an Employee.

For the following sections, it is crucial to understand and to clearly distinguish

- inheritance and subclass, as well as
- class and object.

We will see more formal structures that refer to both class and object levels. There is an instantiation relationship between those levels. Subclassing occurs only on the class level. In many tutorials, levels are not clearly separated, which causes a lot of confusion (Fig. 3.12).

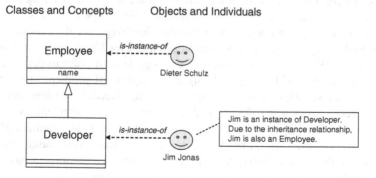

Fig. 3.12 Subclassing and inheritance – two different relationships

3.7 Patterns as Experience Representation

Knowledge allows knowledge workers to deal with problems and difficult situations. Facts can be stored in glossaries. Relationships may be expressed in mind maps or domain models. And use cases are one option to describe requirements and knowledge about interactions.

Experiences often come in a slightly different format: An observation and an emotion lead to a conclusion. This conclusion may include one or more of the following elements:

- A hypothesis about the reason or trigger for the observed event.
- A hypothesis about the consequences of the observed phenomenon.
- An assumption on how a problem could have been avoided.

In general, an experience often implies a pattern of a problem and a solution. When the same problem is encountered again, the same solution is recommended. Because the observation was made in a certain situation and context, a new situation and problem will never be exactly the same. However, because a pattern abstracts from irrelevant details, chances are good for identifying "similar problems," which imply trying "similar solutions." This conclusion is confirmed by each new experience that includes similar situations and consequences. On a more abstract level, they represent similar problems and solutions – confirming the pattern.

Variants of patterns: Definition of terms and relationships were more or less formalized using the above-mentioned approaches. Along the same lines of thought, the description of a pattern as an experience representation can be more or less formal.

- Least formally, a sentence with an IF/THEN clause implies a correspondence between a situation (IF) and a consequence (THEN). Natural language can be used to phrase the conclusion of an experience. In this interpretation, patterns resemble rules.
- A little more formally, a template can be created that highlights the IF and THEN parts. If a form is used at all, it will often contain several classifying attributes. The attributes help to characterize relevant situation properties. This also facilitates matching a given situation with the situation triggering the pattern.
- At DaimlerChrysler, some experience packages (see Chap. 6) were described in 13 facets (Fig. 3.13). Those facets were organized in order to describe more and more details, with the core being a description of problem and solution. This concept was illustrated as "pyramid structure." Because the domain of those experience patterns was software quality and process improvement, the patterns were named "quality patterns." If a subset of the facets are formalized (e.g., only certain entries are allowed in a defined grammar), case-based reasoning can run on the patterns [109]. Case-based reasoning is explained in more detail in Chap. 6. All other facets may remain semiformal or informal.

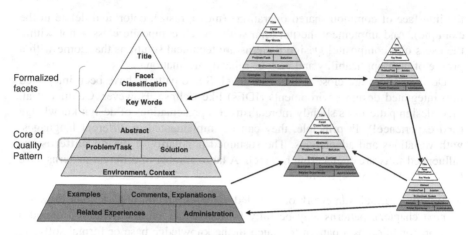

Fig. 3.13 Quality pattern pyramid structure and relationships to other quality patterns [54]

Design patterns are well known in software engineering. Like the above-mentioned informal pattern types, **design patterns encode experience**. In particular, a design pattern describes a solution to a frequently recurring implementation problem [46]. Because design patterns describe program structures, they represent low-level software design experience. Most patterns are associated with a UML diagram (e.g., composite design pattern in Fig. 3.14). However, Gamma et al. present several pages with about a dozen facets for each pattern. For example, a composite pattern is appropriate IF several types of elements and groups of elements must be treated in the same way. In a graphical editor, a complex group of symbols should be moved, resized, colored, and deleted like a single circle or rectangle. Obviously, a loop is required. However, the pattern says in its THEN part: Provide a common superclass to all elements and the composites (groups). Let this superclass define

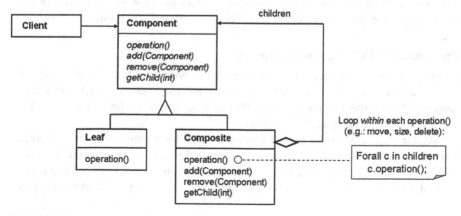

Fig. 3.14 Composite pattern [46]. Printed with permission from: Pearson Education Deutschland GmbH, Martin-Kollar-Str. 10–12, Munich, Germany

the interface of common shared operations (move, resize, color, and delete in the example). And implement the iteration within each composite class – not within the users of a composite! Design patterns are technical solutions that come with a profile of their applicability and various related information.

Design pattern are close to the code level. Some patterns have been integrated into integrated design environments (IDEs) like Eclipse. However, Gamma et al. view design patterns as slightly more abstract representations of design knowledge (and experience!). In principle, they can be implemented in different languages, with variations and adaptations. The sustained popularity of **design patterns** has influenced software engineering research. A large number of different patterns have been published [45, 54, 67, 88].

- Within a formal framework of knowledge representation (e.g., an ontology, see next chapter), patterns may be fully formalized. A precise definition includes a precondition as a pattern to match in the knowledge base or formal software engineering model. If this precondition can be matched, the formal pattern needs to formally describe the reaction this will trigger. At least, a notification can be sent ("the inheritance depth of the design exceeds five levels"). In more complex cases, the respective formal model can be modified.
- For example, class hierarchies can be rearranged to avoid excessive inheritance hierarchies. Graph grammars are a formal mechanism for replacing subgraphs based on rules (i.e., patterns). Formal representations of patterns are usually difficult to write and understand for humans. This is an old tension. In the realm of experience management, the opportunity to pin down patterns formally is rare.

3.8 Problems for Chapter 3

Problem 3.8.1: Pattern

What is a "pattern" with respect to knowledge and experience management? What are the core elements of a pattern and what are they used for when describing and reusing software engineering knowledge? Give an example from software testing.

Problem 3.8.2: Defining quality aspects

Finding a common language with the customer is important in software engineering. Assume you are defining quality attributes for a new piece of software with a customer from a medical background. Why is it important to define key terms like "reliability" or "ease of use" explicitly?

Assume you are developing a banking system for teenagers on the Internet. This program is supposed to target young, inexperienced banking customers. They should be offered basic and additional information on the banking products, and each of their interactions should be explained in detail if they wish. Also, teenage customers should not be allowed to overdraw their account. This example is used for the following problems.

Problem 3.8.3: Mind map

In the process of developing the system, innovative ideas and important reminders are collected in a mind map. The intention is to gain an overview of important and "cool and catchy" concepts that should be taken into account in order to make the teenage bank account system a success. Draw a mind map of a teenage bank account with at least four directly related concepts and about two to four comments each. Comments should explain the innovation or importance of each concept.

Problem 3.8.4: Brainstorming versus mind map

When you drew the mind map, you were not performing brainstorming, although some people might call it so. What are the main differences between drawing your mind map and "real" brainstorming?

Problem 3.8.5: Glossary entries

Provide glossary entries for "graphical user interface," "bank account," and "ATM card" (no debt allowed for teenagers) with respect to the teenage bank account.

Problem 3.8.6: Typos

Typos (incorrectly spelled words) are more common in mind maps than in glossaries. Why is that so and why is it usually not a problem for mind maps?

Problem 3.8.7: Domain model

What happens when a teenage customer turns legally adult? How can you find out what is supposed to happen then? Write a use case for this operation and highlight two pieces of "domain knowledge" it contains.

Problem 3.8.8: Use case

Describe the use case of "changing the PIN" using the use-case template shown above. Make sure to address the characteristic need of young customers to learn about permitted PIN formats and the implications of changing a PIN (and maybe forgetting it). What happens when they enter incorrect input?

Problem 3.8.9: Writing a pattern

Let us assume the company developing the teenage banking system has gathered experience with many other systems for young people. During those projects, there was a recurring misunderstanding: When young customers were interviewed for requirements, they rarely checked "intuitive interface" as a high priority. Nevertheless, customer satisfaction seemed to depend on ease of use. Structure this observation as a pattern, and describe how the teenage banking project can make use of it.

Chapter 4
Formal Representations and Structures

4.1 Objectives of this Chapter

After reading this chapter, you should be able to

- Define an ontology for a given application domain and explain how it can be used in software engineering.
- Describe facts and information statements in RDF.
- Implement an ontology in Protégé, an open-source tool for ontology development.
- Carry out basic reasoning strategies manually and explain how they work.
- Name and briefly describe well-known approaches in the area of structuring knowledge for reuse.

This chapter describes core techniques that are part of most knowledge management initiatives. According to Earl's classification scheme, they qualify as "technocratic" approaches. In this chapter, knowledge is described in a more formal syntax. A system of languages and tools is available to access knowledge on the World Wide Web and to feed it into tools that take advantage of a clearly defined structure.

Recommended Reading for Chap. 4

- OpenGALEN Foundation. OpenGALEN, *http://www.opengalen.org/*
- Protégé. *http://protege.stanford.edu/*
- A collection of many different ontologies: http://www.schemaweb.info/
- Software engineering ontology based on SWEBOK: http://www.seontology.org

4.2 Concept and Purpose of Ontologies

Initiatives like Semantic Web [17] pursue the vision of a distributed knowledge base. If meaning can be encoded in structures and syntax, tools can reason on the semantic level. We should keep in mind our primary goal: Managing knowledge in software engineering for the purpose of supporting software engineering activities. A rich and accessible knowledge base can contribute to that purpose.

K. Schneider, *Experience and Knowledge Management in Software Engineering*,   99
DOI 10.1007/978-3-540-95880-2_4, © Springer-Verlag Berlin Heidelberg 2009

Within the ontology community, Gruber's definition is widely accepted: "An ontology is an explicit specification of a shared conceptualization." [49]. Everyone dealing with ontologies should know this definition. For applying ontologies in software engineering, our definition should focus on guiding activities:

Definition 4.1 (Ontology)

An ontology is a data model that represents a set of concepts within a domain and the relationships between those concepts. It is used to reason about the objects within that domain (Wikipedia, August 30, 2007).

This pragmatic definition will be used below. Ontologies are created as a basis for automatic interpretation of the data model. This allows tools to refer to the meaning implied by the ontology. The above definition is specific for computer science. The same term is defined in a more generic way within philosophy or within other domains.

At first glance, this definition may remind a software engineer of UML domain models. A domain model or UML class model contains classes, which are similar to concepts. They have attributes and there are relationships between them. Instances are created from classes, and individuals are created from concepts in an ontology. At first glance, there are many similarities. As we will see, there are also several differences between domain models and ontologies.

Ontologies can be represented in a graphical notation. According to the above definition, this notation must provide symbols for concepts (classes) and for relationships. In addition, there will be mechanisms for expressing attributes, rules, and queries for reasoning. Fig. 4.1 shows a small part of an ontology for a medical problem domain.

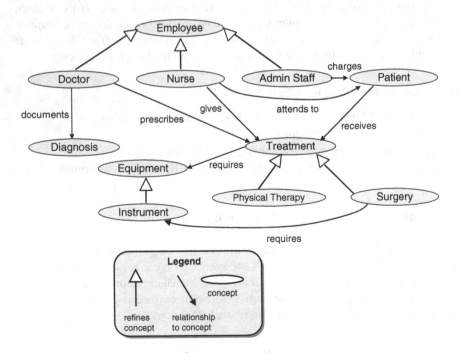

Fig. 4.1 Excerpt from a medical ontology

Like any of the above-mentioned semiformal notations, problem domain ontologies help software engineers to better communicate with domain experts. Communication between software and domain professionals will be improved by defining essential terms (as concepts or classes) and their relationships.

In complete domain ontologies, there will be hundreds of classes and highly specific concepts.

Example 4.1 (OpenGALEN medical ontology)

OpenGALEN is a well-known ontology in the medical domain [80]. It provides an extended glossary including relationships and the opportunity to use that structure in an automated way. Fig. 4.2 displays an example of a symptom, "pyrexia," informally called "fever." The browser on the left-hand side allows the user of this open-source ontology to search terms and symptoms in a systematic way, with definitions, formal value descriptions (like *BodyAsAWhole*), and relationships (e.g., *isSyndromeElementOfInfluenza*). Such a definition may look like a normal glossary entry at first. However, the predefined set of available attribute values and relationships are a clear indication of a more formally defined vocabulary and a formally structured body of knowledge. OpenGALEN [80] can be downloaded and explored

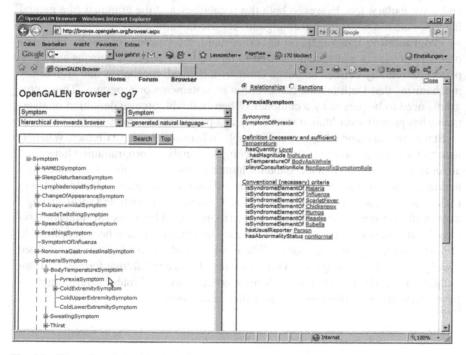

Fig. 4.2 "Fever," as defined in OpenGALEN [80]. Printed with permission from 152 Medische Informatiekunde, PO Box 9101, 6500 HB Nijmegen, The Netherlands

free of charge. You should take this chance to get used to a serious domain-specific ontology.

An ontology can be used to organize knowledge about a problem domain (like automotive or medical systems, see Fig. 4.1 and Fig. 4.2 for ontologies on medical issues).

4.3 Representing Knowledge Items

Knowledge needs to be expressed in statements. A statement can be made in different forms. Natural language is a straightforward format for expressing knowledge:

> George Miller is a Software Engineer who earns € 55,000 a year.
> He designed the XY software product. His boss is Andy Burk.
> His daughter Alice likes chili chocolate.

First of all, not all statements about George may be relevant for a software engineering knowledge base, even if they are true. Usually, a professional knowledge base will not contain personal information about employees' children.

Ontologies support the automatic interpretation of information, which calls for a formally defined syntax for statements. **Natural language** is based on a grammar and a vocabulary, too. However, both the vocabulary and the grammar of a natural language are too wide and too ambiguous for use in ontologies.

Programming languages, on the other hand, are tailored for use by the computer. Their syntax and semantics need to be understandable for humans and compilers. A formally defined language contains a defined vocabulary and structuring mechanisms that facilitate the composition of statements or programs. Those programs need to be parsed by a compiler. When in doubt, precise definition of statements has priority over human readability in a programming language.

Statements in **an ontology** typically reside in between the two extremes. Whereas natural language is too vague to support computer analysis, programming languages are considered difficult to understand for human users. In the realm of software engineering, however, the threshold for using a formalized language should be lower than in an application domain like medicine. Computer scientists and software engineers will not have major difficulties using a more formal language. Several attempts have been made to bridge the gap: Vocabulary and grammar have been simplified to almost-natural language statements. The result is readable for humans and defined clearly enough for ontologies and for reasoning. There are different formats and languages for describing an ontology: Among others features, Protégé offers template-based interaction for defining classes, slots, and properties.

4.3.1 Resource Description Framework

The Resource Description Framework (RDF) is a general-purpose language for representing and referencing information on the Web. It is intended for representing metadata about Web resources, such as the title, author, and modification date of a Web page, copyright and licensing information about a Web document, or the availability schedule for some shared resource. RDF is intended for situations in which this information needs to be processed by applications rather than be presented to people directly.

RDF provides a common framework for expressing this kind of information. It can be exchanged between applications without loss of meaning. RDF is based on the idea of identifying things using Web identifiers (called *Uniform Resource Identifiers*, or *URIs*) and describing resources in terms of simple properties and property values. This enables RDF to represent simple statements about resources as a graph of nodes and arcs representing the resources and their properties and values [114].

An ontology (residing on the class or concept level) describes *potential* structures and elements in a knowledge base. The knowledge base itself is a collection of concrete instances that is conformant to those structures. A fact in a knowledge base is an instance of a class in its ontology.

Example 4.2 (Concept)

The class represents a concept (e.g., "Software Engineer"). The concept of a Software Engineer is defined in the ontology by combining and naming several slots (attributes) and properties (relationships to other objects). Software Engineers are described in an abstract way on this level.

If we want to express a statement about a particular Software Engineer, we need to instantiate the class and fill attributes. For example, George Miller may be an instance of the class Software Engineer, with a salary (attribute) of € 55,000 and a relationship to the design document (object) of project XY. These statements look straightforward. They are almost ready for processing by a computer.

4.3.2 RDF Triples for Simple Statements

If knowledge engineers want to work independently of a specific tool, they need to use a standardized exchange format. RDF is such a format. It can be used across a number of tools to write parseable statements. The syntax of parseable statements can be read and analyzed by a computer. Basically, simple statements are expressed as RDF triples in RDF.

Example 4.3 (George Miller)

The RDF triple in Fig. 4.3 represents the statement:

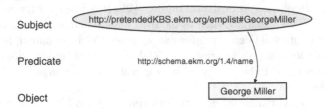

Fig. 4.3 RDF triple stating the name of a person

- There is someone identified by the URI of his entry in the employee list of a knowledge base system: *http://pretendedKBS.ekm.org/emplist#GeorgeMiller*. This knowledge base is fictitious; we just pretend it exists for our example.
- The individual George Miller has a slot "name," which is filled with the String literal "George Miller."
- The relationship between a Person and his or her name is assumed to be defined in the schema (version 1.4) *http://schema.ekm.org/1.4/* via the slot "name."

Resources (individuals) are denoted by ovals, attributes and relationship slots are denoted by arcs, and literals are denoted by rectangles in RDF triples. In RDF, there is no notion of classes for organizing resources, just a very simple type concept. Further concepts are provided by Resource Description Framework Schema (RDFS) and Web Ontology Language (OWL), which are presented below. Please note: All URIs in the examples containing the *ekm* substring are for illustration in examples only. Do not try to find them on the Internet.

Obviously, RDF was made to refer to resources on the Web. An **RDF triple** in Fig. 4.3 has three grammatical constituents: subject–predicate–object. They are the basis of simple statements in English or another language.

- **Subject**: Someone or something considered a "resource." Resources are often Web pages but may be any persons or items represented by a URI.
- **Predicate**: Indicates how the subject is related to another concept. This relationship may either be static in nature ("name" or "worksFor") or it may indicate an activity of the subject ("writes-...").
- **Object**: Defines what the subject is related to or what the subject is doing. In the above examples, "George-worksFor-Bill" or "Bill-writes-moduleXY" are complete statements including a subject.

Each of the three constituents is identified by a URI but does not have to reside on the Web. In our simple example, George Miller is a living person. The URI representing him within the knowledge base may point to his homepage, for example.

From the perspective of the ontology, only the concepts modeled in the ontology are meaningful: The few statements about George Miller are all the knowledge base "knows" about him. In the closed world of the ontology, we *define* the meanings of ontology elements rather than "reconstructing their real-world meaning." There are deep philosophical discussions about this seemingly subtle difference [82]. Although a software engineer interested in knowledge management support might not be interested in all those arguments, it is important to keep this so-called **closed-world assumption** in mind.

Mnemonic 4.1 (Ontology as a model)

An ontology is a model of reality but not reality itself. It is a simplified selection of aspects that are mapped to formalism convenient for management.

Eliciting and representing knowledge are challenging tasks. In Chap. 5, this issue will be discussed in more depth focusing on experience elicitation. However, acquiring knowledge and presenting it in a knowledge base is an equally challenging task. It is called **knowledge acquisition.** Asking an expert to type in knowledge manually is unrealistic. There should be semiautomated support to infer knowledge from the activities experts perform anyway.

Example 4.4 (Predicates)

As in Fig. 4.4, *predicates* can be rather simple: George has a name. His daughter likes-to-eat chili chocolate. George earns a salary of €55,000. **Predicates** describe the relationship between subject and object. Therefore, they are graphically expressed as an arrow or a line. In RDF, not only **subject** and **object** are identified by URIs: Properties and relationships between subject and object are also defined by URIs. In the case of a property, the URI points to a definition of the respective relationship. Meaningful concepts and relationships are defined in schemas. An ontology can be a specific schema for knowledge items.

Mnemonic 4.2 (Relationships in a schema)

A relationship (e.g., of type "daughter-of") with a URI connects individual relationships to relationship classes defined in a schema or an ontology that is referenced by the URI.

Therefore, URIs in RDF often point to a property class in an ontology or a schema. Assume the "daughter-of" relationship has a URI pointing to a Family

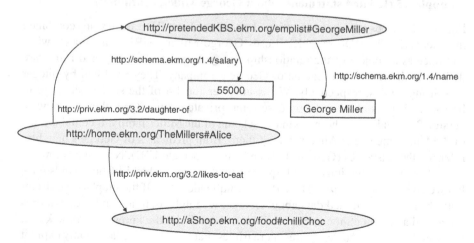

Fig. 4.4 RDF graph of the George Miller example

schema, which means: "This individual relationship of George to his daughter Alice is an instance of the relationship 'daughter-of,' which is being defined in the Family schema." For example, the Family schema could specify the "daughter-of" relationship only between a Person and a Female Person (the daughter). No instance can be established between a Person and a Male Person. The relationship can have attributes and properties such as a "quality of relationship." The relationship defines its relationship instances.

The terms *schema* and *ontology* are treated as synonyms here. Many existing schemas and ontologies define their respective domain in a generic way. Specific classes and relationships can be added in order to define domain particularities for a specific project or environment. This extends the schema. Medical treatments, for example, can be represented by a medical ontology such as medSchema (see Fig. 4.1) or OpenGALEN (Fig. 4.2 [80]). Each company working in the medical domain may use existing schemas and extend them.

In our software engineering example, the relationship "name" was assumed to be defined in the `schema.ekm` ontology. In Fig. 4.3, the URI of the predicate name (`http://schema.ekm.org/1.4/name`) points to that schema, and in particular to the name-relationship defined in it. Through this mechanism, the property is clearly defined.

4.3.3 RDF Graphs for Multiple Related Statements

A single RDF triple expresses an atomic statement. However, even the short natural language expression above contains several related statements. They can be expressed by a number of related RDF triples. In Fig. 4.4, we describe all facts expressed in the introductory sentences on George Miller by overlapping RDF triples. Subjects and objects are used for several simple statements in one combined graph.

Example 4.5 (Related statements about George Miller, continued)

Fig. 4.4 describes the above-mentioned situation: Four RDF triples are combined in a network. The RDF graphRDF uses George Miller's URI as a subject twice, and once as an object of the relationship `daughter-of`. `Salary` and `name` are defined in the (fictitious) schema of George's company. They are filled by integer and String literals, respectively. We assume version 1.4 of the schema.ekm.org to be used. There is also a schema describing private entities (priv.ekm.org, now in version 3.2), and even a home.ekm.org schema of the Miller family. It contains a list of the family members. Alice is one of them. Both predicates of George's daughter refer to other instances (George- URI and chili chocolate URI). Note that we might *guess* from the expressions what http://eShop.ekm.org/food#chilliChoc stands for – but we do not *know for sure*. The URI is a unique identifier. If the graph is consistent with the above-mentioned data about George, we might assume that his daughter is Alice and a certain eShop carries chili chocolate. To let the knowledge base know, we would have to add at least three more triples that encode those facts. Only explicit statements represent knowledge in the knowledge base.

```
<http://pretendedKBS.ekm.org/emplist#GeorgeMiller> has
<http://schema.ekm.org/1.4/name>
"George Miller".

<http://pretendedKBS.ekm.org/emplist#GeorgeMiller> has
<http://schema.ekm.org/1.4/salary>
"55000".

<http://priv.ekm.org/TheMillers#Alice> is
<http://priv.ekm.org/1.4/daughter-of>
<http://pretendedKBS.ekm.org/emplist#GeorgeMiller>.

<http://home.ekm.org/TheMillers#Alice> is
<http://priv.ekm.org/1.4/likes-to-eat>
<http://eShop.ekm.org/food#chilliChoc>.
```

Fig. 4.5 N3 representation of RDF graph above

RDF graphs may remind you of mind maps or domain models. However, they differ in notation and meaning. All concepts expressed by those graphs can be expressed in textual notations as well. Berner-Lee's "Notation 3" (N3) just lists the three URIs of a triple. Instances are represented by their URI. They are literals included in quotes. Additional comments may be inserted for better readability (like "has" and "is" in the example). Those comments are ignored by the ontology (Fig. 4.5).

eXtensible Markup Language (XML) can be used to represent this information as well: Fig. 4.6 shows an equivalent representation in XML/RDF. Despite

```
<?xml version="1.0" encoding="UTF-8" ?>
<rdf:RDF
    xmlns:rdf="http://www.w3.org/1999/02/22-rdf-syntax-ns#"
    xmlns:work="http://schema.ekm.org/1.4/"
    xmlns:george=
        "http://pretendedKBS.ekm.org/emplist#GeorgeMiller"
    xmlns:food="http://eShop.ekm.org/food#"
    xmlns:private="http://priv.ekm.org/TheMillers#"
>

<rdf:Description
    rdf:about=
        "http://pretendedKBS.ekm.org/emplist#GeorgeMiller">
    <george:name>George Miller</george:name>
    <george:salary>55000</george:salary>
</rdf:Description>

<rdf:Description
    rdf:about="http://eShop.ekm.org/food#chilliChoc">
</rdf:Description>

<rdf:Description
    rdf:about="http://priv.ekm.org/TheMillers#Alice">
    <priv:daughter-of rdf:resource=
        "http://pretendedKBS.ekm.org/emplist#GeorgeMiller"/>
    <priv:likes-to-eat
        rdf:resource="http://eShop.ekm.org/food#chilliChoc" />
</rdf:Description>

</rdf:RDF>
```

Fig. 4.6 XML/RDF representation of above RDF graph

its popularity, XML is not well suited for human readers. Do not expect software engineers to encode or decipher knowledge from a lengthy XML file. The XML format works well as an intermediate exchange format for tools. People should not be expected or forced to read it.

Fig. 4.6 reads as follows:

- After providing XML versioning information, the RDF part is opened.
- There are several shortcuts to other namespaces, indicated by `xmlns`. For example, `work` is defined to point to a namespace that describes George's work environment.
- In each Description clause, one subject is described. The `about` clause points to that subject by providing its URI. In the above example, the URI points to `#GeorgeMiller` in the `pretendedKBS` schema.
- All lines down to the next `</rdf:Description>` contain the description of the subject: its predicates and objects. Each statement describes one arc in the RDF graph. Every subject needs its own Description clause.

RDF triples have a very simple structure. Unfortunately, they are not powerful enough to express all statements one might want to make. Even overlapping triples as in Fig. 4.4 are not sufficient to express many statements a useful knowledge base should be able to express.

Several tricks have been invented to circumvent the restrictions imposed by the triple structure. Unnamed objects, blank nodes, and datatype extensions are among these tricks. Because RDF lacks datatypes, they can be mimicked as in the following example: `"55000"^^xsd:integer` stands for an integer value of 55,000. The XML datatype in the xsd namespace is referenced, and the awkward notation provides a technical bridge between the value (55,000) and a datatype in xsd.

However, this level of technical detail and trickery is a clear indication that we are operating on an inappropriate level. Software engineers building a knowledge base need abstraction layers to protect them from this low-level notational jungle. We will not pursue this aspect further.

4.3.4 Ontologies, Schemas, and Namespaces Provide Structure

As we have seen above, RDF triples often refer to one or more schemas. A schema is an ontology that is "imported" when the schema is referenced. Technically, the schema is declared as a namespace. The elements (objects, predicates, etc.) of that namespace are accessible for reference after that declaration of the namespace is "opened". Shortcuts make references easier to read.

In the above example, different namespaces were defined (Fig. 4.7).

This example opens XML/RDF and assigns five namespaces (rdf, work, george, food, and private).

```
<?xml version="1.0" encoding="UTF-8" ?>
<rdf:RDF
   xmlns:rdf="http://www.w3.org/1999/02/22-rdf-syntax-ns#"
   xmlns:work="http://schema.ekm.org/1.4/"
   xmlns:george=
      "http://pretendedKBS.ekm.org/emplist#GeorgeMiller"
   xmlns:food="http://eShop.ekm.org/food#"
   xmlns:private="http://priv.ekm.org/TheMillers#"
>

</rdf:RDF>
```

Fig. 4.7 Importing schemas and namespaces and defining shortcuts for them

4.3.5 Semantics Through Resource Description Framework Schema (RDFS)

Resource Description Framework Schema (**RDFS** or **RDF-Schema**) is a generic extension of RDF containing ontology concepts for reference. Further schemas can be defined in order to provide custom-made ontologies for custom-made knowledge bases. A schema adds meaning or semantics to the syntax provided by RDF. A reference to a schema links a syntactic statement to a semantic knowledge item.

A vocabulary is defined as a set of associated URIs. The union of the concepts "imported" through those URIs defines the terms in the vocabulary.

Definition 4.2 (Namespace)

A namespace is a technical concept. It is used in XML to refer to the names visible and usable. Syntactic constructs of namespaces in XML/RDF provide access to the semantic concepts in the vocabulary of that namespace.

A popular schema among the ontology community is known as the "**Dublin core**" [57]. It is a schema or ontology defining the concepts and relationships within the area of documents, electronic sources, books, and libraries. Web crawlers are autonomous tools that can use this ontology to search information on huge collections of documents. The knowledge about documents and their relationships is encoded in a machine-readable format; this was the initial intention of building an ontology. Tools built on the Dublin core can provide services to the users that benefit from "semantic knowledge" in that domain. Because documents are ubiquitous in a knowledge society, the Dublin core is an important foundation for many tools that go beyond syntactic (keyword or full-text) search.

RDFS can be referenced in the same way as other resources. URIs pointing to RDFS need to start with the prefix:

$$rdfs = "http://www.w3.org/2000/01/rdf-schema#"$$

By convention, this prefix should be associated with the rdfs: shortcut. This has been expressed above by assigning the URI to the shortcut. With that shortcut, a reference can be written as:

home:Customer rdf:type rdfs:Class

Customer is defined to be a Class. In other words, the RDF type is set to the refs concept "Class" for our own (home) concept Customer. rdfs was defined above as a shortcut to the RDFS schema. We can now instantiate the new class for individuals like "Jerry Stuart" or "Eva Meyer."

The option to import schemas and namespaces is a powerful concept. It helps knowledge engineers to reuse concepts far beyond their own creations. However, this flexibility comes with potential confusion:

- *Orientation*: How can a knowledge engineer know all the schemas and ontologies he or she could use?
- *Synonyms*: What if different people associate different schemas with properties that stand for the same semantic relationship?
- *Homonyms*: What if different imported schemas use the same name for different semantic concepts?

Detecting and harmonizing **schema conflicts** are difficult tasks that require skilled knowledge engineers. For software engineers who just use a knowledge base, those fundamental difficulties will be less relevant. In a large organization, dedicated knowledge engineers will be in charge of resolving those problems. In smaller organizations, software engineers in charge of knowledge management should select a small set of schema references. It is advisable to limit the scope of associated namespaces. Many problems from theory are less pressing in practice as long as a few guidelines are followed. After all, the purpose of knowledge and experience management in software engineering is to empower software engineers in their jobs. They should not have to serve as knowledge administrators instead.

RDF supports encoding of information into triples and RDF graphs. During reuse, information must be retrieved. For that purpose, tools and languages have been built that allow applying common retrieval languages to RDF. SPARQL [118], for example, is an database query language for information retrieval in RDF. It was SQL statements. RDF statements are considered a data storage, and SPARQL provides well-known SQL query mechanisms for searching and modifying those data. Technically, SQL is an existing mechanism that has proved its usefulness. Semantically, SQL databases do not provide sufficient support for queries and knowledge management. Therefore, the content and structure of knowledge bases are defined in ontologies rather than databases.

4.3.5.1 Summary: Sharing Semantics

Concepts and relationships of an ontology need to be defined in an unambiguous way. RDF is a format that facilitates the inclusion of Internet resources. RDF triples are basic grammatical constructs for making statements. RDF-Schema (or RDFS) serves for assigning meaning to the elements of an RDF statement by pointing from individuals to their "classes" in the schema. Elements in the RDF triple refer to a schema, such as RDFS or the Dublin core ontology. Tools that use the ontology can refer to the same schema, and, hence, the same semantics. Thus, they can reason on a semantic level: Instead of reasoning on things and properties, their rules and queries can refer, for example, to classes of software engineers, product versions, and relationships such as writes-relationships, and so forth.

4.4 Defining Ontologies with Web Ontology Language (OWL)

We will now see how an ontology is described using the Web Ontology Language (OWL). OWL is a markup language for publishing and sharing ontologies on the World Wide Web. OWL is built on RDF and, in principle, extends its vocabulary. However, OWL is not simply an extension. To maintain computability and efficiency, not all RDF operations are permitted in OWL.

Definition 4.3 (OWL variants)

In fact, three variants of OWL have been defined that address different needs:
OWL-Full: *A full extension of RDF that grants downwards compatibility to RDF and RDF schema. In that variant, all RDF statements and operations are also permissible in OWL-Full. The downside is a loss of computability. That means that some derived facts in an OWL-Full ontology cannot be proved, although they may be true. This is a severe setback for the purpose of making logical inferences on the ontology.*
OWL-DL: *A subset of OWL designed to stay computable. OWL-DL supports the same language constructs as OWL-Full. However, some usage restrictions apply in OWL-DL.*
OWL-Light: *Yet a more restricted subset of OWL-DL. Those further restrictions were not made out of theoretical considerations (as in OWL-DL) but as a convenience for different kinds of users.*

OWL-DL requires classes, properties, and individuals to be disjoint. OWL-Full allows overlaps. A precise definition of all differences between OWL-Full and OWL-DL is provided in the Semantics and Abstract Syntax document [117]. Those restrictions ensure computability, which is important for the use of an ontology. For example, powerful reasoning tools can exploit the expressive power of OWL-DL and exploit computability at the same time. Authors and readers of OWL-Light work with a simpler language subset, so they can master it faster. What may be even more important: OWL-Light is a convenient platform for tool builders who are not willing or able to support OWL-DL.

If in doubt, OWL-DL is the variant to work with. Its restrictions are less severe than those of OWL-Light, and its formal semantics are computable.

Mnemonic 4.3 (Purpose of OWL)

OWL is intended to serve as an exchange format between tools that use and exploit information on a semantic level. OWL is not a language designed to directly communicate with human users.

Not all language constructs can be explained in this book; resources on the Web contain hundreds of pages to introduce syntax and semantics of each construct

[117]. Interested readers may find it helpful to read more about the foundations of RDF first [116] and the OWL Guide [115] afterward. There are many examples and more specific resources available that are linked to those documents. However, before digging into the details and special cases of the Web-based material, it is recommended to finish this chapter of the book. Its main purpose is to provide readers with a profound overview of the most relevant aspects of OWL as a language for describing ontologies. This will make it easier to read and understand more detailed documents.

4.4.1 Ontology Metainformation (Header)

Example 4.6 (OWL)

An ontology is described in an XML document. It contains tags specific to OWL (such as <owl:Ontology ...>) and starts with metainformation about the ontology itself. An ontology is itself a resource, so it may be described using properties from the OWL and other namespaces, for example:

```
<owl:Ontology rdf:about="">
  <owl:versionInfo>... </owl:versionInfo>
  <rdfs:comment>    ... </rdfs:comment>
  <owl:imports rdf:resource="..."/>
</owl:Ontology>
```

At the core of an OWL-described ontology are classes, properties, and attributes.

4.4.2 Creating Classes in Class Axioms

OWL classes can be described in six different ways. Each variant of describing a class can be embedded in the OWL language construct of a "class axiom." The class axiom creates the class. There are different ways of describing a class through class axioms. For each variant, there is a short example given below.

Example 4.7 (Classes in different class axioms)

- *A class identifier*. Because OWL refers to Web-based resources, URI references are used as class identifiers. Only the existence of the class is defined. We know nothing about the class or its elements. All we know is its name.

  - <owl:Class rdf:ID="Version"/>
    defines a class of software versions.

- *An extensive enumeration of individuals*. In this variant, a class is considered a collection of predefined individual instances instead of a mechanism for creating instances.

- The list of employees in the George Miller example is an enumeration of employee individuals.

- Defining a class as an *intersection of two or more existing classes*. This implicit definition is an alternative to defining class instances explicitly, like in an enumeration of its individuals. The elements of an intersection class may vary over time: If a new element is introduced into both referenced classes, this new element automatically becomes an element of the intersection class. That one element belongs to more than one class!

  - All Software Engineers who are also (`owl:intersectionOf`) Testers could be defined to form a new intersection class "SoftwareExperts." It contains those software engineers who also work in testing.

- Defining a class as a *union of two or more classes*. This is yet another alternative to defining the individuals of a class implicitly.

  - Managers and Software Engineers together may be considered Staff. Staff would be a new class populated by the union operation (`owl:unionOf`). Staff and a common superclass "Employee" of Managers and Software Engineers can be defined as different classes. However, those different classes may contain the same elements.

- A class can be defined as the *complement of another class*. Again, this variant uses a set-specific operation to derive one class description from another one.

  - Supporting Staff could be defined as a class of all Employees who are not Software Engineers, expressed as (`owl:disjointWith`).

- A *property restriction* implicitly describes the set of individuals: All individuals that satisfy the restrictions described in the property. Restrictions can be either value or cardinality constraints.

  - Senior Engineers can be defined as all Software Engineers with more than 5 years of experience. Experience is treated in this example as a property with numeric value.

Instances of classes are the individual "things" that populate a knowledge base. OWL provides two useful predefined classes:

- **Thing** is the most general superclass in the inheritance hierarchy. All OWL classes must be (direct or indirect) subclasses of Thing. As a consequence, all individuals of any class are also individuals (instances) of Thing. Everything is a Thing.
- **Nothing** is the complement of Thing: Nothing is a class that does not have (and cannot have) any individuals. Vice versa, Thing is the complement of Nothing. Everything is a Thing.

Because many operations in ontologies treat classes as sets, the full and empty sets are important.

4.4.3 Properties

Properties are the constructs used in OWL to describe relationships and attributes. There are two different kinds of properties:

- **Object properties** relate individuals to individuals. They link objects to objects.
- **Datatype properties** relate individuals to data values. They attach a label to the individual or assing a value to an attribute.

OWL classes inherit their features from RDFS. Both kinds of OWL properties are subclasses of rdf:Property. When we talk about "rdfs resources," we mean both classes and properties (Fig. 4.8).

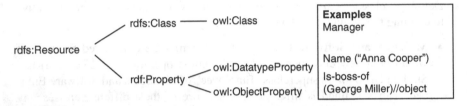

Fig. 4.8 Constructs in OWL and where they come from

4.5 Ontologies and Object-Oriented Terminology

At first glance, ontologies and object-oriented languages seem to be very similar: Classes, relationships, attributes, and instances can be found in both worlds, with only slight variations in terminology. However, the overview discussion about class axioms showed a number of differences you should be aware of.

Table 4.1 shows a comparison of terms and meanings in different contexts. Not all comparable terms refer to identical concepts, and some differences are more important than others. The last column comments on differences between terms. Those differences are explained below. Note the two variants provided for Protégé. Older versions (up to version 3) used a proprietary format to represent ontologies newer version use OWL. The terms on the left-hand side of the slash were used in older versions, whereas the newer (owl) versions of Protégé use the terms on the right-hand side of the slash. For example, what used to be called a "slot" is now either called "Object Property" or "Data Property."

Example 4.8 (Independent attributes)

In a programming language class description, an attribute like author is part of the description of the class SoftwareDocument and applies *only* to instances of the class SoftwareDocument. Another class (say, ProcessModel) might also

Table 4.1   Comparison of terminology for related concepts

OO Term	Ontologies	Protégé(old/owl)	Comments
Class	Concept	Class	Ontologies treat classes/concepts as sets of individuals
Instance	Individual	Instance/individual	
Relationship	Property (ObjectProp.)	Slot/object property	Slots pointing to other individuals
Attribute	Property (DatatypeProp.)	Slot/data property	Slots pointing to literals
Class model	Schema or ontology	Ontology	Model on the class level
Object model	Knowledge base (KB)	Knowledge base	Networks of instance-level pieces of knowledge need to comply with class-level models
–	Search in KB	Query	OO models are usually not queried, but code may be generated from UML models

have an attribute called `author`, but this would be considered a *different* attribute. In other words, the *scope* of an attribute description in most programming languages is restricted to the class or type in which it is defined. In RDF, on the other hand, property descriptions are, by default, *independent* of class definitions, and have, by default, a *global* scope. They can be explicitly declared to apply only to certain classes using domain specifications.

As a result, an RDF schema could describe a property within the software engineering terminology schema "seterms": `seterms:author` can be specified without indicating a domain. This property can then be used for instances of any class that have an author. One benefit of the **RDF property**-based approach is that it becomes easier to extend the use of property definitions to situations that might not have been anticipated in the original description. At the same time, this is a "benefit" that must be used with care, in order to ensure that properties are not applied in inappropriate situations.

Classes as descriptions or prescriptions: RDF-Schema provides schema information as additional *descriptions* of resources but does not *prescribe* how these descriptions should be used by an application. In programming languages, a class description prescribes exactly what all its instances will look like, what attributes and methods they will have, and how they will behave. Classes in ontologies are tightly associated with the set of their individuals rather than with a template for creating instances. From this perspective, it is straightforward to apply set-operations such as union, intersection, or selection.

Convenient additions: RDF lacks even basic mechanisms like cardinalities or a type system. RDF-Schema adds a semantic layer on top of RDF but still lacks expressive power. OWL contains constructs for handling cardinalities and several other aspects. OWL is a richer and more specific language than RDF (Schema).

4.6 Software Engineering Ontologies

There exist ontologies that model and support different aspects of software engineering. Because software engineering is a knowledge-intensive discipline, it can be worthwhile capturing concepts and relationships in order to encode and manage related knowledge.

4.6.1 Software Engineering Ontologies on the Internet

A well-known collection of ontologies can be found and browsed at www.schemaweb.de. Ontologies reach from wine-tasting over software projects to knowledge management issues. Not all ontologies in this collection are very complete or useful. Some ontologies related to software engineering are offered at www.schemaweb.de, too. A slightly older ontology was built on SWEBOK: www.seontology.org. It offers definitions of general software engineering terminology as its concepts. Those concepts are refined and instantiated to store concrete project artifacts in the knowledge base. A purpose of this ontology was to support collaboration among distributed teams. Happel and Seedorf [51] provide a concise overview of existing ontology approaches in software engineering. In analogy to our overview of software engineering activities presented in Chap. 2, Happel and Seedorf identify existing ontologies proposed by researchers for many aspects, ranging from requirements engineering terms and document structures to fine-grained structures of individual requirements. In this phase, they claim improved traceability for ontology-based requirements engineering as opposed to semiformal approaches.

In design and implementation, a challenge lies in the combination of UML models, model-driven architecture (MDA), and ontologies. Their structures are not intrinsically compliant. However, because both model-driven and ontology-based approaches apply strict formalisms, there are chances for mapping and merging. Although this is still a research issue, documentation and maintenance are obviously areas for practical application of knowledge bases and ontologies. According to Happel and Seedorf, software engineering ontologies can be classified by the way they are used in software projects: Development time versus run-time and for modeling software versus infrastructure.

Calero et al. [23] present an introduction to the use and construction of ontologies in software engineering. They assume the same benefits from using ontologies: More consistent use of terminology and a basis for automation. They also use SWEBOK as reference and try to merge concepts of ontologies with aspects of model-driven architecture.

4.6.2 Small Software Engineering Ontology for Exercise

For the purpose of getting a good overview, we build our own software engineering ontology in the following sections. It will be very small and rudimentary, but it enables us to see it grow in terms of concepts, and within a tool. Of course, the same mechanisms can then be used to extend an existing larger ontology.

Example 4.9 (Software engineering ontology)

We will use the simple software engineering ontology as a running example for the remainder of this chapter. This ontology considers Managers, Software Engineers, and Quality Agents as Employees of a company. Much of their work is related to Documents in one way or the other. Software Engineers write Documents, Quality Engineers review them, and only Testers may test Code. Please note that some individuals may belong to more than one concept, like a Software Engineer who is acting as a reviewer every now and then. However, a Programmer who is not a Tester at the same time cannot test, according to this ontology. An ontology serves to clarify concepts and their relationships. A model-driven code generator, for example, is modeled as a tool that uses UML specifications as input and generates code as output.

Fig. 4.1 and Fig. 4.9 illustrate the definition of an ontology as "a data model." Basic building blocks of an object-oriented class model look similar to an ontology as sketched above, but they serve different purposes. Whereas class models **prescribe** future software systems like a blueprint, ontologies **describe** the structure of a knowledge domain. When class models are implemented during a software

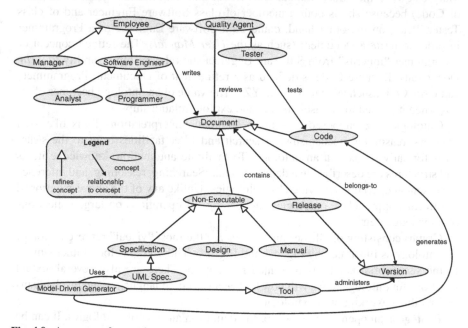

Fig. 4.9 An excerpt from software engineering example ontology

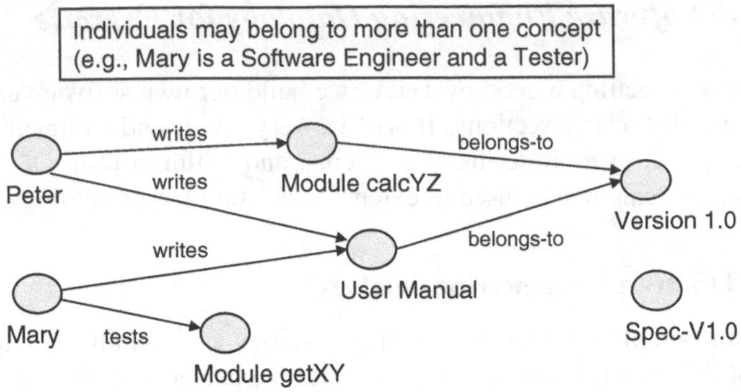

Individuals may belong to more than one concept
(e.g., Mary is a Software Engineer and a Tester)

Fig. 4.10   Graphical model of some knowledge items (instances) that conform to the above ontology

project, they evolve from prescriptive to descriptive roles. Each successfully implemented prescriptive model can act as a description of its implementation.

Concepts or classes of an ontology need to be instantiated just like instances of classes in Java or UML. There are several subtle differences. In UML, there are object diagrams to depict the interaction of instances during execution. Instances of an ontology represent formal pieces of knowledge. All items and relationships together make up a "knowledge base." Fig. 4.10 shows individual instances of the concepts depicted in Fig. 4.9. Knowledge is represented by individuals and their concrete individual relationships.

The instances and their relationships must conform to the ontology. In Fig. 4.10, Mary can *write* the "User Manual" Document and *test* "Module get XY" (a piece of Code) because she is both a member of class Software Engineer and of class Tester. Peter, on the other hand, could be a Software Engineer or a Programmer in order to *write* a Document (such as the *User Manual*). The refined concept of Programmer "inherits" from Software Engineer the relationship or ability to *write* Documents. Because Code is defined as a refinement of Document, Programmers can *write* Code, such as "Module calcYZ." The value of an ontology becomes obvious when it is used to precisely define and explore relationships.

Ontologies are supposed to support automatic interpretation. Tools like Web crawlers, reasoning mechanisms, or search and filter facilities refer to the structures formally defined in an ontology. To facilitate automation, knowledge items and structures are described in a defined syntax. Searching, reasoning, and inference are essential operations provided by ontologies. Unlike any of the above-mentioned semiformal approaches, ontologies support logical operations on large collections of knowledge items.

Graphs consisting of ellipses and arrows are the most "visual" representation of an ontology as illustrated by Fig. 4.1 and Fig. 4.9. Those graphs look rather similar to the semiformal notations presented in Chap. 3. There are also several textual notations for ontologies. We will now look at a variety of languages and mechanisms that facilitate working with ontologies.

Protégé is an open-source tool for the definition and use of ontologies. It can be downloaded and used to explore ontology building.

- We will first use the most easy-to-use view of Protégé to build a sample excerpt of our software engineering ontology. Simple examples will provide hands-on-experience. You are encouraged to follow the examples using Protégé yourself.
- Above, the languages promoted by the W3C (World Wide Web Consortium) were introduced:

- **RDF** allows integrating Web resources into ontologies.
- **RDF triples** are the basis of formal descriptions of concepts and relationships.
- **RDF/XML** is an XML representation of RDF instead of a graph.
- **RDFS** serves as a metamodel for defining domain-specific concepts. When tools can reference the semantic domain relationships, they can also exploit them for specific functionality. For example, SWEBOK can be described in RDFS. This would allow software engineers to refer to its terms when they describe software engineering knowledge in their ontology.
- **OWL** is built upon RDF. It extends its generic modeling capabilities toward ontology functions. This includes easier access to data types, cardinalities, and other advanced mechanisms.

- Using standardized languages helps to share ontologies. Because many information and knowledge exchange tools use the World Wide Web, the above-mentioned languages (RDF, RDFS, and OWL) help to make an important step toward a meaningful interpretation of subwebs. This is at the core of the Semantic Web initiative [17].
- Protégé supports its proprietary format as well as OWL. There are many other tools for creating and editing ontologies. Ontoedit [2], for example, is a commercial tool for that purpose.

When you download Protégé, you can get *extensive documentation* together with it. There are examples to practice ontology lessons (e.g., on pizzas, travel, or cameras). As Fig. 4.11 implies, there is a complex collection of Web-based documents provided to study ontology construction in Protégé. In this book, you will see enough of the languages to build your own ontology. For further details, please refer to the available material that comes with Protégé.

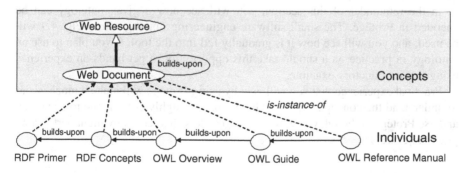

Fig. 4.11 Related documents on the Web, presented as instances of a simple ontology

Remember we are interested in reusing knowledge in software projects. This is the reason for us to use an ontology: It allows combining and searching the knowledge base. We also want to detect inconsistencies. We will use inference and other formal mechanisms to check the knowledge base. In the remainder of this chapter, we will always keep in mind that we are not artificial intelligence experts looking for a challenge; we are software engineers searching for a mechanism to support our software work.

4.7 A Tool for Working with Ontologies: Protégé

Ontologies facilitate automatic interpretation of information. There are many tools on the market that claim to support ontologies, and a company may decide to invest in a powerful and expensive tool. Many tools are built on similar concepts as the tool we will use here: Protégé.

Protégé is an open-source tool that is available free of charge [86]. It comes with online help and a manual. Links to basic reading material are included. Protégé contains an editor for building ontologies and for creating individual instances of knowledge items. They are called "instances" in older versions of Protégé and "individuals" in newer versions and in tool-independent terminology. Queries represent the reasoning mechanism for exploiting the knowledge base.

The material attached to Protégé exceeds this entire book in size. It is neither possible nor desirable to cover all concepts and details of RDF, OWL, or the Protégé system in this book. The selection presented here was made for software engineers who will work in a knowledge-intensive environment. You should understand the principles and foundations of ontologies, and you should be empowered to build and use a simple ontology for a new domain. Based on this expertise, you will be able to extend your insights when you have the opportunity to contribute to a knowledge management initiative in practice.

You will need to structure knowledge in an application domain of your future software projects. In addition, you can structure your own domain of expertise: software development. Successful knowledge management in software engineering builds on those two pillars.

In the remainder of this section, you will see how a given ontology can be encoded in Protégé. The small software engineering ontology from Fig. 4.9 will be used, and you will see how it is gradually fed into the tool. If you plan to use an ontology in practice, you should take this opportunity to get hands-on experience using this introductory example.

Practical experience that you will gain by using Protégé will make it much easier to understand the concepts presented here. You are highly encouraged to download and use Protégé, although you will be able to follow this section without performing practical exercises.

1. **Download Protégé from http://protege.stanford.edu/**

   - You need to register as a user.
   - Download is free and there are no strings attached.
   - Requirements to run Protégé are specified on this page.
   - A current version of Java (e.g., Java 1.5) is required.
   - Download a version that can handle OWL.

2. **Install Protégé**

   - You receive a self-extracting file for your computer and platform.
   - Install Protégé by executing that file.

3. **Open Protégé**

   - Double-click on the created icon to start Protégé.
   - Choose one of the provided projects from the Web using "Open URI" (e.g., project "pizza").
   - Select the "Classes" tab and open subclasses of Thing until you see a view like Fig. 4.12. To open a class, press the small triangle before its name.

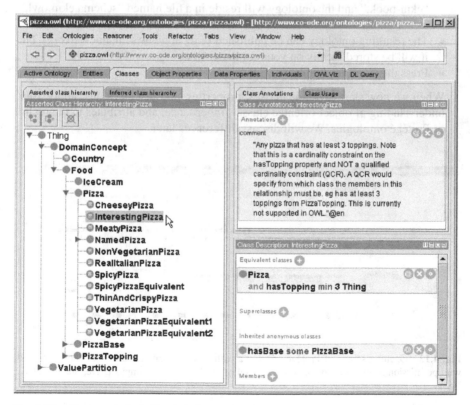

Fig. 4.12   Pizza example in Protégé. Interesting pizza has at least three toppings and a pizza base. Printed with permission from Stanford University School of Medicine, 251 Campus Drive, Stanford, CA, USA

- Online help is provided for all details of the tool.
  - We will use only fundamental operations in this chapter.
  - Refer to online help for further details.
  - This chapter shows screenshots from Protégé as illustrations. Of course, the look and feel of Protégé may differ in future versions.
  - Other tools use similar mechanisms. The discussion in the remainder of this chapter is considered an introduction to the concepts, supported by a tool. It should not be misunderstood as a full step-by-step tool introduction. We will see the main road but not all the options, exceptions, and variants.

4. **Create a new ontology**

   We create the small software engineering ontology of Fig. 4.9 for exercise. It contains only a few classes, subclasses, and properties (attributes and relationships). We call the ontology schema.ekm, the example schema for this book on experience and knowledge management (EKM).

   - When Protégé opens, replace the given default ontology name and path by a more specific path and name. In our example, the subdirectory was named "ekm-book," and the ontology will reside in a file named "schema.ekm.owl," as in Fig. 4.13.
   - The resulting ontology can be published (e.g., at www.semanticweb.org), but it will be stored locally on your computer first.
   - Press the Continue button.

   When we now start to define classes, properties, and instances, just apply your understanding of object-oriented classes, inheritance, and attributes to the realm of Protégé ontologies. We will discuss differences later.

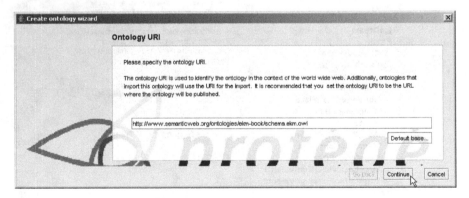

Fig. 4.13 Opening screen of Protégé offering a path and file name for a new ontology. Printed with permission from Stanford University School of Medicine, 251 Campus Drive, Stanford, CA, USA

5. **Insert a few classes and subclasses**

   Create the class structure depicted in Fig. 4.14:

   1. Select the Classes tab.
   2. Select a class (i.e., a concept) with the left mouse button. When you start with an empty ontology, only Thing exists to start with.
   3. Press the left icon 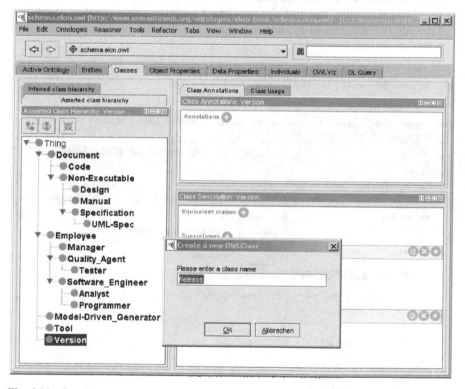 to create a subclass or the middle icon to create a same-level class. Thing is the root of the class hierarchy.
   4. Type in a class name in the appearing class creation box.
   5. The created class is inserted as a subclass of the initially selected class. In Fig. 4.14, class Version was selected; the left icon was pressed (and is still gray). The new class is called Release. When the OK button is pressed, the new class will occur indented under the Version class.
   6. By nesting class definitions, a hierarchical subclass structure can be created.

Fig. 4.14 Creating a subclass of Version by using small icons over "Thing". Printed with permission from Stanford University School of Medicine, 251 Campus Drive, Stanford, CA, USA

6. **Create a few properties (or "slots") using the** 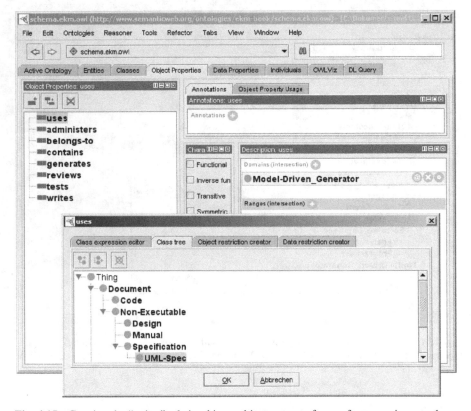 ﹍ ﹌ ⊠ **buttons**

Properties represent attributes and relationships of instances. In Fig. 4.15, the relationship "writes" is selected. Its domain is set to `Software_Engineer`, and its range is just being set to `Document`. This complies with the ontology where Software Engineers can write Documents.

- Select the "Object properties" tab. All relationships are displayed. They are not filtered by domain or range.
- Select an "add property" symbol (left or middle symbols above).
- Type in the name (e.g., writes) and select the domains and ranges by pressing the ○ symbol next to those labels. In Fig. 4.15, the domain has been set already to `Software_Engineer`. The range is just being selected from the hierarchical class list.

Relationships were shown in the schema of Fig. 4.9, but no attributes. Useful attributes may be the name and salary of an employee. They are introduced under the "Data properties" tab, just like the Object properties were inserted above. So far, only the structure of the ontology has been defined, including classes and

Fig. 4.15 Creating the "writes" relationship as object property from software engineer to document. Printed with permission from Stanford University School of Medicine, 251 Campus Drive, Stanford, CA, USA

properties (relationships and attributes). Attributes may now be added. If a super-class has a property, all subclasses will inherit that property. For example, every Employee has a salary. Therefore, a Programmer has a salary, too. Of course, attribute values may vary between individual.

7. **Create individual instances as knowledge contents**
   In the next step, concrete individuals are instantiated. They represent facts or statements in the knowledge base. This is done under the "Individuals" tab. A few instances of our ontology were shown in Fig. 4.10. We create individuals in Protégé to populate the ontology. This will turn it into a simple yet complete knowledge base.

In Fig. 4.16, the individuals depicted from Fig. 4.10 were encoded in Protégé. Each was assigned one or more "types" by selecting classes. A comment for Mary was provided, stating that she is both a Programmer and a Tester. She has those two types. Therefore, she can `write` the `User_Manual`, and `test` `Module_getXY`. Those object properties state relationships between individuals. They represent statements in the knowledge base. In addition, Mary's `salary` attribute has the value of 55,000 euro or dollar, which should be declared in the data property defini-tion of that attribute. The attribute was assigned to Employee on the class level, so that each instance of Employee or one of its subclasses has a salary.

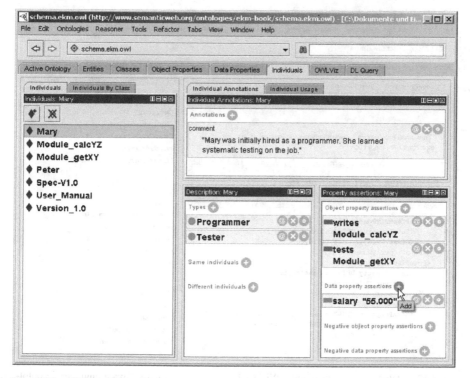

Fig. 4.16 Filling the ontology with knowledge items (individuals of classes and properties). Printed with permission from Stanford University School of Medicine, 251 Campus Drive, Stanford, CA, USA

For exercise, model the entire situation depicted in Fig. 4.10 and invent a few attributes.

- Add individuals by pressing the 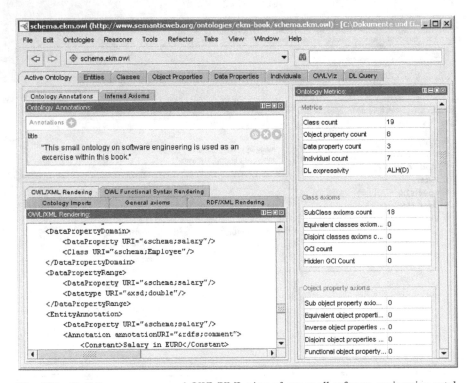 button. Provide a property name.
- Insert a relationship by pressing ⊕ next to "Object property assertions" and select a relationship and target instance.
- Add an attribute value by adding a "Data property assertion" in the same way.

Properties are not tightly or exclusively connected to one class. Instead, the same property (e.g., name) can be assigned to Software Engineers, Documents, and so forth. This is different from assigning attributes in UML or Java.

At this point, we saw all screens and features required for implementing the entire software engineering ontology example of Fig. 4.9 and the individuals depicted in Fig. 4.10. This is sufficient to construct and fill an ontology and fill the knowledge base.

After this construction phase, we can look at the "cover page" of our small software engineering ontology ("Active Ontology" tab in Fig. 4.17). A comment can be entered to explain the purpose and status of the ontology. A number of counts and statistics are displayed on the right-hand side. Obviously, our ontology contains only a few elements so far.

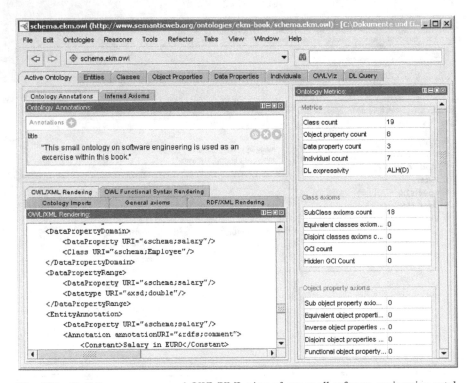

Fig. 4.17 Statistics cover page and OWL/XML view of our small software engineering ontology. Printed with permission from Stanford University School of Medicine, 251 Campus Drive, Stanford, CA, USA

The lower left part is particularly interesting: It provides different views of the ontology. For example, Fig. 4.17 shows a part of the RDF/XML presentation. There are OWL-views, too. This mechanism can be used for comparing different formal representations and for exercising their usage. By extending our small example, you can experiment with Protégé and investigate in detail what impact your changes have on the formal textual transcripts.

Once you have managed to create a class structure and individuals for schema.ekm, you have created a new ontology with Protégé. In previous sections, you saw different representation formalisms such as RDF and different kinds of class descriptions. Many of those concepts can be tried out using the above simple example.

4.8 Benefits from Using Ontologies

Creating an ontology is interesting and challenging. Benefits are only realized, however, when ontologies are actually used. The features offered by an ontology can be used in different ways. Its formally defined structure enables knowledge engineers to query the knowledge base along semantic relationships. Unstructured collections of information can only be searched for keywords; similar or related concepts are not considered. Reasoning uses those structures to answer complex questions.

On the way to queries and reasoning, vague and uncertain information needs to be clarified and formalized. This difficult process has a valuable side-effect: it forces participants to reflect on terminology and concepts. Assumptions need to be made explicit. Knowledge is externalized and discussed. This process will never be complete under the constraints of a software company. But it will increase the awareness for knowledge sharing and resolve some unspoken misunderstandings. In addition, externalized and formally coded knowledge can be stored and exploited automatically.

Results must be presented or even visualized in order to reach intended users.

There are several existing ontologies on the Internet. By reusing existing ontologies, software engineers get a better start in their knowledge management initiatives. Of course, any source needs to be evaluated before it is adopted.

4.8.1 Semantic Queries and Reasoning

The formal structure of an ontology facilitates semantic search. It goes beyond syntactic full-text search of keywords by using thesauri, similar terms, and semantic relationships.

Example 4.10 (Queries about George Miller, continued)

The first and most striking benefit of an underlying ontology is the ability to search for information by referring to its semantic meaning. A picture is either a JPEG file (technical) or it is the picture of George Miller (semantic). It is meaningful to ask `George Miller` (the individual in the ontology) about his `boss` or his `salary`. On the level of JPEG files and numbers, this level of search and navigation is impossible.

Meaning or semantics is provided by a link from syntactic structures (classes, properties, etc.) to URIs and real-world objects. That link establishes "meaning"; semantics are assigned by mapping a symbol or string to the entity it represents. Charles Sanders Peirce [52] laid the foundation for semiotics, the science of signs, symbols, and their meaning. He is one of the forefathers of modern ontologies. Semiotics asks how meaning is constructed (i.e., created!) and understood when using signs and symbols. The operations on a knowledge base create and manipulate classes and instances that can be interpreted as signs and symbols.

Roughly speaking, a symbol or a sign stands for an object and is being interpreted by an **interpretant**. This establishes a triangular relationship of object, symbol, and interpretant. Meaning is established when someone can construct or reconstruct the triangle.

Example 4.11 (Meaning in semiotics)

An emergency exit is a door. It is represented by a symbol (with or without text). When the same symbol is used throughout a company or even a country, all citizens or customers can interpret that symbol. They act as interpretants and will run to the door in case of fire. They know that it will not lead into a dead end.

Meaning is often the result of a negotiation and discussion process in a community. A single individual defining the meaning of a term or a sound, or an icon, or any other symbol is a rare exception. The processes of agreeing on meaning and communicating it to others is at the heart of building knowledge bases and ontologies. Software engineers using a knowledge base will often use queries. A query is a specified search statement in the set of Things that are the individuals of an ontology.

Example 4.12 (Query)

Searching for a software module that was used in a particular software release calls for a semantic query. Full-text search of module names will not do.

Mnemonic 4.4 (Class extensions and membership)

There is more potential in ontologies: Formal reasoning can exploit formally defined knowledge beyond direct queries. Class extensions and membership of individuals in classes offer interesting opportunities for further semantic reasoning.
Example queries include:

- **Class membership**. Does an individual qualify as a member of a given class? In a knowledge base, class membership is not a static aspect and may change due to dynamically changing properties and attributes.

- **Equivalence of classes**: Have all modules been tested? Or, in ontology terminology: Is the class of code modules in project XY equivalent to the class of tested code modules? This question can be answered by checking class equivalence. Because of the descriptive nature of classes in ontologies, members may shift in and out of a class. A class is like a view on Things: It contains all individuals that happen to fulfill all restrictions defined in its class description.
- Ontologies can be checked for **inconsistencies** (i.e., errors) due to their formal properties. For example, an individual cannot be in a class and in its complement. Nor can an individual be in two classes that are defined to be disjoint. All those incidents indicate modeling errors. Removing the errors will make the knowledge base more useful.
- Besides uncovering outright inconsistencies, reasoning can help to detect **derived relationships** or class memberships that occur due to the implicit definition of classes. When several people maintain a knowledge base, unintended connections are easily entered and need to be identified before they mislead users. In particular, Web-based multiauthor ontologies need powerful mechanisms for identifying inconsistencies and unintended consequences. Importing and sharing ontologies or their knowledge bases is an opportunity. However, it also poses a threat to validity.
- Uncovered errors can be removed, thus improving the quality of a knowledge base. An error may reside on the ontology or schema level or it may be due to faulty knowledge items on the instance level.
- **Reasoners** are tools that apply logic to an ontology with its knowledge base. Usually, an ontology is represented in an intermediate format like XML and interpreted by the reasoner like RACER (http://www.sts.tu-harburg.de/~r.f.moeller/racer/) or FaCT + +(*http://owl.man.ac.uk/factplusplus/*).
- Other tools can make extended use of semantic information. Because many generic tools exist for searching and reasoning, custom-built tools will usually extend this functionality and combine it with other features: Project management mechanisms can use knowledge about the status of deliverables. It can be analyzed and presented in a highly customized way. Heuristics on error density and test techniques could use knowledge about tested modules in order to derive warning lists for modules that "look suspicious" from the perspective of a heuristic knowledge query.

4.8.2 Preserving Knowledge for the Organization

An important class of benefits goes beyond technical opportunities. Handling a knowledge base and managing knowledge explicitly stimulates learning and reflection in participating software engineers. Those benefits may have equally important impacts on software projects:

- Knowledge encoded in ontologies and knowledge items is explicit knowledge. According to Chaps. 1 and 2, knowledge management has to deal with the tension between tacit and explicit knowledge. When software experts leave the company, or when they are assigned different responsibilities, their treasure of knowledge is endangered: Everything that is implicit and tacit can easily be forgotten. New employees do not have access to it, which makes reuse impossible. As we will see in subsequent chapters, it is not trivial to make knowledge explicit – or to reuse explicit knowledge. But in many cases, explicit information has a much better chance of getting used by more people.
- There is something like a "critical mass" effect in knowledge bases. During the early 1990s, the World Wide Web reached only a small fraction of the information available on computers worldwide. When you tried to book a hotel room or a movie ticket in 1994, many attempts would fail. Not all hotels had Web sites. Only a few movie theaters offered online booking at that time. This experience did not encourage users to try it again. Today, the Internet has reached and exceeded a critical mass: There is now a high coverage of resources on every aspect of our lives. It is very likely to find useful information on the Internet. The "critical mass" was reached several years ago. The increased likelihood of finding relevant documents has pushed the benefit of the World Wide Web to a new level.

Today, there is a complementary challenge: How to find the few meaningful chunks of information in the huge pile of links delivered in response to a query? This is when Web-based ontologies come into the picture: They add semantic search and reasoning capabilities to tools. By going far beyond keyword search, the precision (i.e., percentage of relevant hits) can increase. It can make the smaller number of delivered links more beneficial.

4.8.3 Benefits Through Adequate Presentation

The result of a query can be a simple list of objects that match that query. The immediate result of semantic reasoning may be difficult to read for software engineers without in-depth knowledge management expertise. Often, an adequate presentation of results adds significant value to the practical use of an ontology.

A knowledge base and an ontology offer formally defined structures and contents. Tools can be built that follow relationships, generate queries, and display results in a domain-specific way. There is a wide range of possible presentations that exploit the knowledge base. In this section, a few examples will give an impression of this important field.

Example 4.13 (Domain-specific interface)

Protégé offers a generic interface for working with all kinds of ontologies. However, domain-specific browsers and editors can turn a Protégé ontology into a more domain-specific tool. OpenGALEN [80] provides an interface that is tailored to the needs of medical experts. It considers their way of looking for information and highlights some of those links and relationships that are meaningful to them. For example, consultation roles are given without any search needed (Fig. 4.18).

Presentation can go beyond textual browsers. In many cases, a visualization of complex information will support software experts better than will a heap of relationships buried in OWL, RDF, or XML. RDF graphs are a conceptual step toward visualization of knowledge statements. There is more one can do.

Protégé offers interfaces for extending its capabilities. They are implemented as plug-ins that are integrated into the Protégé system. One of the widgets available is the GraphWidget. A tutorial for using that widget can be found on the Protégé Web site [86]. Fig. 4.19 is taken from that online tutorial.

GraphWidget's main purpose is to support visualization of knowledge bases. A network of instances and their relationships is drawn in a simple notation. The cognitive abilities of human experts are challenged and exploited: Humans are good at pattern matching in complex visual scenes. Ontologies are good at storing large amounts of data. Presentation widgets like this example can bridge the gap between a rich base and convenient access.

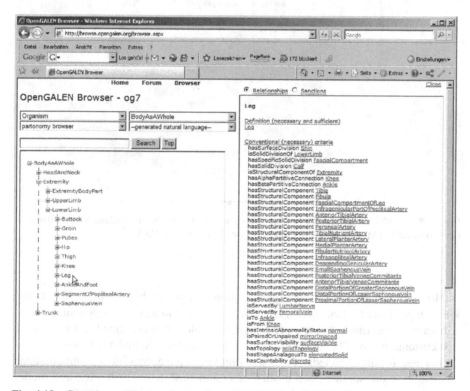

Fig. 4.18   Domain-specific interface in OpenGALEN: OpenGALEN Foundation. http://www. opengalen.org. Printed with permission from 152 Medische Informatiekunde, PO Box 9101, 6500 HB Nijmegen, The Netherlands

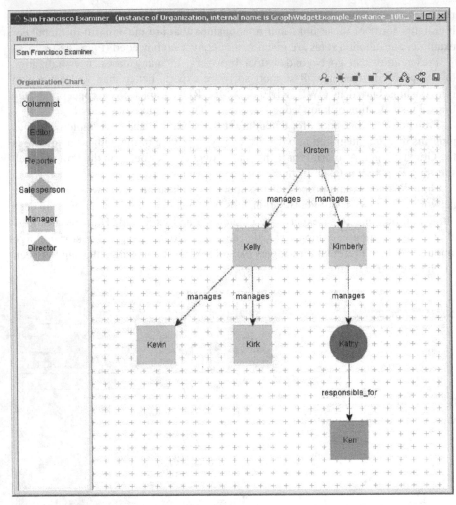

Fig. 4.19 GraphWidget from the Protégé Web site [86]. Printed with permission from Stanford University School of Medicine, 251 Campus Drive, Stanford, CA, USA

Both editors and graphical representations empower human users and bring knowledge closer to their mental models. Knowledge in a complex domain such as software engineering is much more comprehensible if it is presented and visualized in a customary way. The impact of presentation must not be underestimated!

Because formal knowledge bases and ontologies are accessible to computational extensions, more sophisticated evaluations (statistical, heuristic, etc.) and modifications can be implemented. In many cases, agents (semiautonomous programs) can operate on a large knowledge base. When the World Wide Web is considered a distributed knowledge base, Web crawlers search through large amounts of distributed information. Only the imagination of knowledge managers is the limit to the potential applications of those agents.

4.9 Problems for Chapter 4

Problem 4.9.1: Definition and purpose
What is the definition and the purpose of an ontology?

Problem 4.9.2: RDF graph
Use the ontology sketched in Fig. 4.1: Describe a situation as an RDF graph in which Dr. Dieter Drew prescribes "weight lifting" as a physical therapy to patient Peter Painful. Nathalia Newton is a nurse who assists Peter in doing the weight lifting in a health-stimulating way. Treat names as string attributes defined in that same ontology.
Use http://ontoMed.schema/ as the name for the ontology shown in Fig. 4.1. Assume that the hospital maintains a list on the intranet. Employees, patients, and treatments offered are listed in http://hospital.mainList, with the subcategories /doctors, /nurses, /patients, and /treatments. A specific entry (e.g., XY) is accessible at #XY.

Problem 4.9.3: Inheritance
Explain what happened to the inheritance relationships in Fig. 4.1 when you drew the RDF graph, and why.

Problem 4.9.4: Multiple roles
Looking at the RDF graph above: Can an individual or instance have multiple roles (subject, predicate, object)? Substantiate your answer with an example.

Problem 4.9.5: xmlns
What does the statement (xmlns:medSchema= "http:// ontoMed.schema/") mean and how can that be used in subsequent statements?

Problem 4.9.6: Attributes
What is the difference between an attribute "name" in a Protégé ontology versus that in an object-oriented class model? How are attributes assigned in both environments?

Problem 4.9.7: OWL-DL
OWL-DL is often used as the variant for ontologies applied in practice. Name the two other variants available and provide reasons that make OWL-DL preferable.

Problem 4.9.8: Test ontology
Construct a simple ontology in Protégé with six classes. Sketch the ontology first using the bubble notation of Fig. 4.1 or Fig. 4.3.
The purpose is to collect knowledge on test strategies. A test strategy determines what test cases look like. A test case is characterized by the provided input values

(parameter values) and by the expected outcome or reaction. A test strategy is considered successful if it helps to find many errors. The test cases used as a reference are combined in a test suite. After this sequence of test cases has been performed, the number of errors detected is recorded.

Problem 4.9.9: Knowledge acquisition

Who could provide what part of the knowledge you need to populate the above-mentioned knowledge base? Outline a plan for how you could get all required data into the knowledge base with the lowest possible effort.

Chapter 5
Experiences: Beyond Knowledge

5.1 Objectives of this Chapter

After reading this chapter, you should be able to

- Define experience as opposed to knowledge.
- Draw and explain the experience life-cycle.
- Give examples of activities carried out in each part of the life cycle.
- Analyze your own experience with respect to the concepts presented.
- Decide what needs to be done next when a fellow software engineer turns in an experience report.
- Name several techniques and tools that support activities in the life cycle.
- Map experience to a simple ontology or a case-based reasoning system.
- Discuss advantages and loopholes of explicit experience exploitation.

This chapter builds on the knowledge management issues presented thus far. It goes into more depth about mechanisms for acquiring knowledge and experience and describes how to process them during their life cycles. It might come as a surprise how much effort and sophistication are required to extend knowledge management toward systematic exploitation of experiences.

Recommended Reading for Chap. 5

- Davenport, T.G.P., *Knowledge Management Case Book – Best Practises*. 2000, München, Germany: Publicis MCD, John Wiley & Sons
- Schneider, K. and T. Schwinn, *Maturing experience base concepts at Daimler-Chrysler.* Software Process Improvement and Practice, 2001. 6: pp. 85–96

5.2 What is Experience, and Why is it Different?

The previous chapter explained how knowledge can be encoded in different representations and stored in ontologies. The instances of an ontology make up a knowledge base, which can be searched and used for reference. Advanced mechanisms for information retrieval and presentation can make use of the semantic annotations that come with an ontology. Semantic searches on the World Wide Web are at the

K. Schneider, *Experience and Knowledge Management in Software Engineering*,   135
DOI 10.1007/978-3-540-95880-2_5, © Springer-Verlag Berlin Heidelberg 2009

core of the Semantic Web Initiative [17]. Those mechanisms can also be used for building a new ontology for your company.

According to the introductory chapters of this book, information turns into knowledge when it is related to a person's preexisting knowledge. From that perspective, knowledge is always bound to brains and people. We have suggested interpreting the term *knowledge transfer* as a layered protocol of data, information, and (virtual) knowledge flows. Knowledge management alludes to a similar mechanism: By collecting, refining, and distributing information to those people who can extend their preexisting knowledge, it is fair to call this process (indirect) management of knowledge. Ontologies are among the most sophisticated mechanisms for supporting formal encoding, exploitation, and use of knowledge. There are exchange formats like OWL and tools like Protégé to implement ontologies in practice.

In Chap. 1, essential concepts were defined. Core aspects include:

- Knowledge resides in people only.
- Experience is a subset of knowledge.
- Each experience can be viewed as a three-tuple of observation, sensation, hypothesis, or conclusion. All three components are necessary to gain authentic, impressive, and useful experience.
- Knowledge can be built by learning from experience. Some authors even regard this as the only possible way to acquire knowledge; others see reading and listening as other options.

The informal and semiformal techniques in Chap. 3 were introduced to elicit ideas and experiences. They also show how to formalize them. Ontologies are among the most formal representations of knowledge in software engineering – many companies have not yet reached that level in their knowledge and experience management endeavors. Nevertheless, all projects can build on their own experiences.

Experiences are a particular subset of knowledge in software engineering. Experiences have a number of properties that make them special and that require special treatment. Experience management has never reached the same level of public attention as that of knowledge management. At the same time, there has always been high appreciation for "experienced" software engineers. Experience is held in high esteem in most environments; but the associations related to experience diverge drastically. In this chapter, we will need to narrow the definition of a useful experience in order to handle it more effectively.

Let us look into a few examples of what might be considered "experiences" in a software engineering environment. All examples are taken from real projects. Each of them is briefly discussed to gain a better understanding of relevant properties.

Example 5.1 (Experienced architect)

Alex is an experienced software architect. She has participated in four large projects and a few smaller ones in the role of an architect. When she is confronted with a requirements specification, she always looks at quality requirements first. Those requirements have always had the biggest impact on architecture and design. When Web systems are to be developed, Alex asks for frequency of use and reliability requirements, whereas many of her junior colleagues never think about those issues until the very end of the project – when it is almost too late.

When people talk about experience, a story like this could be told. In the perception of colleagues and co-workers, experiences are not distinct items of knowledge but an attribute of a person. As such, experience does not describe a very specific ability but refers to a wide and vague spectrum of tasks someone performs very well. In experience management, however, it is often advantageous to look at distinct pieces of experience rather than a vague fluidum of a person. This perspective is dictated by our professional desire to manage, spread, and exploit experience systematically. In private life, a different perspective may be more adequate.

Describing experiences as three-tuples may help when we analyze a situation. In the above-mentioned scenario, one might note one of Alex's *observations*: "Junior colleagues asked for user volume late in projects X, Y, and Z." She obviously remembers that this was "almost too late." In more concrete terms, Alex might have *observed* last-minute changes in architecture, causing errors and long working hours. Alex did not like that (*emotion*), as she prefers a regular family life. Therefore, she has decided for herself to ask for frequency of use right away – hoping to consider those quality requirements in the first place and to avoid overtime work (*hypothesis and conclusions*). Note how some of the aspects in the three-tuple were not explicitly presented in the original story. How do we know Alex observed overtime work and did not like it? In most reports on experiences, the observations are cut short, and emotional aspects are omitted altogether. Unfortunately, only a blend of selected observations, conclusions, and biases is passed on to others. We consider them incomplete experiences.

Alex can act according to her experiences without ever making them explicit. She just does what she has concluded to do. In fact, experiences tend to be tacit. Making them explicit requires a trigger and a motivation. Why should Alex talk about her feelings? And who would care to listen in a professional environment? Transferring experiences effectively is rather difficult. This is the main reason why experience management calls for techniques that go beyond knowledge management.

Example 5.2 (Terrible experience)

Kevin had a terrible experience in his last project: Mary and Dieter may be great software engineers, but they are not team players. Whenever Kevin asked one of them to explain a design concept, they would look at each other and start to giggle. Kevin just joined the company half a year ago, and their reaction drove him crazy. What kind of knowledge management could force them to help Kevin when he needs it?

From our experience management point of view, the experience reported above is neither complete nor useful. There is a full observation and a definite emotional response. However, a conclusion is missing. Should Kevin conclude not to ask co-workers for help? Is it an adequate conclusion to blame the problems on poor knowledge management? None of those are conclusions worth managing. Although a "bad experience" can be a source of rewarding insights, it may also be distorted by anger and overreaction. Only when Kevin's boss learns about the situation may there be a well-tempered conclusion. This example shows how formally well-structured experience can either be inadequate or only appropriate at a different level.

Example 5.3 (Testing experience)

In the next story, Tom is testing code. He had been a developer for many years and only recently started to focus on testing. During a 1-week seminar, Tom has refreshed his knowledge on testing techniques. That helped him to create test cases in a more systematic way. In particular, he has learned to distinguish black-box testing that is driven by the specification and white-box testing that is driven by code structures and coverage. After the seminar, he is highly motivated to apply those concepts. When he finds a bug in a module ABC, he remembers a similar bug he had to fix as a developer: He had forgotten to initialize a variable. Out of curiosity, Tom checks the initialization in ABC – and there is the error! Tom is thrilled about his finding and eager to tell others about it. He is full of excitement when he talks to four of his co-workers over lunch. He emphasizes that he has invented a new testing strategy: checking for missing initializations. One of the colleagues is responsible for experience and knowledge management. He interviews Tom and captures the experience as long as it is fresh.

In this scenario, fine-grained experience is transferred orally when it is fresh and full of emotion. Tom does not fill in a boring experience report form half a year later; he passes on orally and informally what he has just experienced. Chances are good for his co-workers to pick up Tom's excitement together with his advice. They know the kind of module Tom was working on, and they trust him as a modest and responsible person. In this scenario, all three aspects of an experience are present, and they are transferred over lunch. When Tom is later interviewed by the experience and knowledge management (EKM) personnel, more details come up. However, in an official setting, Tom might be reluctant to show his emotions – too bad for the written account of his experience. The transition from implicit to explicit representation of experience is even more delicate than with knowledge.

Conclusions: The three stories illustrate three different kinds of "experience" that we know from daily life. The term *experience* is used intuitively with very different connotations and different associations. By analyzing all three stories with respect to reusable experiences, we try to identify the three-tuple of experience aspects. Although all stories talk about "experience," some aspects were missing in the first story; overwhelming emotions distorted the experience in the second story; and the status and freshness of experience presentation had a major impact on its usefulness in the third story. In the following sections, we will address several activities in the experience life-cycle. Each of them needs to consider the delicate nature of experiences.

Experience versus knowledge: With knowledge, neither observations nor emotions are required. According to Definition 1.7, knowledge is related to other pieces of knowledge in the brain. In theory, it does not matter where knowledge came from or how people liked it. Everyone can learn facts and even relate them to other facts he or she knew before. However, knowledge is often less authentic, convincing, or impressive than experience. Smart experience and knowledge engineers will target a balance of simple, factual knowledge with a more powerful and more expensive complement of experiences.

5.3 Valuable Experience in Software Engineering

The stories in the previous section showed different interpretations of experience in a software engineering environment. Obviously, both content and presentation of an "experience" are important for its reusability and merit. The three-tuple of observation, emotion, and conclusion provides a first template for experiences. If any of these content aspects is missing, the experience is not complete. In many cases, knowledge is the conclusion aspect of experiences.

What is good and valuable experience in the realm of software engineering? It is impossible to list all content areas; the SWEBOK [56] mentioned in Chap. 2 is a good reference for an overview. However, we might be able to identify certain criteria that specify intentionally what makes a good experience. This characterization will be used as a reference for all activities in experience management: How do they attract and preserve the right experiences?

Criteria for valuable experiences in software engineering from an experience management perspective follow:

Related to a task at hand. Experiences that are not related to the job or the activities carried out in a software project may be emotionally loaded and very authentic. However, they do not contribute much to the success of the company or the business unit. This criterion may sound trivial, but when experiences are collected, it is often violated. People forget to focus.

Related to a frequently recurring task or situation. Experiences related to a unique event are less valuable than those related to a daily situation. The potential reuse frequency of an experience depends mainly on the frequency of the respective situation. Supporting daily tasks just a little may pay off more than a significant improvement or saving in a rare activity.

Containing all three aspects of an experience: observation, emotion, and conclusion. The above-mentioned stories illustrate this point: It helps to understand better what happened, and it helps in memorizing and applying the experience. The three aspects refer to contents, not to format. It does not matter how an experience report organizes the aspects, nor whether they are neatly separated. The challenge related to this criterion is rather to encourage experience holders to make all aspects explicit – in a professional environment. For the experience manager, the main challenge is to keep experiences "fresh": analysis, storage, recombination, and delivery must not lose any of the three aspects – or a part of the experience is lost.

Experience made in a similar context. Experiences may be highly context-dependent. What might be working in a strictly hierarchical company could be counterproductive in a small team (e.g., quality assurance procedures). The issue of identifying and matching contexts is a major challenge for experience exploitation. There are basically two alternatives for picking only appropriate experiences:

(1) Specifying context attributes and characterizing new situations by those same attributes. Similar attribute values indicate highly related experiences. (2) By limiting the scope of many experiences to a common context, all experiences are more or less related to that *same* context and can be reused. The second approach is easier to implement but has fuzzier borderlines: Very specific experiences might not be transferable based on the common context. It might be best to adopt approach (2), but enrich it with optional attributes to describe specific context constraints. This minimizes effort without limiting the ability to be more specific when needed.

Fresh and authentic. Originally, experiences were exchanged orally. Stories were told over a cup of coffee. When they became boring, the experience would no longer be mentioned. In experience management, the quality criterion of "freshness" is still important. An experience conclusion is more likely to be reused when the audience can relate to the observation. In that case, they will "feel the emotions" and feel as if they were in the shoes of the original experience holder. This emotional link provides authenticity and a better chance for reuse. On the other side, experiences that are outdated, incredible, or from a totally different background are less valuable.

Suggest actions for reusers. The conclusion or hypothesis of an experience may be abstract or concrete. It can explain the reasons for a situation to occur, or it can provide advice on how something can be achieved or avoided. Although all variants of conclusions and hypotheses can make valuable experiences, those that provide concrete advice for action are often more valuable. However, experience engineering is an activity that tries to rephrase and rearrange experiences. Therefore, experiences can be improved later on.

Short and easily comprehensible. Like the previous criterion, size and style can be reworked afterward. In the end, however, a short experience report or presentation is more valuable. When someone needs to find experiences related to his or her own situation, the experience report should allow finding out quickly. It is not only the length of the document that counts: Clear and concise writing style, structure, and overview elements (figures, tables) add to this aspect.

Appropriate granularity; smaller, when in doubt. Some experiences do not even need a full experience report. They can be stated in just a few sentences. This is even more true when unrelated experiences are reported separately. Smaller chunks of experience are easier to read and to understand. However, there are good reasons for not dividing each experience into very small experiences. The lower limit of valuable experiences is defined by their context dependencies: If a small-grained experience is reusable only in a very limited context, it may be more laborsome and less reusable to describe in that context – better leave the experience within its natural context of the longer story. This criterion is more difficult to apply: As small as possible, but as large-grained as dictated by the original experience context.

Reliable. Different people can interpret the same observation very differently. Depending on their own private prior experience and prior knowledge, they may reach different conclusions. Therefore, experience three-tuples may be contradictory or outright wrong. Everyone managing and reusing experiences should be aware of that risk. It comes from relying on all the tacit background of those making the experience. Nevertheless, experience holders should not be encouraged to make up highly speculative hypotheses or draw unlikely conclusions.

Levels of Exchange

Experience exchange can occur on different levels of an organization. Each level has its advantages for certain kinds of experiences.

Personal communication. This can hardly be called experience management, but it is the most common and most effective way of reusing experiences. Experience management should not object to it but add other opportunities that are less confined to a personal relationship.

Exchanging experiences within a team, group, or department. A small environment offers the advantage of familiarity. It is easier to foresee who might eventually receive an experience report and what may be the reactions. As opposed to a very large, anonymous community, a small group can build on trust and exchange more delicate experiences. Critical conclusions and errors are delicate.

Large collections of experiences and knowledge (e.g., in an ontology) are usually established by central units in a company. Factual and procedural knowledge that is independent of context details can easily be shared within a larger group of knowledge workers. This is the level of company knowledge management initiatives. Merging knowledge and experiences from more people has a better chance of exceeding the critical mass. The more a repository can offer, the more likely it will have something to offer for any given requestor. Return on investment for experience and knowledge management will grow when reuse is facilitated within a larger community. However, context-sensitive issues, unreliable or contradictory experiences, or delicate details about individuals must not be spread beyond a small, trusting circle.

Some initiatives have been established among a group of companies (e.g., DaimlerChrysler in the Software Experience Center [95]). They avoid competitive issues but exchange information and highly aggregated experience on software engineering issues, such as the adoption of the Capability Maturity Model CMM [83], the European initiative for software maturity, SPICE (ISO 15 504), or the Capability Maturity Model Integrated CMMI [1]. The CMMI contains concepts inspired by SPICE and CMM. At this level of abstraction, strategic decisions and experiences can be exchanged.

At the highest level of congregation, conferences, user groups, and professional community meetings (e.g., organized by the Association for Computing Machinery, ACM [110], or the German Society for Computing, "Gesellschaft für Informatik" GI [47]) serve a similar purpose: exchanging experiences and insights. On this level, some experiences are conveyed in experience reports. Others are transformed into conference papers and contributions that emphasize an insight. In our terminology, this may be either a conclusion from an experience or a deeper insight gained by relating experiences with previous knowledge. On this level, experiences have mostly lost their authentic quality. When sufficient experience engineering and peer reviewing has been done, some new "knowledge" may emerge from the experiences – and knowledge is treated differently.

This section and the previous sections have set the stage for the experience management activities presented below. You should keep example stories and criteria in mind when we now walk through the different steps of experience engineering. Knowledge management follows a similar life-cycle, as discussed in Chap. 2. We will mainly look at experience engineering but also point to some differences in the respective activities of knowledge management.

5.4 Experience Life-Cycle

In Chap. 1, an overview of knowledge management was given. Fig. 1.8 summarized the activities in knowledge management. Managing experience is a special case of managing knowledge. The activities of Fig. 1.8 are, therefore, mapped to the activities of the so-called experience life-cycle. The activities of experience and knowledge management are not a one-shot task. Instead, they need to be repeated over and over again. The end of a cycle prepares the organization for the next cycle. The iterative nature is just alluded to by the cycle on top of Fig. 5.1. At the bottom,

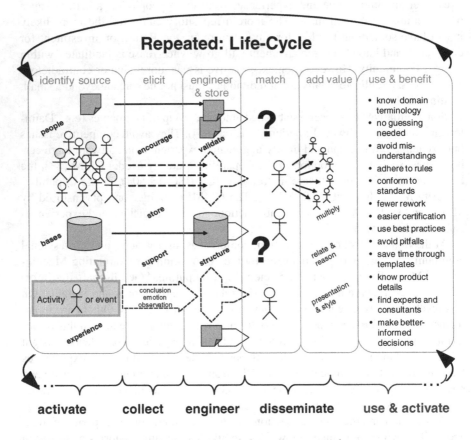

Fig. 5.1 Experience life-cycle as iterative knowledge management tasks

knowledge management steps are mapped to slightly different terms and activities. The latter will be used below to describe the experience life-cycle.

The different wording indicates different challenges. In experience management, a source of experience needs to be identified and activated: We need to take action in order to make experience holders aware of the asset they have. Often, experience is tacit and must be made explicit. This happens during the collection or elicitation activity. Very important is the engineering activity that compares and validates, refines, and turns experiences into best practices. The aspect of storing experiences and intermediate products of experience engineering is a more technical issue that is often overrated. The importance and difficulty of matching existing experience to current needs is often underestimated. Experience can be reused only when the last step of experience management (dissemination) is also carried out effectively.

Actual reuse is not considered part of the experience management life-cycle. In fact, new insights are gained and new experiences are made during the usage of previous experience. Experience management needs to identify new experiences, thus closing the cycle. Actual usage is considered the glue between delivering stored knowledge and experience – and reacting to it, based on new experiences. A slightly more abstract view of the experience life-cycle is presented in Fig. 5.2. As opposed to Fig. 5.1, inner details of the activities have been omitted. In turn, the iterative nature was emphasized, and the experience management terminology was used.

The cycle shows experience management tasks. According to the above argument, it is a special case of the knowledge management life-cycle, as depicted in Fig. 2.5. Application and use of experiences during software projects need to be synchronized with the experience life-cycle. From our perspective of experience and knowledge management, experience-related tasks appear in the foreground. The entire life-cycle is needed to provide software engineering. Application and use are not considered experience management tasks themselves.

Experience Management Tasks and Activities

The following sections describe activities and approaches in experience management that help to instantiate the tasks in Fig. 5.2. The task bubbles are clus-

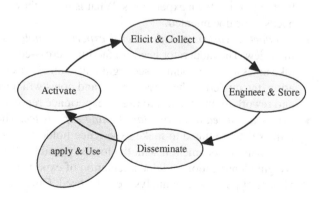

Fig. 5.2 Tasks in the experience life-cycle

tered by logical coherence: Activating experiences is a logical prerequisite for collecting them. Elicitation is a specific subtask of collecting experiences. Instead of simply storing data, experiences must be compared, validated, and reformatted before they are stored. Again, storing is a rather simple subtask of experience engineering. Subsequent sections are grouped by activities: For example, an interview is an experience activity. It performs two life-cycle tasks: activation and elicitation of (raw) experience. Both tasks are iterated within seconds. An interviewer should be aware of those two tasks and know that none of them must be neglected.

5.4.1 Activating and Eliciting Raw Experience

If we start walking through the experience life-cycle at the Activate step, we are confronted with raw experience. Identifying sources of experiences and trying to elicit valuable experiences is mostly carried out by an activity like:

- *Interviewing people.* A member of experience management conducts an interview with one or two people who were identified as having valuable experience. Many people seem to be experienced, but the challenge is to identify those with the right kind of experience. Another challenge is to help them make it explicit. As we have seen in Chaps. 1 and 2, tacit knowledge and experience are hard to capture: Because the interviewer does not know exactly what to ask for, an interview may miss the point.
- There are *structured and open interviews*. Structured interviews are guided by a set of questions to answer. Strictly structured interviews resemble answering a questionnaire. In a semistructured interview, a similar list of questions is prepared, but the interviewer does not strictly follow the list. Questions are rather seen as a checklist that can be addressed in any order and even without asking explicitly. Open interviews leave the initiative completely to interviewer and interviewee.
- *Asking experience holders to write down their experience.* This is a popular approach but a problematic one. Experience holders have little reason to do their best in writing down experiences. What is more, they can often not imagine what needs to be documented.
- *Conduct a workshop with several experience holders.* This is a variant of an interview. The moderator needs to facilitate cross-communication. Someone will take notes and document raised arguments and experiences. In a multiperson situation, the moderator has less control, and notes will need substantial engineering and rework to turn them into useful experience reports.
- *Try an advanced technique for eliciting experience.* There are a number of techniques that are tuned to make experience holders aware of what they know and help them to document it with the lowest possible effort. For example, the lightweight identification and documentation of experiences (LIDs) technique [90], a variant of post-mortem analysis can be used. Others use tools and technology to

facilitate note-taking or recording. A small number of sophisticated techniques apply dedicated software tools in specific situations to capture experience in a light-weight way [112, 113].

- *Studying existing documents.* Initial elicitation does not always imply talking to people. Sometimes, there are traces in documents pointing to an interesting event. For example, two versions of a specification that differ completely might indicate a problem in between. When one document (like a manual) is supposed to build on another one (a design or specification), but there are obvious differences, this can be a good trigger to ask very specific questions.

Mnemonic 5.1 (Raw experience)

No matter what technique is applied during the identification and activation step, the result will be raw experience. Notes, records, and initial experience write-ups will need cleaning and engineering. Raw experiences are rarely fit for reuse. Many raw "experiences" do not even qualify as experiences. According to our definition, they are missing an aspect, or they do not fall into the category of valuable experiences.

Raw experiences usually have deficits:

- Observations and conclusions are too specific for reuse by someone else.
- Conclusions are unclear and either too abstract (what needs to be done?) or too specific (how would that translate to a slightly different situation)?
- Conclusions may be unreliable. A single observation or conclusion will hardly make someone make a drastic change. Confirmation by others is lacking.
- Stories, statements, or experiences are confidential, contain names and secrets, or could be seen as personal attacks. All these cases require careful cleanup and checking. Often, company names, project titles, or individual names should not be disseminated beyond a very restricted circle of team members.

During elicitation, an interviewer or moderator cannot check the quality of the experiences that might or might not be hidden in the raw material collected. Sorting out raw experiences is inevitable. Disseminating unchecked raw material can do severe damage to an experience management initiative.

Many of those phenomena are typical for experience; they would not occur in knowledge acquisition.

5.4.2 Experience Engineering and Storing

Definition 5.1 (Experience engineering)

Experience engineering is an activity that improves experiences or related material by applying systematic procedures, similar to engineering.

Tasks Within Experience Engineering

In particular, experience engineering includes:

- Cleaning, sorting out, and rephrasing raw experiences.
- Technical reformatting and preparing for storage and retrieval (indexing, short description, evaluation, transfer to an exchange format like XML).
- Constructing more valuable experiences by comparing and aggregating several experiences and deriving a common overview or conclusion: Contradictions, inconsistencies, and confirmations are uncovered. There may be problem-specific relationships between experiences, too.
- Reformatting or rephrasing experiences or derived material. Not all experiences are documented in a highly readable and reusable style. Experience engineering should remove typos and mistakes, rephrase overly complex sentences, and facilitate understanding by deriving figures, tables, or visualizations from given material. Material may include other experiences or knowledge.
- Harmonizing experience and derived material in style and granularity.
- Turning textual experience reports into presentation material like slides, diagrams, or short reading material.
- Turning experiences into procedures to follow. They are often called "best practices." In a project situation, software engineers usually do not care to learn about experiences made by others. They need to know what to do in their own project. Therefore, experience engineering should turn one or more experiences and related material into hints for action. In the ideal case, a complete process or procedure will be described that reflects the experiences made.

Storing the results of experience engineering is a logically separate task. Of course, it will be carried out every time a result is created. At this point, storing can be considered a trivial "save" operation that does not require any in-depth discussion. Preparing for appropriate storage, however, is less trivial: Examples in Chap. 6 show how storage structures (databases, Web sites, files) need to follow intended dissemination strategies. Once they are in place and the experience cycle is turning, storing has become an easy operation (Fig. 5.3).

The term **"best practice"** is often used in a euphemistic way. Strictly speaking, a best practice would need to be derived from practice or practical experience – with no speculation or theory involved. This degree of experience coverage is rarely achieved. Mostly, conclusions from experiences will be bundled with common knowledge or some of the experience engineers' convictions. Calling a documented procedure a "best" practice logically seems to imply it has been compared with some other, less suitable practices. Again, there will rarely be a set of competing practices that failed to win the title of the "best of all practices".

In most environments, best practice indicates a procedure that is based on experiences from practice. Some mistakes were identified through experiences and are avoided by that procedure. Further conclusions from experiences have been taken

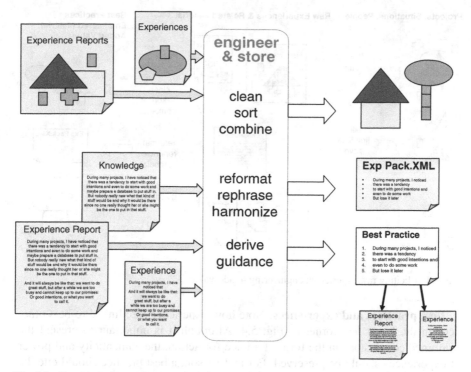

Fig. 5.3   Overview of experience engineering tasks

into account, and gaps have been filled with existing prior knowledge or other experiences.

Although it is not customary to apply very strict criteria to what is called "best practice," this term should be more than a marketing label. We should not accept calling a prescribed procedure a "best practice" that has never been tried and proved its value in practice. This is a reasonable criterion for using the term "best practice" for practical purposes.

Experience engineering can be carried out by dedicated experts in the field of experience and knowledge engineering. However, even lay persons will add value to their own raw experiences when they review them in a separate cycle. Peer reviews of experiences will produce even better results. An essential point is: No matter how the raw experience was collected and no matter who does the job – **experience engineering is crucial** for the success of an experience management initiative! If you doubt the necessity of this step, think about the above-mentioned list of potential deficits in raw experiences. Collecting and cleaning are two contrary modes of operation. From a cognitive point of view, it is impossible to carry out both in parallel. Therefore, they cannot be carried out on the side while raw experiences are reported. A separate step is required

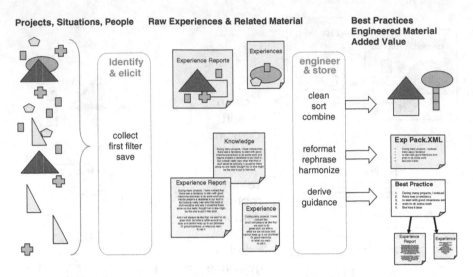

Fig. 5.4 Eliciting raw experience; engineering to add value

Best practices and experiences: Note how experiences are linked to best practices in the lower left corner of Fig. 5.4. Although it is important to present the combined conclusions in the form of advice for action, the authenticity and power of experiences should be preserved. For that reason, a best practice should cite the experiences it was derived from. This allows readers to (1) quickly find out what to do and to (2) learn more about backgrounds and related experiences. Even better: it should provide hyperlinks to allow direct access from the best practice to related experiences. The second case will be especially important if a best practice does not seem to fit their current situation. A project manager or software engineer needs to find out the rationale behind the best practice advice and derive his or her own conclusions.

Experience engineering itself is a highly knowledge-intensive task that requires expertise and experience in the field. Because many of the experience engineering operations listed above require filling gaps or interpreting material, experience engineers cannot be replaced by mechanisms or administrative clerks who are foreign to the software discipline. Therefore, an appropriate representation of experience, knowledge, and related or derived material is crucial for experience engineers to elicit ("activate") ongoing feedback from the projects. It is in experience management's best interest to encourage critical reflection and feedback (see Sect. 5.4.4). A format like Experience Reports invites detailed comments on rationale. This is a good opportunity for the refinement of experience and best practices. As we will see, it may be a necessary but not sufficient precondition for closing the experience learning cycle.

5.4.3 Dissemination

Novices in the field of systematic learning from experience often forget or underestimate this task. They will often neglect the matchmaking task and consider their job completed when experiences or best practices have been stored and "made available" at some Web site. This is a fundamental mistake.

It has been shown in many practical knowledge management initiatives [9, 12, 39, 92] that an active and explicit effort is needed for matching the derived material to those who might need it and to help them use it. We call this step *dissemination*.

Distribution is a related term, but dissemination emphasizes the challenge of actively distributing material *to the right person at the right time in the right format*. This task is far from trivial. Without effective dissemination, all previous activities for identifying sources, eliciting and activating experiences or knowledge, and all effort spent on knowledge and experience engineering and storing will be wasted. This claim holds for the entire field of knowledge and experience management: Failing to deliver results to the software engineering practitioners in an appropriate way turns the entire organizational learning initiative into a failure.

Acknowledging this challenge is probably the most important step. Experience management needs to carefully consider how to address the following issues with each given piece of experience or related material:

1. Who is the potential addressee of an experience or a derived best practice?
2. What is the situation in which this kind of material would be most helpful, and are any other reuse scenarios imaginable?
3. What material and advice would a software engineer or addressee need most in that situation? Are there any documents, templates, data, or experiences that would assist them efficiently? Can they be derived or engineered from the material?
4. How do we know who is doing what in a current project situation, and how do we know this across multiple projects that may even be distributed in a large organization?
5. How do we know what situation people are in and when they will reach a status that matches the reuse situation anticipated above?
6. How can they articulate what they need – which might or might not differ from the anticipated needs?
7. How can someone find and reuse material such as experiences, best practices, or parts thereof. In most cases, neither the person nor the situation will match the exact profile of a given experience. The only communality may be a similar challenge in a different context. How can different contexts be considered?

Dissemination must take into account the individual situation and needs of those software engineers who are supposed to benefit. Chapter 6 discusses several examples and options for concrete implementation. Some of them can be reused. However, each new situation calls for careful consideration of the above-mentioned questions.

Example 5.4 (Order is important)

The above list is numbered because we need to refer to some of the above-mentioned issues. The numbers do not necessarily imply a *strict* order, but it may be useful to use it as a checklist for each experience or derived result. Moreover, the order of issues can guide dissemination. For example, there is no use in contemplating exceptional reuse (7) as long as regular users (1) and scenarios (2) have not been identified. Each issue will have consequences for dissemination: Where, how, and when should what material be presented or even sent directly to someone?

As software engineers, you are used to planning. Planning is based on information and estimations. Issues 1, 2, and 3 have to do with anticipating users and situations where that reuse may occur. We need to guess what the reuse situation might look like and optimize the engineering and dissemination efforts for that purpose. If we have good and valuable information on reuse situations, chances are better to meet the needs. Therefore, experience management needs information on how the material might be reused. A good approximation is to look at how it has been reused in previous cases. For that reason, dissemination needs to be a two-way road: While reusers receive material, experience management needs to get back information on usage. As we will see, both directions need to be made as easy and painless as possible.

Issues 4, 5, and 6 address a different problem: In order to match profiles, how do we know about all current activities? If experience management takes these issues seriously, keeping track of projects and status information is obviously important. As a direct consequence, experience and knowledge management should be linked to planning and tracking information held in software management tools. If automated matchmaking is desired, profile information needs to be formal enough for automated comparison and evaluation.

Issue 7 goes beyond making anticipated matches. Many artificial intelligence researchers and even some knowledge engineers dream of the "magic match" when a piece of previously engineered experience or knowledge is combined and delivered in a nonanticipated way, making a big improvement. Software engineers will be delighted if they encounter this rare phenomenon – but they should not rely on "surprise matches" (Fig. 5.5). We should plan for planned matches and welcome all others as an extra bonus.

Some knowledge engineers argue: "We can never know all the situations in which a piece of knowledge can be reused – so it is counterproductive to plan and think about it for long." Although they may be right in some situations, software engineering is a domain too sophisticated to expect emerging matches. Obviously, there are different opinions on this point, and you should make up your own mind when you implement experience and knowledge management in software engineering practice.

Fig. 5.5 Magic match: unanticipated use of an experience report

Experience   Surprising reuse of experience

Example 5.5 (Expecting an emerging match)

A software company sells computer games. Sometimes customers called in and wanted to buy gaming hardware with the games. A knowledge engineer was just about finishing an ontology on the company games. Instead of providing a simple Web interface with a list of links to the games, the engineer provided a natural language interface for customer requests that could search for all potential future devices and services and features imaginable.

There is usually a huge gap between the potential power and the actual usefulness of a system that waits for emerging matches. It is often better to optimize for a set of matches that are required.

5.4.4 From Dissemination to Activation (Next Cycle)

Dissemination is closely tied to experience engineering. The goal of engineering a certain type of experience should be specified by looking at the material needed for dissemination. As a rule of thumb, engineering refers to adding value by working on contents, whereas dissemination refers to presentation, advertising, and distribution.

As issues 4, 5, and 6 have indicated, dissemination also extends into the use of experience-based material: The more experience management knows about the actual use of the delivered material, the better it can focus future engineering and dissemination. The experience life-cycle is a two-layered learning cycle: Software projects learn by reusing experience-based material, and experience management learns to handle experience-based material better. In the terminology of Chap. 2, these two layers resemble single-loop learning (project level) and double-loop learning (both project and experience management levels).

How can we **establish feedback** from using material for activation of new experiences? Fig. 5.6 illustrates the idea.

- There are several options for eliciting feedback, and one or more of them need to be implemented.
- *Do nothing and wait.* Why should a project manager or a software engineer spend her time on providing feedback? As we will see below, appealing to altruism is

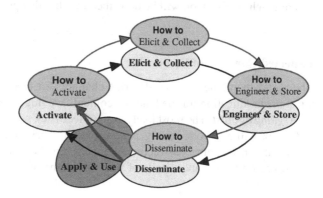

Fig. 5.6 Double-loop learning in the experience life-cycle

not a good option. Often, software engineers do not even know who to contact. And they do not know whether their feedback will be welcome. Only when people are really angry and dissatisfied will they complain on their own initiative. This is only a small fraction of the feedback you should be interested in.

- *Distribute questionnaires with the material.* This is a simple and straightforward but not necessarily the most effective approach. The entire experience (or knowledge) management life-cycle is brittle and always at risk of being interrupted. If you rely on volunteer activity like completing a questionnaire and sending it in, you are running the risk of losing potential feedback. At least, software engineers know you are looking for feedback, and where they could send it. However, you might go one step further in assisting them.
- *Web-based feedback.* At first glance, this approach looks similar to questionnaires. However, electronic feedback often poses a lower threshold to software professionals. They are used to working on the computer anyway, so a few additional keystrokes are not as bad as completing a paper form and putting it in the mail. There are several variants of Web-based feedback.
- *Contextualized feedback opportunities.* When you provide feedback over the Internet, you might have encountered the need to describe your problem or situation. This is tedious and error-prone for both sender and receiver. There are several approaches to sending e-mails or messages directly from a work environment that you might want feedback about. In that situation, the environment can add tags to indicate the position you were in when you wrote the message. Different levels of sophistication are possible. This is a research issue. Ontologies and semiautomated techniques can help to lower the threshold and improve feedback quality and quantity.
- *Calling in.* Using a phone number instead of a Web address will be appealing to some people who prefer talking to typing. Also, the receptionist can ask back and clarify things during the first contact. However, calling somebody requires time and initiative, too. If you reach a helpdesk that knows nothing about your context, this will discourage you from calling again.
- *Talking to somebody.* Experience is usually transferred by talking to people. Informal lunchtime conversation is an important channel. Direct communication is time-intensive, but for some environments and kinds of experiences, it may be worthwhile having experience and knowledge brokers. In the final chapter, an approach by Ericsson will be described that builds upon this concept [36].

Expected Contents of Feedback

The above-mentioned options describe channels for feedback. We can also provide a rough classification for the kinds of contents we might expect.

Arguing against. The most likely kind of feedback will be reasons why something did not or will not work exactly as described in a best practice. Ideally, this kind of feedback can contain constructive elements that help experience management to refine preconditions and details of use. All channels listed above can be used for arguing against a recommendation. Experience management should not defend its material but accept this feedback as a serious and valuable contribution.

Positive feedback. In rare cases, projects will thank experience management for material like templates, hints, or warnings that helped them to work better. Of course, this kind of feedback raises confidence in experience-based material. Besides that, it usually does not contain any new details or information.

Additional experiences. When the culture in a software company is mature enough, projects will capture post-mortems or LIDs – experiences of different kinds. They send results to experience management. In this scenario, experience is not really activated by previously disseminated material; project participants carry out their duties independently.

Additional support material. Highly committed software engineers will volunteer to "improve" a best practice by sending their own templates, procedures, and support material. Experience engineering should again take those contributions seriously and make sure to thank the senders. However, sent-in material needs to be checked and evaluated before it is disseminated. Was this material ever used in practice? Is there an experience related to it or does the sender simply assume the template or process "should be better for obvious reasons"? If an experience repository contains many elements that lack an experience background, authenticity and reliability will suffer. Experience engineering will at least compare volunteered material with other experience-based results.

Cases. Sometimes, a project or person has collected rich data on a project or a certain activity. That data may be in a different format than that of experience three-tuples, hence, it may not be directly usable. However, a skilled experience engineer will gladly accept those send-ins and visit the sender. Often, there is more useful material in an environment that has realized the value of collecting case studies or data.

In general, experience management should take each contribution as a trigger to reflect on the validity of material. Those who showed commitment and contributed once should also be remembered as potential contributors in the future. Experience engineering needs to match people as well as contents.

5.4.5 Software Engineering Specifics

Note that the discussions above referred to software engineering contents. Experience and knowledge management might look very different in different domains such as insurance marketing or repair of Xerox machines.

Example 5.6 (Xerox machine: A different domain)

Xerox maintenance personnel can benefit from knowledge and experience management: Each problem encountered with a certain copier model can be stored together with the symptoms and the solution used. In all future incidents, similar symptoms can be mapped to suggest trying that solution again. Because of the large number of incidents, statistical effects may help to see repeating success or failure. Because of the simple nature of symptoms and solutions, there are good chances to map experiences and proposed solutions to an ontology. This ontology will probably describe the structure of a Xerox machine and provide experience-based patterns matching symptoms with solutions. In this case, many of the challenges of activation, elicitation, and dissemination do not occur: A technician must provide information on each problem he worked on – regardless of motivation or activation. Dissemination can be facilitated by ontologies or other knowledge bases. This is difficult and requires good skills in the knowledge management area. Experience engineering in the Xerox machine example is still important: All formalisms used to match and deliver patterns of symptoms and solutions rely on a well-formed knowledge base. Feedback from the field of the technicians must be engineered into that format. However, Xerox-type experience management faces none of the social problems that come with software engineering experience.

Example 5.7 (Helpdesk: A different domain)

A similar situation occurs with the helpdesk of an insurance company. Agents need to search and access huge amounts of information fast. Like the Xerox technicians, however, they face numerous cases of a similar nature. The problems reported by calling customers can be indexed via their insurance products. Therefore, rather small, recurring, and similar-looking pieces of knowledge and experience need to be managed.

In software engineering, we are usually not dealing with so many, so small, or so similar incidents. A big problem in a software project may evolve over weeks or months and then lead to a long and complex experience report. Despite our definition of the experience three-tuples, software engineering observations and emotions can hardly be formalized to the same degree as in the case of insurance products or Xerox machines (Fig. 5.7).

There are examples of small-scale knowledge management in software engineering. Jäntti [58], for example, reports on knowledge management that resembles the Xerox example: There is a repository of problem reports and suggested diagnoses.

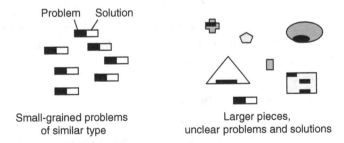

Problem Solution	
Small-grained problems of similar type	Larger pieces, unclear problems and solutions

Fig. 5.7 Granularity and size of experiences: similar in routine tasks (*left*), different in software engineering (*right*)

When a program does not print, for example, an experience-based hypothesis may be: The printer module has a software bug.

The extra-fine granularity in this example might encourage a large number of small entries. However, because there is no mechanism or task for combining the microscopic "knowledge entities," this example is not very likely to fully exploit the potential of knowledge management.

5.5   Challenges to Software Engineering Experience Reuse

Before we discuss a few more misconceptions about reusing experiences and knowledge in software engineering, you should keep in mind why we tried to reuse it in the first place: If we can avoid a mistake based on previous experiences or best practices, we will gain a lot in software engineering.

Example 5.8 (Avoiding mistakes)

There are many cases in which mistakes are avoided:

- A project manager who considers a risk he might have neglected otherwise. When she is prepared for the risk, the project may take precautions. For example, an unreliable subcontractor might not be hired despite a cheaper price if he caused trouble in another project.
- Reusing a good test strategy may help a software engineer to find three errors in the code that might have gone undetected otherwise. Each error popping up at the customer costs 100 to 1000 times as much as an error fixed in advance.
- A team that finds a detailed prescription (best practice) of how to carry out reviews in a certain situation will save time and avoid failure. If the best practice does not only offer an experience report, but also all templates, procedures, and hints for an efficient review, the savings are enormous.

Benefits are multiplied if more than one project can reuse experiences. Software engineering often deals with bigger chunks of material. Matching is more difficult, and psychological barriers exist. However, even a few successful attempts pay for quite some effort invested.

At face value, experience exploitation is supposed to provide benefit for new projects based on the insights gained in past projects. However, there are several other expectations and assumptions, some of them hidden or implicit. During the **Software Experience Center (SEC)** project at DaimlerChrysler, we could often identify those expectations only when we faced them the *second* time. The most important ones of those findings were reported in [92]. The following list of expectations is taken from that publication.

The assumptions and misconceptions are clustered. They are briefly described, discussed, and a piece of advice is given on how to handle the challenge that arises from that assumption.

5.5.1 Can Experience Management Replace Experts?

When you carry out an experience management initiative, you may meet people who believe you will extract and dump all relevant experience into a repository.

This expectation is unrealistic and should not be nurtured.

It implies valuable experience is around everywhere and just needs to be put into a repository. However, eliciting, collecting, and engineering *useful* experience is not trivial. Stories about projects are often mistaken for reusable experience.

In most environments, there is a lot of experience residing in people. At first glance, the problem just seems to be picking up all that experience so it does not dissolve into vague rumors or oblivion. However, it is a popular misconception that there is much value in *raw and superfluous* experience. Not everything that comes to anybody's mind is a valuable and reusable piece of experience. A lot of experience elicitation effort is wasted when only this thin and unsettled spread of "experiences" is captured. We learned that the assumed and the perceived values of those "experiences" often deviate drastically: The bearer of the experience considered a story highly relevant experience, whereas experience managers could not translate it into anything reusable. Much more effort must be spent on analyzing raw experiences than on getting them in the first place. In the 5 years of SEC, thin-spread observations were almost never reused, whereas deep experiences going beyond rumors could effectively be turned into best practices and were actually reused.

The misconception also implies that anybody could tell all of her or his experiences. Again, this is not true. As we have seen in Chaps. 1 and 2, a lot of experience and knowledge is tacit. Experts are unaware of it. Experts often have several layers of knowledge and experience, each building on many others. There are also psychological barriers: Who wants to give all his or her knowledge away? As a consequence, a highly ambitious experience management initiative will not be able to "extract it all." A more modest attitude is more likely to succeed.

Identifying a misconception is an opportunity: We know what mistake not to make. Concrete consequences for an experience manager in the field of software engineering should be:

- Do not claim or nurture the vision of "extracting all knowledge or experience" from anybody.
- Treat experts with respect and be aware that you will still need them after an experience repository is built.
- Plan more time for engineering raw experiences into reusable material than for the elicitation of raw experiences.
- Interviews and workshops are important, but do not expect them to uncover huge amounts of valuable experiences during the first cycle. Allow for several experience life-cycles to build up, validate, and consolidate.
- Elicitation requires sophisticated approaches. A simple interview will not reach the depth of experience you might be interested in. By exposing experts to previously collected and engineered material, they can argue on a more profound level. Act as a facilitator.

5.5.2 Do Not Rely on Altruism

In the field of experience and knowledge management, many people assume others will act altruistically: For the benefit of the company or the team, they are supposed to invest time and effort but do not receive any immediate reward. You will find a number of unconscious assumptions at the root of many techniques or procedures:

- "People will fill an empty experience base."
- "Experts will document their knowledge or experience."
- "Busy experience holders will take time to talk to interviewers."
- "Experts will be glad to answer all questions, repeatedly."
- "Software engineers will encode their insights in OWL."
- "Contributors will check whether experience engineering has correctly presented their (previously donated) raw material."

Some of these assumptions sound appealing, but they are often wrong. Researchers and managers both tend to assume that business unit employees see the need for putting experiences into a repository or telling an experience management support group before they can get something back from there – later.

This is sometimes true, but often it is not. We met a few employees who had embraced the concept of experience exploitation. They accepted to talk to experience management several times just to provide information – and they did not expect to get something back in return. At the same time we had drastically overestimated the patience of many employees. Even those willing to contribute limit the amount of effort spent.

There are two obvious reasons against sustained altruism:

- Sheer amount of work. Software engineering is a busy field, and there are always deadlines and time pressure. Squeezing in even a few extra minutes is a luxury. When we reach overtime – and we always do – the question boils down to: Why should an expert spend 20 minutes on unpaid, volunteer experience validation rather than on playing with his children?
- Loss of status. Knowledge is power, and so is experience. Giving away knowledge or power means lowering one's own value. Who knows who will be laid off when business is slower? This is a classic dilemma hampering knowledge management. It has many facets, and it cannot be honestly resolved. There is some truth to the concerns, but in most cases, experts do not suffer disadvantages when they give some of their knowledge away – they are recognized as experienced and knowledgeable experts which often raises their status.

Both reasons need to be considered. A successful initiative needs to find an individual, tailored answer to these concerns. The workload of experts must be minimized, at least for the experience management work they do: Use assistants and tools and sophisticated techniques to save hours and even minutes. The second problem will always require management commitment. Volunteer contributors must (must!) not have disadvantages. Details cannot be solved in general.

Incentives are often proposed to provide rewards. If a contribution to a knowledge base or an experience repository is paid in money, there is an obvious reward. The balance of effort and reward can be restored. This is a good idea and should be considered. However, incentive systems can become counterproductive quite easily, and in a surprising way, as Davenport [26] describes: At Siemens, there were different incentive systems.

- It turned out that low incentives might not convince people to do extra work if they would not do it anyway and without incentive.
- However, generous financial incentives evoked incentive-optimization strategies by some employees. When packages were counted, they tended to contribute two small experience packages rather than a big one. They wrote sloppier reports when contents were not evaluated. In short, substantial incentives corrupt the system as many software metrics do: People are intrigued to optimize their income, not the value they add.
- One attempt was to reward both experience contributions and the usage of experience – those packages that were reused more often received higher incentives. But reusers had advantages, too. You can imagine the consequence: Downloads soar and circles of friends cross-optimize their benefits. None of those phenomena needs to be criminal or even mean in nature. Optimizing advantage is a part of human nature. However, experience managers should exploit that trend in a responsible way, not deny it or complain about it.
- Not all incentives need to be financial. It is a breakthrough to include social recognition like awards and honors into the reward system. More than many managers might think, social recognition can be gained when experiences are not disseminated anonymously. Ambitious experts like to be recognized as the author of many contributions. They would never turn in bad quality under their own name.

The open source or Wikipedia community seems to operate on a similar basis. Altruism occurs, and it is an important ingredient of open platforms. However, altruism is associated with volunteer activity. By definition, no one can be forced to volunteer information. It cannot be part of a job description to work without reward. In fact, open contribution systems provide **social recognition as a valuable reward**, together with complete flexibility of work. A good experience and knowledge management initiative will learn from those communities and build a similar reward system.

Mnemonic 5.2 (Altruism)

We should be glad to receive altruistic contributions. But an experience and knowledge management initiative cannot rely on it. Plans and operations should be designed to run without altruism.

Again, there are concrete consequences for experience management:

- Consider efforts and rewards carefully. When you plan procedures for elicitation and dissemination, make sure each role and person has a fair balance of investments and benefit.

- When you design an elicitation technique, make sure to optimize it for individual effort! Those providing input must be saved every single unnecessary task and step. Administrative tasks should be shifted to the experience personnel instead of "asking the experts to classify. . .," and so forth.
- Rethink each and every procedure that will not work without altruism. Essential procedures that build on altruism are bound to fail [50].
- Experience managers are paid for running the initiative. Their reward for eliciting, engineering, and fine-tuning activities lies in a successful operation of the initiative. For this group, effort and benefit appear in different forms than for participating software engineers.
- Install a moderate incentive system. Incentives should appeal psychologically, but high financial benefits may be counterproductive. Reward contributions by making them public.
- Consider carefully what material you want to identify by author: It may provide social rewards, but some experiences need to remain anonymous. Others will be absorbed into best practices – maybe main contributors should be listed on the derived document.

The problem of motivation and incentives is delicate. After looking into concerns and problems, we should mention one more element that is crucial for experience reuse: **intrinsic motivation** of talented and committed software engineers. No extrinsic (coming from the outside) incentive or reward system can compensate for missing intrinsic (internal) motivation. Intrinsically motivated employees are among the most valuable assets a company can have. Implications cannot be discussed in detail in this book. Nevertheless, intrinsic motivation is a good starting point for effective experience work. The above-mentioned considerations and pieces of advice will help to sustain it.

5.5.3 Barriers to Experience Flow

Those interested in experience management assume: "Some people document their experiences, others read and reuse them." Surprisingly, even this basic assumption is often not fulfilled.

Example 5.9 (Fears and barriers)

As we have seen above, effort may be a barrier to documenting experience. There needs to be some incentive or motivation. One of the barriers mentioned above was a reluctance to give away experience and knowledge. Software engineers may fear losing some of their value for the company when they give away their experience or knowledge. There are also concerns on a psychological level concerning power and influence. Rare knowledge or experience can be a source of power, and experts can receive advantages and benefits in exchange for sharing their knowledge. What happens if that knowledge is now stored in a repository? Those concerns are easy to understand.

There are also barriers to reusing experience. This is more surprising, as the intention of reuse is to save time and effort. Who would not want that?

Information overflow. Many researchers and authors of experience-based material consider their task completed when they have inserted their contribution into a database, experience base, or intranet page. This assumption is widespread, but it is tragically wrong. As others have pointed out in their domains [80], there are so many sources of information on a wide variety of media that most people suffer from an information overflow. As a consequence, most "available" information must be ignored.

Not aware of matching information. Making information "available" is just not good enough. Software quality agents really need a piece of experience at the time and in the way they can best integrate it into their respective work assignment. The tragic element lies in the fact that excellent material can sleep on a wonderful experience base system – without ever being found and used by those who desperately need it. In SEC, we reacted by not only advertising our experience bases but also by tightly integrating them into a system of training courses, newsletter notes, and information briefings for the subject conveyed (e.g., risk management) [65].

Doubt about reliability/not invented here syndrome. Researchers and managers assume that the need for experiences is obvious. Reuse seems to be the obvious solution, and experience exploitation seems self-supportive in nature. However, some people do not believe in the quality of material they do not know.

Example 5.10 (No reuse)

It came as a surprise to us in SEC when people were often very open and giving in interviews but reluctant to search, read, or apply any material we had retrieved from others. Our conclusion was that they did not trust the quality of the offered experiences. This phenomenon is well-known as the "not invented here syndrome."

Reuse needs to be encouraged actively. There are different approaches to implementing this attitude: Incentives for reusers is one. Using existing personal contacts for recommending reusable material is probably more effective. In this perspective, workshops, quality circles, and, in particular, coaching and consulting situations can be used not only to *capture* experience but also to discuss and to *spread* it.

5.5.4 Essential: Management Support

When there is not sufficient support from management, some software engineers consider starting knowledge management initiatives bottom-up. They hope that small and local successes will grow into a big initiative and incur increasing management support.

Management support and commitment are essential in many activities. Experience and knowledge management is impossible without strong and visible management backing. Financial support and resources are important. If there is not sufficient money for hiring experience managers or experience engineers, respective activities fade away. While writing an experience report could be done on the side, experience engineering is a serious and demanding job that requires time, dedication, and qualification as an experience and knowledge manager.

Management *backing* is equally important: There will be times when experience management seems to delay a project or an activity. Benefits will not arise instantaneously, as experience engineering needs to collect some experiences before it can compare and disseminate them. Initial effort to start an initiative is high, and it requires some patience. Impatient management that withdraws resources and trust will kill each initiative.

It is sometimes difficult to convince higher management to spend money and free valuable resources for the sake of "cross-functional" activities like experience exploitation. Business units tend to start with bottom-up activities (e.g., quality circles, volunteer documentation, etc.), hoping for more management commitment later. Beginning successes are supposed to open the door for larger-scale activities. In SEC, many of those basic support activities were rather successful (i.e., produced benefit for the business unit).

However, bottom-up activities seldom exceeded local impact. Management commitment rarely grew gradually. Local activities were welcome but not perceived as a first step toward a bigger initiative. They differed in scope, goals, participants, and structures.

A pure bottom-up approach will hardly exceed its initial level. There seems to be a critical mass of investment in experience exploitation. With a small number of potential experience reusers, success is much less likely. Investment, effort invested into discussions, and strategic attention are also needed. Below a certain threshold, most activities will vanish. Above the threshold, there is a tendency for mutual reinforcement.

The conclusions from this challenge sound straight-forware, but are difficult to follow:

- An experience and knowledge management (EKM) initiative will not succeed if there is no real and active management commitment.
- When starting bottom-up, activities will most probably remain on the initial level and may be hard to sustain, due to a lack of critical mass.
- Management commitment can be measured by resources assigned to the initiative and by explicit public statements made to the employees supporting the initiative.
- If you do not have management commitment and do not want to shift to bottom-up software process improvement, you should not attempt to start an EKM initiative. It is not worth the effort.

Personal commitment will work on a small scale: If you are happy with a Web site or a Wiki for exchanging news and opinions, you may generate substantial benefit for yourself and some co-workers. However, this hardly qualifies as experience or knowledge management.

When you join a working EKM initiative, you are much better off. A working reuse cycle does not need as much energy to sustain. Also, individuals may decide to run a very modest and small-scale initiative just for their own benefit. Countless examples show that the (moderate) effort invested is often rewarded by reasonable benefit. The concerns about building an EKM initiative bottom-up are mostly associated with a large scale and with critical mass effects.

5.6 Problems for Chapter 5

Problem 5.6.1: Life cycle

Draw the experience life-cycle and briefly explain each activity.

Problem 5.6.2: Experience engineering

Assume your team is using a new framework for software development. Programmers report problems they have had. If possible, they also report how they solved them in the end. What should experience engineering do with those reports and what roles can patterns play?

Problem 5.6.3: Experience three-tuple

Describe one of your own experiences in software engineering as an experience three-tuple. Make sure you do not neglect the emotion!

Problem 5.6.4: Best practice

All projects in a business unit need to follow a new process. The first project using it reports some experiences. Why can experience engineering usually not be shortcut by asking the projects to provide best practices right away?

Problem 5.6.5: Contradictory experiences

Two testers report experiences on a test tool. Tester A is happy, because the tool helped him to create far more test cases than usual. A larger number of errors were found early in the testing process, and late testing phases were far more relaxed. Tester B, however, was disappointed because the tool provided only "trivial test cases," as he puts it. Assume you are an experience engineer and need to make sense of those contradictory experiences. Give at least two potential explanations for the different experiences! If both testers A and B are equally competent, what could experience engineering ideally try to derive from their experiences?

Problem 5.6.6: Delicate experience

Why is experience an even more delicate matter than factual knowledge? Describe two different kinds of experience: (1) one highly critical kind of concrete experience that would be very helpful to reuse, but that will be very hard to elicit; (2) one kind of knowledge that should be easy to get (and useful to reuse). As an experience engineer, what kind of experience would you focus on first?

Problem 5.6.7: Argue well

How do you react if your boss asks you to start developing a knowledge-building strategy for your team of eight people – with the option of spreading it across the entire business unit if it really provides substantial benefits. Once you reach that level, he promises to provide additional resources and promote you to "knowledge expert." Sketch your argumentation!

Chapter 6
Experience and Knowledge Management at Work

6.1 Objectives of this Chapter

After reading this chapter, you should be able to

- Explain several techniques for supporting experience management tasks.
- Describe in detail how the light-weight identification and documentation of experiences (LIDs) technique works.
- Relate a given experience or knowledge management technique to the classifications and experience management tasks described in the previous chapter.
- Evaluate a given experience and knowledge management (EKM) technique with reference to the framework described in this book.
- Contribute to an EKM initiative by pointing out weak spots and making suggestions for improvement – with respect to the principles described above and by comparing them to the cases presented in this chapter.
- Conceive a knowledge and experience repository that avoids known mistakes.
- Describe to management what a repository or IT solution can do for an EKM initiative and what it cannot achieve.

This chapter provides case stories on three different levels of granularity.

In the first section, specific techniques are discussed. A technique is a concrete sequence of steps supported by tools, checklists, or the like. Techniques may work better in certain environments, but they are rather generic in nature. A technique could be transferred and used in a different environment. A core component of most experience and knowledge management (EKM) initiatives will be a knowledge repository or experience base – or both. From a computer science perspective, building such a repository may be an interesting intellectual and technical challenge. There are a number of issues that need to be taken into account when you plan to build an effective repository. In the third section, we will take a look at some large-scale initiatives and discuss their design and particularities with respect to the principles laid out above.

K. Schneider, *Experience and Knowledge Management in Software Engineering*,
DOI 10.1007/978-3-540-95880-2_6, © Springer-Verlag Berlin Heidelberg 2009

Recommended Reading for Chap. 6

- Johannson, C., P. Hall, and M. Coquard. *Talk to Paula and Peter – They are experienced*. In *International Conference on Software Engineering and Knowledge Engineering (SEKE99). Workshop on Learning Software Organizations*. 1999. Kaiserslautern, Germany: Springer
- Kerth, N.L., *Project Retrospectives: A Handbook for Team Reviews*. 2001, New York: Dorset House Publishing Company
- Schneider, K. *LIDs: A light-weight approach to experience elicitation and reuse*. In *Product Focused Software Process Improvement (PROFES 2000)*. 2000. Oulu, Finland: Springer
- Wenger, E., *Communities of Practice – Learning, Meaning, and Identity*. 1998, Cambridge, England: Cambridge University Press

6.2 Specific Experience Management Techniques

There are a number of techniques devoted to capturing knowledge or requirements. Within the discipline of knowledge management, *knowledge acquisition* is the term referring to that task. Similar techniques can be used for experience elicitation.

Experience tends to reside in the heads of people, where it was created by observing an interesting and emotionally moving situation or process. The challenge is to make tacit or vague experience explicit and to capture it in a format that can be reused by others. Challenges were described above. In this section, we will see different attempts to deal with the challenges.

6.2.1 Interviews, Workshops, and Post-Mortems

Glossaries are important for better understanding, but they are not a specific knowledge management tool. Along the same lines, interviews, workshops, and project post-mortems are not only used in the context of EKM, but EKM needs to use them, too. When we use them in this context, we need to take the previous section into account. A special variant of interviews, workshops, and post-mortems may better serve the needs of elicitation or knowledge acquisition.

Classical interview: Single individuals are interviewed. One or two interviewers prepare for the interview by preparing questions and conceiving the course of the dialogue: They introduce themselves, ask an open question to start the conversation, and then try to get a confirmation in the end. An interview is a more or less structured conversation. Several elements, like open or closed questions or cross-checking questions, are scheduled to elicit a certain kind of information. The initiative in a structured interview lies in the hands of the interviewer. By following a list of questions, the process is predefined, too.

Closed questions have a limited, enumerated set of possible answers: A yes/no question is the extreme form of a closed question. Asking for "the most successful project" is also a closed question when there is only a limited set of projects to

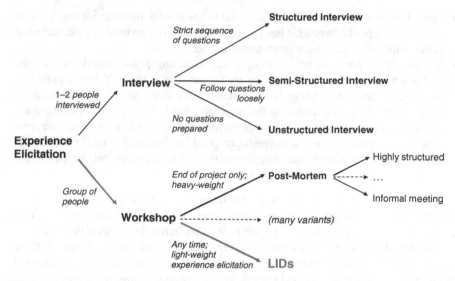

Fig. 6.1 Basic and generic elicitation techniques compared with LIDs as a specific experience elicitation technique (as described later)

choose from. Open questions, on the contrary, allow interviewees to speak freely. Open questions can usually not be answered with a single word or sentence. Asking for opinions, definitions, or suggestions leads to open questions. Open questions with an unanticipated answer transform an interview into a dialogue. However, interviewers will consult their prepared list of questions even in a semistructured interview and check whether they get enough answers while the interviewee talks freely (Fig. 6.1).

Good interviewers plan an interview like a movie: There is a story line guiding the interview. This preparation makes sure the interview is making efficient use of the resources and time devoted to it, in particular interviewee time. Deciding about closed and open questions is a means of minimizing the participants' cognitive effort. When planning the interview or workshop, software engineers need empathy with their counterparts. If we want to capture experience in an interview or a workshop, we must enable participants to talk about their experiences.

Although it is not easy to define what makes an interview or workshop successful, it is rather easy to spot a number of mistakes that might ruin the attempt. A number of **recommendations for interviews** can be derived:

- There should be two interviewers: One asking questions and maintaining the communication while the other tries to capture, document, and support the exchange. If there is a single interviewer, writing must be minimized, as it is idle time for the interviewee. On the other side, the interviewer must memorize exactly what the interviewee said. In that situation, a voice recorder is often used. It is sometimes difficult – and always time-consuming – to search or transcribe a record.

- Interviewers must be prepared: They need to know what this interviewee has said about their topic before, what has been documented or captured before, and what others think who have been interviewed earlier.
- Usually, there needs to be an opening and a closing phase. Interviewees need to "warm up" and must be brought up to speed in a topic. When a person is supposed to talk about his or her experiences in a field, an interviewer needs to spend some minutes introducing the respective field. Through the opening statements, interviewers will be able to set the tone and expectations for the interview. Both opening and closing statements are good opportunities to tell the interviewee about the mission of the interview and what future steps will happen to the experience he or she raises (Fig. 6.2).

Interviews are very popular as a knowledge acquisition or experience elicitation technique. Tacit knowledge and experience needs to be made explicit. This can be achieved by questions and a story line that helps the interviewee to access unconscious knowledge. In the case of experience, it is helpful to address all three aspects (i.e., observation, emotion, hypothesis) whenever one of them is mentioned in an answer. As always, a good interviewer may extract those three aspects from an answer to an open question. In standard interviews, only and explicit conscious knowledge or experience is usually communicated. This is a severe limitation.

Workshops are used for a wide range of purposes during a project. They can be used to capture knowledge or experience from more than one or two individuals at a time. Depending on their application area, workshops will vary even more than

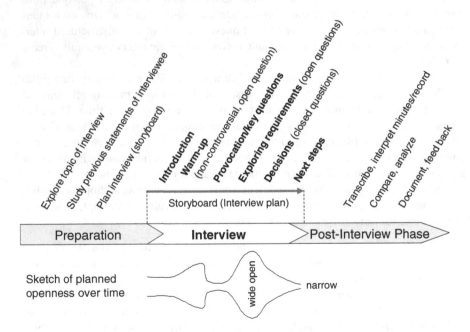

Fig. 6.2 Dramaturgy and tasks around an interview (example)

interviews. In general, a workshop should not just be seen as a set of parallel interviews: Less attention can be paid to each participant, and speaking time must be shared by more partners. In return, statements by one person may remind others of insights they had forgotten. Tacit knowledge or experience can be activated better in a well-moderated workshop. Like an interview, a good workshop should be planned with a story line; it underlies the agenda, but is far more fine-grained. It is an internal plan the interviewers want to follow which takes into account the expected reactions of the participants. There must be a person assigned to take notes; in a surprising number of workshops, so many insights are mentioned but never get documented. A special acquisition or elicitation variant of a workshop needs to emphasize activating those insights, making them explicit – and documenting them.

Definition 6.1 (Post-Mortem)

Post-Mortem workshops are a technique for capturing project experiences for the benefit of future projects. The purpose is to elicit those experiences after the end of a project ("post-mortem") and to document them in a form appropriate for later reuse.

In our terminology of experience exploitation, a post-mortem tries to cover activation, collection, and a part of experience engineering. Dissemination needs to be arranged separately.

6.2.1.1 Techniques for Post-Mortems

There are several specific techniques for post-mortems, as described in [19] and [63].

- In simple variants, a post-mortem is little more than a meeting in which all participants can talk about their observations and evaluate and criticize them. This kind of unstructured post-mortem is not expected to deliver much value. However, participants often feel better when they had a chance to raise their concerns and talk about problems they have encountered. Such a meeting has a cathartic impact, which frees the minds of people for coming challenges. It provides little support for EKM.
- Highly sophisticated post-mortems follow longer processes that include one or more workshops but also require participants to prepare or document for the purpose of reuse. Kerth [63] describes variants that require each participant to spend several days on a post-mortem. Such an amount of effort is only justified if it creates substantial benefit.

In many organizations, new project teams are assembled directly after or even while a previous project still runs. Many participants are eager to push the new project forward and perceive a lengthy post-mortem as a burden. Under these conditions, it is difficult to activate as many insights as needed for high benefit.

Obviously, post-mortems are a natural source for experiences. However, when the usual constraints of experience management are considered, the requirements for an adequate post-mortem workshop are as follows:

- short and easy to perform (light-weight);
- held at the end of the project or immediately after it;
- conducted by a group of co-workers in order to cross-activate experiences;
- has a clear perspective for reuse, maybe after a little experience engineering.

There are not many techniques that match all those requirements. For that purpose, the light-weight identification and documentation of experiences (LIDs) technique was developed during the DaimlerChrysler Software Experience Center (SEC) project. Its basics are sketched here as an example of a light-weight technique that has been carefully optimized for experience elicitation and documentation.

6.2.2 Light-Weight Identification and Documentation of Experiences

LIDs is a light-weight experience elicitation and documentation technique. After 3–5 months, a group of co-workers can use LIDs to produce an experience package within just half a day.

Definition 6.2 (Light-weight and heavy-weight techniques)
There are two ways to optimize the perceived value of a technique: Either the benefit is increased or the effort is reduced. Heavy-weight elicitation techniques invest more and expect more benefit. Light-weight techniques limit time and effort invested. In exchange, they accept limited benefits.

Software engineers can be expected to spend some additional effort as part of their job responsibilities. However, experience management is often perceived as an add-on. Keeping extra effort low is crucial. Therefore, light-weight techniques appear as an interesting alternative: They are optimized for minimal cognitive load and effort and still produce reasonable results.

LIDs stands for light-weight identification and documentation of experiences. The English word *lid* is also a metaphor for the desired result: A group of people who have carried out an activity together "collect their experiences in a pot and put a lid on it." This act provides closure and releases participants from the duty of remembering what happened. Many software engineers appreciate the opportunity to talk about their observations, experiences, and recommendations. However, they do not like to write them down, review, compare, and rework them.

The LIDs technique is designed to support a small to mid-sized group of co-workers. They may have played different roles in their common activity. One facilitator is needed who knows how to carry out LIDs. The facilitator can be an EKM supporter or a group member who knows LIDs. A computer projector is required. No sophisticated tool is needed.

The results of a LIDs session are useful even without any further processing or engineering. At the same time, they are ideal material for experience engineering. Again, nothing needs to be done (low threshold), but much can be done (high ceiling) with the outcome of a LIDs session. Low threshold and high flexibility makes LIDs a good example of an optimized experience management technique.

There are some **assumptions associated with LIDs**:

- During an extended activity, several documents are written, revised, and used. There are plans, checklists, deliverables, and sometimes even essential e-mails that determined the fate of a project or an activity. They are a part of the project the participants "observed" during the project. We want to save and reuse a subset of those documents when we capture experiences.
- Some time after the activity, participants will forget what version of a document was actually used; why they made a decision at this point; who received that important e-mail, and so forth. Without this information, all follow-up comments and recommendations are decontextualized.
- Responding in a group helps participants to remember the activity better than in a separate interview. As discussed above, a remark by one person often provokes replies by others. This is fast experience activation built into human nature.
- People talking and the above-mentioned documents need to be related. Not all versions of all documents must be stored, however. It is better to save only those few documents and versions that made a difference and were part of the "observation" that led to some "emotion" and "conclusion." Documents no one remembers immediately after the event or activity should not be collected.
- Many people like talking, but not writing. A single 2- to 3-hour meeting seems acceptable to most if (and only if!) this is all they need to do for experience documentation.
- People need help to remember events and dependencies. An elicitation session needs structure and documentation support, like templates.

There is no magic. The written experience package must be created somehow. In this case, the facilitator carries the burden of typing what people say while they are saying it. To make this task easier, the facilitator starts with a given template (Fig. 6.3).

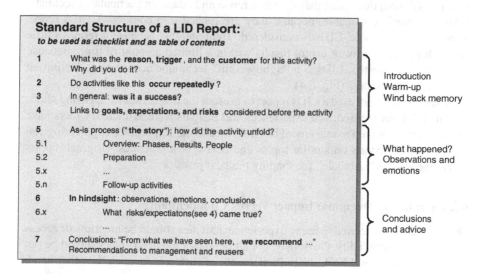

Standard Structure of a LID Report:
to be used as checklist and as table of contents

1	What was the **reason, trigger**, and the **customer** for this activity? Why did you do it?	Introduction
2	Do activities like this **occur repeatedly**?	Warm-up
3	In general: **was it a success**?	Wind back memory
4	Links to **goals, expectations, and risks** considered before the activity	
5	As-is process ("**the story**"): how did the activity unfold?	
5.1	Overview: Phases, Results, People	What happened?
5.2	Preparation	Observations and
5.x	...	emotions
5.n	Follow-up activities	
6	**In hindsight**: observations, emotions, conclusions	
6.x	What **risks/expectiatons** (see 4) came true?	Conclusions
	...	and advice
7	Conclusions: "From what we have seen here, **we recommend** ..." Recommendations to management and reusers	

Fig. 6.3   LIDs template, used as storyboard and table of contents [90]

The core of the LIDs template is a table of contents that guides the group through their common activity. This table of content acts as an agenda for the LIDs elicitation session. It starts with a few questions about the reported activity. When the LIDs report is completed, answers to those early questions will help reusers (i.e., readers) to contextualize the information. Experience engineering may use it to index or classify or to attribute LIDs results. At the same time, those questions discreetly lead participants into the mood of remembering how everything started and what had initially been expected. At the end of the session, those expectations are checked again. This comparison serves as a reference for recommendations.

At the core of each LIDs, there is a chronological story of the activity. "What happened next?" is the question the facilitator will ask when the group gets stuck. The facilitator types as fast as possible. The typed "transcript" is projected, and participants may correct misunderstandings immediately. This short feedback cycle saves a correction cycle after the session, which would have taken days. Typos are not corrected during the session.

Marking and linking documents: When a document is mentioned and seems to play an important role, its name is underlined. This helps to find those document names afterward. After the LIDs session, all mentioned and underlined documents must be sent to the facilitator (only the relevant version), who will copy them all into a new directory. This is "the pot." Then, the facilitator creates hyperlinks from underlined names to the files in the pot. In the next pass, the facilitator corrects obvious typos. The LIDs report with its hyperlinks turns into the lid that can be put on the pot. Both together are a self-sufficient experience package that can easily be transferred, e-mailed, read, and further engineered.

Results and deliverables of LIDs: A typical LIDs report is about 6–12 pages long, has 5–15 files of different kinds attached to it, and is usable for many purposes. Mainly, software engineers starting a similar activity in the future should read through related IDs reports. Often, they are inspired by an experience or by an attached (linked) document that they can reuse and adapt. In particular, checklists, hints, or plans are valuable, because they are related to a context. A LIDs report may be rather sizeable. LIDs is considered "light-weight" because it requires little effort. It produces a lot of useful results within a limited amount of time. Because little effort is invested, LIDs is a "light-weight" technique according to Definition 6.2 of light-weightness (Fig. 6.4).

Some people have used a LIDs report to present the project status. Existing slides and material were reused, and experiences and insights were extracted. Others have used information for a management briefing, and so on. Experience engineering can compare LIDs reports on similar topics and derive best practices. Original reports should be kept as "rationale" for shaping the best practice.

6.2.2.1 Inherent Dilemma: Impact Versus Confidentiality

One delicate issue related to many experience activities should be mentioned: access rights and confidentiality. Obviously, not all details of a failed project should be put publicly on the World Wide Web. Participants of such a failure, on the other hand,

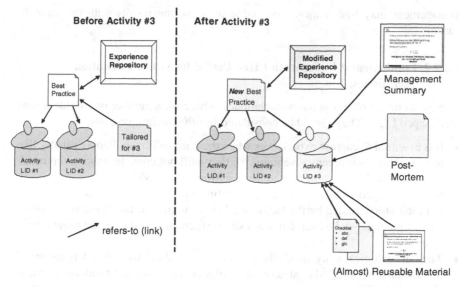

Fig. 6.4 Snapshot of using two existing LIDs reports (#1 and #2) for preparing Activity #3 (*left*) and for deriving additional material (*right*)

should have an opportunity to learn from their own experiences. To remember better and draw more profound conclusions, participants should be encouraged to reflect and to externalize their insights. In accordance with Schön's terminology [98], they need an artificial breakdown.

There are two related aspects that need to be considered:

- Participants should provide names and details without worrying about privacy when they talk. However, the facilitator may take out names in the final pass or not even write them down.
- There must be a clear definition of the recipients that will be allowed to access the LIDs report and the pot. It is not unusual to keep the circle very small, such as the participants and the experience engineering group. Experience engineers must carefully remove confidential elements. In extreme cases, even experience engineering will be excluded. When in doubt, recipients should be more restricted. Even in the smallest circle of participants, the value of preserving your own experiences for your own later use will exceed the effort of a 3-hour meeting.

There is an inherent dilemma between the high impact by spreading experience and a threat to confidentiality. Post-Mortems, for example, face that same dilemma. LIDs builds trust: (1) Participants see the projection and may veto anything written. It will be deleted without discussion. (2) Facilitators should not even note names, so they cannot forget to remove them later.

After a time-consuming elicitation event, management will insist on exploiting results widely. If only very little effort has been devoted (e.g., in a LIDs session), management may find it more acceptable to leave the results with the team of participants.

6.2.2.2 Fundamental Concepts in LIDs: Useful for Other Elicitation Techniques, Too

One could invent other elicitation techniques. There are a number of considerations that shaped LIDs. They should be considered in other techniques, too:

- It is essential to capture experiences when they are still fresh. People usually like to talk about their recent adventures, so they will not consider talking too much effort. A checklist is important to avoid getting lost in war stories.
- It is advantageous to have a facilitator writing the online report. Participants just tell their story, guided by the facilitator. When no trained facilitator is available, a participant may take over. LIDs is a simple technique and does not require long training.
- The chronological story should be good to read and not too long. Any technical details must be deferred to attached documents. The story must stay comprehensive and should avoid inside slang.
- Templates are among the most reusable documents. Therefore, they deserve special attention. Even documents that are not templates, but generic enough to be easily reused, should be marked as "low-hanging fruits" for reuse.
- Putting everything together in one storage location (directory or "pot") makes it easier to compress, copy, and transfer the material in one piece. Readers will find all related material in one place. They will not have to worry about versions and outdated garbage.
- A LIDs report also protects the "pot contents" from being modified or deleted by others. Therefore, the LIDs must implement a restrictive access mechanism. According to Fig. 6.3, it provides searching and output operations but not modification or direct input. This makes LIDs a read-only access.

Summary: If you want to try LIDs in an appropriate situation, use the table of contents in Fig. 6.3. Guide participants through the chapters and let a facilitator take notes. Copy the documents mentioned into the "pot" directory, and hyperlink them to the report (after the session). Distribute lid and pot to the defined list of recipients.

6.2.3 Case-Based Techniques for Dissemination

Experiences and knowledge need to be prepared for matching with the needs of new projects. This step is very important for turning the potential of a knowledge and experience base into a concrete benefit.

The approach of case-based reasoning can be applied to dissemination. Tautz et al. [109] describe applications of this approach. The principle of case-based reasoning resembles pattern matching. In general, a "case" is described by a number of attributes. In experience management, a case may be an experience or an experience package. Larger experiences with a defined structure are often called "experience packages" [13, 18]. An experience package contains several interrelated experiences. Together, they represent an insight, based on an observation, with associated material.

When a project searches for related experience, case-based techniques will require that project to specify its search query in terms of the attributes describing the cases. A soft matching algorithm on the vector of attributes is supposed to deliver the "closest" matches, or best-fitting cases. A soft matching algorithm not only considers exact matches but also takes into account fuzzy or partial matches. Different *closeness measures* can be defined as matching criteria.

As Fig. 6.5 indicates, a case may consist of attributes and other parts like a textual description or full experience package. It is just important to select or define the subset of attributes that are considered relevant for matching. Even free text may be used for matching, using a full-text search in closeness measurement.

On a large set of attributed cases, case-based reasoning is a powerful mechanism for searching – given a good closeness definition. However, if one of those preconditions (large set, attributed cases, good closeness criteria) does not hold, case-based reasoning faces a challenge. In practice, the build-up phase in which cases need to be attributed will be more demanding, as it is not sufficient to document the experience. Someone will need to assign attribute values. This causes additional effort. It is hardly possible to impose that effort on experience owners. Case-based

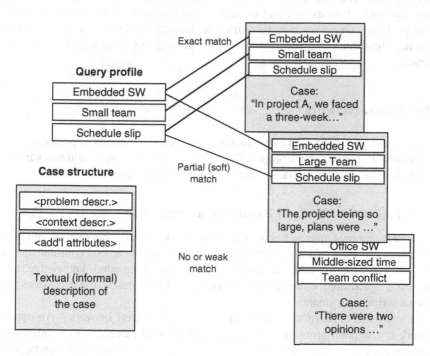

Fig. 6.5 Different case descriptions with formal profiles

reasoning needs dedicated support: A person must be assigned. In addition, matching criteria need to be defined and controlled, which is again a tedious task. Like sophisticated post-mortems, case-based reasoning is a high-effort ("heavy-weight") approach. It calls for substantial start-up investment and continued sustaining effort in an experience engineer. Under certain conditions, this investment may pay off in a software engineering environment.

A good matching algorithm will have high **precision** (i.e., delivering *only* relevant cases) and **recall** (i.e., delivering *all* relevant cases). Those two quality aspects depend on the matching function. In analogy to Fig. 5.7, cases can be small-grained or large-grained.

- Small-grained cases will lead to more matches, but each matching case will make a smaller contribution to the reusing project. When there are many small cases with several attributes, the relative effort devoted to indexing and sorting increases. This is often perceived as bureaucracy.
- In large-grained cases, only a few matching cases will be delivered. A large case tends to contain more relevant information but also more irrelevant information (lower precision). Fewer cases will need to be analyzed and combined, but within each case, not all aspects will be relevant.

During the SEC project, we observed a phenomenon: Initially, there were only a few dozen larger experience packages. At that size and number, a complex matching algorithm may be too much of a good thing. With large-grained experience packages, bureaucracy can be reduced at the cost of precision. A simple list of package summaries may be sufficient. Instead of developing sophisticated matching algorithms, projects may manually browse the short list of experience abstracts.

6.2.4 Expert Networks

Because most knowledge and experience still resides in the brains of people, expert networks try to connect those people. This connection can complement and support other techniques that try to manage pieces of knowledge directly.

6.2.4.1 Experience Life-Cycle Based on Communication

All above-mentioned approaches are intended to make experiences explicit and document them. However, the experience life-cycle also applies to oral communication and even to passing-on tacit knowledge. As long as information, knowledge, and experience is activated, collected, engineered, and disseminated, the cycle does not insist on written documentation.

An important class of techniques in this area are expert networks. An expert network is a defined group of knowledge workers who can reach each other and exchange their knowledge and experience. In a specific domain, the members of that group have expert status; they are trusted and appreciated for their abilities. An expert network is supported by an infrastructure that facilitates searching, contacting, and exchanging information among members.

Depending on the time invested and the organization of the expert network, the expert service might be charged to the requesting team. There must be a balance between excessive prices that prevent projects from using the network and a temptation to shift project effort onto experts that are almost free. Finding a good balance will be a learning experience.

Definition 6.3 (Principle of expert networks)

An expert network is defined by the following characteristics:

- *A team has a problem or question but no expert to answer it quickly.*
- *A member of the team (who is an expert network member) searches the expert network directory to identify an expert who might help with the question at hand. This search procedure may include direct attribute matching, full-text search, or more sophisticated soft matching algorithms. In smaller expert networks, there may be a number of expert profiles for reading.*
- *The directory includes all available contact information: e-mail address, phone and fax numbers, room number. The team contacts the expert and schedules a meeting. Short questions will be solved on the phone.*
- *The expert usually does not write or prepare anything. The team asks and receives feedback and answers. The team is responsible for taking notes and documenting according to their needs.*

The **tool support** typically provided for expert networks includes:

- Web-based search facility. Depending on environment and country, there are different limitations to the possibilities of such a mechanism. In Germany, for example, trade unions and workers' council will not accept highly detailed, personalized records of abilities and tasks carried out.
- Yellow pages are a good metaphor for the interface of an expert network. They are often available to the entire company, not only to the expert network. As mentioned above, the search criteria may be restricted in certain environments.
- Sophisticated tools might provide visual representations of the framework, showing certain relationships or abilities graphically. For example, all people with **service-oriented architecture (SOA)** experience may be colored in blue, with lines between those who are currently working on a common project. Those visual hints support searching projects to make an informed choice. This is important for receiving good advice. And it is essential for the experts who will not be bothered with demands outside their expertise.
- If expert services are charged internally, there should be a mechanism for supporting this administrative step. It should avoid bureaucratic tasks as much as possible (like official call for tenders, contract, bill, etc.).

In contrast with seemingly similar groups, an expert network can be characterized as follows:

- An informal group is an expert network only if there is a support structure and explicit membership.
- The potential members of an expert network are selected with respect to an organization, a task, or a knowledge domain. For example: "All software engineers with a quality assurance role assigned in a past or current project of our company." Generic or private networks like XING [121] do not qualify as expert networks by that criterion. Often, a company explicitly lists the members of an expert network (extensional characterization).
- An expert network usually transcends a single project – even a large one. The expert network provides a mix of backgrounds and skills. It is hardly reasonable to call a project team an "expert network." Only in rare cases like a research and development group will each member have deep expertise that his or her colleagues do not have. A project team is not heterogeneous enough to build a diverse and inspiring expert network.
- A community of practice [119] slightly difers from expert networks: it will often not be supported by a dedicated infrastructure. An expert network is not an emerging group that may be facilitated by a corporate group – an expert network is an explicitly created organization with the explicit goal of supporting expertise across projects.
- Despite its cross-project character, there may be clear goals and responsibilities associated with membership is an expert network. Mostly, members appreciate the reputation associated with selection for membership (Fig. 6.6).

An ontology can obviously be a good basis for the infrastructure of an expert network. It combines clearly defined attributes (slots) with reasoning mechanisms and the ability to deal with large and growing numbers of individuals. In ideal cases, the expert network could be linked to an ontology and a knowledge base of software engineering experiences and knowledge. There is potential for synergy, for example,

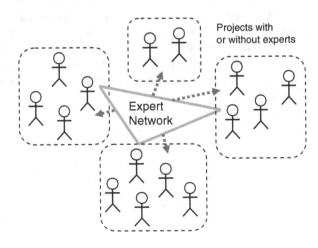

Fig. 6.6 Expert network includes members of several projects and provides support to all projects

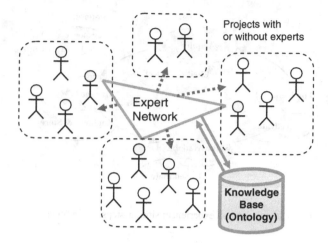

Projects with
or without experts

Expert
Network

Knowledge
Base
(Ontology)

Fig. 6.7 Combining a software engineering knowledge base with an expert network

by defining the content areas and expert domains for common use instead of creating several inconsistent definitions (Fig. 6.7).

One key characteristic of expert networks is the reluctance to elicit or document knowledge and experience. It is considered sufficient to know in which person's head that information is located. An expert and a team in demand can then be introduced to each other. The source of experience is disseminated first. When the expert is identified, he or she needs to be asked. The answers will usually be more or less specific to the target project, requiring neither experience engineering nor dissemination. This cycle started and ended with dissemination, and engineering is happening within the expert's head and the group interacting with him. This mode of knowledge management can be very effective and efficient. Several companies emphasize it. Note that an expert network exceeds random individual contacts among the workforce. It is far more organized.

6.3 Experience Bases

A repository of knowledge is often called a knowledge base. In parallel, a repository of experiences is called an experience base. Both kinds of bases provide more than storage facilities: An ideal base supports all processes and activities of experience or knowledge management.

Example 6.1 (Protégé as a base)

In Chap. 4, we have seen Protégé as an example system for building and using knowledge bases by defining an ontology and populating it with instances. The

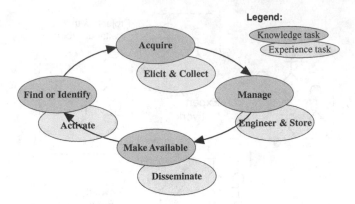

Fig. 6.8 Life cycles of knowledge and experience: similar steps, different emphasis

knowledge management life-cycle resembles Fig. 6.8, following an iteration of knowledge acquisition, knowledge engineering, and knowledge reuse.

The previous section on specific experience elicitation techniques can be adapted for knowledge acquisition, too: There are special interview styles, workshop variants, and combined techniques in which dissemination leads to activating more knowledge. There are more sources to extract knowledge from (documents, books, etc.), and there are some specific sources of experience. LIDs, for example, focus on experience. Case-based techniques stem from knowledge management but can be applied to experiences, too.

There are numerous commercial knowledge management tools. In contrast, experience bases are rarely advertised as such. In many cases, knowledge bases (like Protégé) may be extended to include experiences. However, there are some tools or components that support experience management specifically. This section provides an overview of related functions and features and points out some frequently made mistakes. Respective recommendations are supposed to help you avoid those mistakes and build a successful experience management infrastructure.

6.3.1 Overview of Experience Management Functionalities

Experience management is defined by the experience life-cycle and the need to organize it effectively and efficiently. A tool or technique is considered relevant and related if it either supports one or more activities in the experience life-cycle or if it provides infrastructure and links between those steps.

An ideal EKM tool environment will contain rich knowledge management support (i.e., ontology, presentation, and acquisition tools), dedicated experience management tools, and relationships between the two families of related tools.

Dissemination should not necessarily distinguish between experience and knowledge. It is more adequate to look at EKM from a user perspective: In principle, software engineers do not care who or what helps them to perform their task at hand. In particular, they are not interested in distinguishing between experience and knowledge – and they should not be required to use two different families of tools to handle them. The success of an EKM initiative will not be measured component by component but by its overall contribution to the software engineering capabilities.

For an overview of related functionalities of experience management, the four activities of the experience life-cycle are examined in Table 6.1. Transitions from one activity to the next are added as additional categories, as experience exploitation needs to push forward from one activity to the next. The table simplifies the situation for the purpose of a better overview: For example, a forum can encourage someone who just became aware of an experience (activated it) to provide it to the community.

However, structured elicitation will not be channeled through a forum. Wikis, questionnaires, or in-depth e-mails to experience managers will be more appropriate tools. Tools in the different categories should be integrated or orchestrated to feed into each other for an ideal tool support. The same is true for all activities and transitions in Fig. 6.1.

In Table 6.1, *generic kinds of tools* are related to those categories. New products that fit the types of generic tools pop up and disappear at a fast rate. An Internet

Table 6.1   Types of tools

Activity	Transition	Relevant types of tools
Activate		FAQ, newsgroup, Wiki
	to elicit	Any kind of backwards channel (phone, e-mail response, forum, helpdesk, evaluation form) will encourage people to send activated experience.
Elicit, collect		Wiki, database, e-mail, Web questionnaire.
	to engineer	Tools for knowledge acquisition, form-based Web browser, interactive rating and evaluation tool, package for statistics.
Engineer		Ontology, case-base tool, experience base.
	to disseminate	Visualization tool for contents, rating, and illustration of dependencies. Scientific as well as promotion-oriented illustrations. Flexible Web site structuring tool.
Disseminate		Dedicated Web site, Wiki, FAQ, newsgroup, yellow pages.
	to activate	Computer-supported collaboration tools with features for multimedia data exchange in a group. Features in all presentation and dissemination tools that allow direct, immediate feedback.
Tacit experiences	*make explicit*	Interview, workshop, questionnaire, Web questionnaire, creativity technique, glossary, ontology.
Explicit knowledge	*internalize*	Tutorial, example, need to apply.

search provides a timely snapshot. In this book, however, the emphasis is put on understanding functionalities and concepts supported rather than on individual products that may be outdated soon. The transformation from tacit to explicit and vice versa forms an additional dimension. It is a task for experience management to stimulate those transitions in a systematic way. However, very few tools are available – despite highly general teaching and learning tools. Therefore, those transitions are placed below the core activities in Table 6.1.

Table 6.1 can be read as yet another cognitive map – providing an overview of typical support for key experience management activities. Please note that this table contains only computer-based tools. Cognitive techniques and social practices are not listed. Experience bases are constructed specifically for the purpose of managing experiences rather than knowledge. They may contain several of the above-mentioned generic tool functionalities and often try to combine a chain of tools in order to close the life-cycle loop of experience management.

Some aspects have been found to be important when an experience base is constructed. The vision is depicted in Fig. 6.9: An experience base is like the centerpiece in the experience management life-cycle. It stores information gained in each of the four activities and makes the material available in all other activities that might need them. By storing, organizing, and linking all key aspects of experience management, an experience base can turn into an active memory of the initiative. A number of lessons learned for constructing experience bases will now be presented [94].

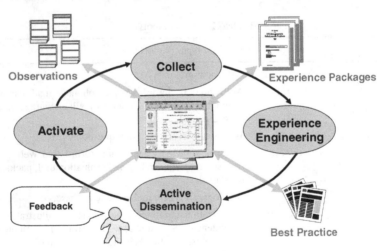

Fig. 6.9 Experience base as a centerpiece of the experience life-cycle [97]

6.3.1.1 Important Quality Aspects of an Experience Base

A number of quality aspects have been found to be particularly important for experience bases:

- Usability

  - Experience organization must correspond with experience volume
  - Focus contents to a limited domain but do not restrict to experience only

- Task-oriented

  - Seed the base
  - Link experiences to a work process or product

- Feedback

  - Encourage feedback and double-loop learning

- Flexibility for change

  - Use an architecture that accommodates all management functions
  - Generate as much as possible

There are issues related to each criterion in the above list. We will look a little deeper into each of those issues. They are turned into advice an best practices here, so they can be considered when a new experience base is constructed.

6.3.2 Experience Organization Must Correspond with Experience Volume

Many initiatives start building a tool to manage the anticipated experiences and experience packages. In most cases, efficient storing and search algorithms are developed to deal with a large volume of experiences. A significant amount of development time can be devoted to those issues. This focus is justified when a large number of elements need to be organized in the experience base. Most initiatives assume this will be the case; but experience needs time to be elicited, engineered and stored. At least for some time, there will be rather limited experience in the base.

We saw a similar example in knowledge management: A large number of small pieces of knowledge can be better organized via a formal structuring mechanism such as an ontology. Searching and soft-matching is facilitated by case-based reasoning techniques. They work well in large and well-attributed collections of cases.

However, experience management often deals with only a limited number of larger experience packages. Attributing or describing them precisely for the purpose of putting them into an ontology is often considered overhead. In that situation, complex classifications, index mechanisms, or search machines might not be the highest priority for a successful experience base. There are simpler mechanisms available for searching experience by association. Task-oriented mechanisms seem to be more adequate for experience bases, as will be described later.

Mnemonic 6.1 (Number of entries expected)

Do not just assume there will be thousands of entries. Experience is slow to harvest, so consider light-weight organizations and search mechanisms.

6.3.3 Focus Contents

In principle, experience bases can hold information, experience and knowledge on a wide range of topics. For example, there could be an experience base on "software engineering." However, when someone has a task to solve, such an experience base will always contain a bit of relevant information – but there will hardly be a lot of information on any topic. Especially during the initial phase, a very broad range of topics tends to lead to shallow contents: There will be a little of everything but not much of anything.

The software engineer in need of advice or experience will probably find no or not much related material. But when should he or she stop searching? It is bad for the reputation of the experience base and the experience management initiative if many people find nothing or little. They will probably not come back.

One way of focusing contents and facilitating a search is to build narrow experience bases. In several situations, single-topic experience bases were far more successful than broad ones [97]. Focus topics were requirements engineering, review and inspection techniques, and requirements engineering in a highly specific domain. Those three topics were focused enough to lead to a "critical mass" of experience rather soon. Because it is easier to structure stored material (according to a task at hand, see later), writing, assigning, and searching material is easier. It is easier to tell whether there is anything useful.

Users appreciate experience bases with a clear mission and scope. They do not like searching related material in different systems or repositories. Therefore, enrich and complement experiences with templates, background information, and all kinds of useful material. From the user perspective, all things that help are welcome. A narrow domain stays manageable even if some additional material is added. Experiences will mostly be turned into best practices. Best practices should contain or link to knowledge, tools, and templates that come in handy when you follow them. Experiences will also be linked as an authentic basis for the recommendations. LIDs [90] is a technique that collects experiences and related material in an appropriate way.

Mnemonic 6.2 (Narrow focus preferred)

Prefer a narrow focus of contents, maybe just one topic. Use simple structuring and search mechanisms that are motivated in the supported tasks of software engineers. Enrich experiences and best practices with different kinds of related information that will help them in practice.

6.3.4 Seed the Base

Many ambitious experience managers plan their initiative as follows:

1. First, there needs to be a powerful tool to hold and search the thousands of experiences.
2. Then, we will make this powerful tool available to the software engineers.
3. They will fill the base by entering experiences. Of course, they need to attribute and classify their contributions.
4. When sufficient experiences have been entered, future software engineers will benefit from the asset of experiences.

We have discussed above that this approach is often unrealistic: The software engineers of item 3 above would face an empty base when they first visit it. Why should they visit an empty collection? Why should they invest time for filling it? Why should they ever come back to it when they know it was empty last time?

This is one of the most frequent patterns in experience and knowledge management: Putting out a "working, but empty" repository. From the viewpoint of users (software engineers, process improvement experts, etc.), such a repository is *useless* – it does not work for them.

The obvious solution is to seed the base before releasing it. A seed is content that has the potential to grow: It must be useful for some purposes of its intended audience, for example review forms or review motivation slides for the review base.

Example 6.2 (Seeding a risk management base)

A company builds a risk management base. To seed it, experience managers collect risk checklists and mitigation activities that worked in the past. Those checklists help review participants and risk managers to carry out their tasks. They are a good and useful seed. But a seed is far from covering the entire topic of risk management. After receiving support, many software engineers may feel inclined to contribute in exchange. At least, many people want to correct what they found inappropriate in the checklists. This closes the experience life-cycle: It starts by dissemination checklists and leads to activation of own experiences.

Obviously, a seed will often consist of factual information, knowledge, or useful presentation of accepted information. A seed does not necessarily have to contain any experience – although experience will increase the potential to grow. When a seed starts to grow, the critical phase of an experience base is over. It is much better to seed the base first and see it grow from the beginning than to start it empty and try to jump-start it later. The first impression it makes on its "customers" is important.

Mnemonic 6.3 (Seeding)

Seed an experience base with information that is useful in practice. It must be sufficient to support practical tasks and should encourage feedback. A seed is successful if it starts to grow by the feedback of software engineers.

6.3.5 Link Experiences to a Work Process or Product

Huge collections of fine-grained and well-attributed experiences or knowledge items are accessible to sophisticated search mechanisms. They must use ontologies, case-based or similar approaches for classification and searching.

6.3.5.1 Do Not Neglect Associated Material

Experiences and related material often come in a far smaller number (below 100) of experiences or experience packages. There may be related material associated with each experience, but there are only few entry points to a search. In that situation, experiences and related material should be linked to a process or a product structure. Organizing experience packages around a given process or product structure provides an opportunity for associative search and indexing: The knowledge workers in a domain (e.g., requirements engineers) will be familiar with that domain. Using a given process or domain structure as a guiding structure often allows software engineers to locate relevant information easily – or to confirm that there is nothing relevant in the experience base.

Example 6.3 (Supported processes)

The supported process may be a software engineering activity like configuration management, testing, or risk management (see Fig. 6.10). A product structure like the architecture of the software is another useful backbone for orientation. Business processes often mediate between the processes of software development and the structure of the emerging software. A business process defines the core of a software product and its functionality. A graphical presentation of the process or product structure is highly advantageous for supporting associative searching and the authoring of new experience packages.

Please note: The visual representation should mainly show the work process or product, not the relationship of the experiences stored. We adopt a user perspective and try to see the repository through the eyes of a process or product expert. Such a person is very familiar with the task at hand – but not necessarily with experience management. Experiences and material must be accessible from the process overview but may even be invisible on the process map.

Mnemonic 6.4 (Visual map)

Humans are good at searching in a two-dimensional space or map. Use a map of their task (a process or product architecture) and link experiences to it. For small to medium-size repositories, this organization has many practical advantages.

6.3.6 Encourage Feedback and Double-Loop Learning

Fig. 6.9 shows the experience base in the center of the experience life-cycle. This vision sets it apart from a generic database, from a mere communication tool, and

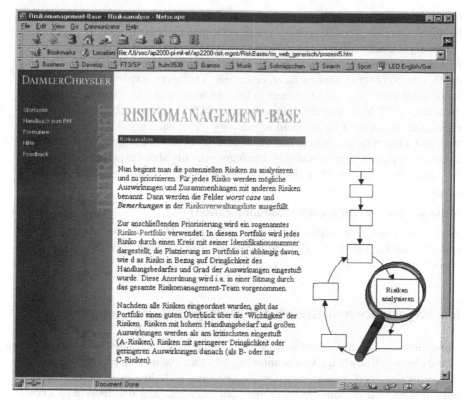

Fig. 6.10 Example of an experience base organized around a process (Risk Management Process at DaimlerChrysler). Reprinted from: Schneider, K. *Experience magnets – attracting experiences, not just storing them.* In *Conference on Product Focused Software Process Improvement PROFES 2001*, Kaiserslautern, Germany, September 2001. Lecture Notes in Computer Science, vol. 2188. Berlin: Springer

from many other types of tools. One of the most important characteristics of an experience base is its support for the *process of experience management*. In short, the experience base should facilitate proceeding from one activity to the next. Activated experience should be easily collected; stored raw experiences should be offered for experience engineering; its results should be forwarded to dissemination.

6.3.6.1 Elicit Experience During Dissemination

As we have discussed earlier, dissemination of experience, best practices, and related information is one of the best opportunities to activate and elicit new experiences. An advanced experience base should contain features to support this transformation, too. Contextualized communication opportunities are among the most sophisticated opportunities for an experience base. If material is disseminated in a form that allows software engineers to respond with a few clicks, chances for feedback increase. Providing many contact channels is another route to feedback.

An experience initiative should expect to continually learn on the level of *experience management* as well as on the *software engineering content level* of risk management, process improvement, or testing. Therefore, experience management tools should remain flexible to react to lessons learned on the experience management level [97]. In his master's thesis, Buchloh [22] developed a construction kit for experience bases built on standard technology. A construction kit approach facilitates fast adaptation and fosters flexible double-loop learning about experience management tools. Experience managers can learn not only about experience content but also about experience methodology and tools. And they can turn lessons learned into adapted tool structures fast.

Mnemonic 6.5 (Contextualized communication)

There are many tools facilitating communication. They can be used as experience feedback components. Providing context information makes them much more powerful.

6.4 Experience and Knowledge Management in Companies

Most large companies started a knowledge management initiative around the turn of the century. Knowledge was acknowledged as an essential asset and as a precondition for sustained success. Software engineering including process improvement was in particular demand. Maintenance, combination, and distribution of knowledge were approached from different angles, depending on the respective company priorities.

A selection of approaches is described below. They will be presented as cases that illustrate certain concepts. Discussion will focus on the remarkable aspects of each respective company.

6.4.1 The NASA Software Engineering Laboratory and its Experience Factory

Software is a key ingredient in NASA projects and missions. The NASA Software Engineering Laboratory (NASA-SEL) is a research and software development organization that provides NASA with high-quality software. Space missions depend on software, so NASA made significant efforts to improve their software engineering abilities beyond usual industry expectations.

Through a long-term collaboration with the University of Maryland [14], NASA-SEL initiated and maintained a process improvement program. At that time, the Capability Maturity Model CMM [83] and its European counterpart, SPICE (ISO 15 504) did not yet exist. It was the intention of NASA-SEL to improve project predictability, efficiency, and product quality by improving software processes. That

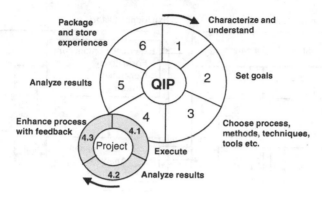

Fig. 6.11 Quality improvement paradigm (QIP) with integrated measurement [10]

same intention was later pursued by several process capability models. However, NASA-SEL used its own data and experience for focused process improvement.

Prof. Victor R. Basili from the University of Maryland introduced two corner-stones of the initiative: the quality improvement paradigm (QIP [10]) and the experience factory [11] concept. QIP is an iterative process of learning in the realm of software quality and software process. QIP (see Fig. 6.11) assumes an iterative process of organizational learning. Quality improvement is achieved by carefully planning improvements, by analyzing results, and by feeding insights back into the next cycle of improvement. Applying the presumed improvements in projects is an integral part of the QIP approach.

QIP is both goal-oriented and measurement-based. After exploring the situation, setting goals is a crucial step. Software quality cannot improve in an abstract and generic way. It is essential to know the direction and criteria for improvement. In step 3, a process and many related aspects are chosen. In this step, a change to the existing situation is planned. However, only future projects can show whether the planned changes will actually improve according to the predefined criteria. In step 4 of QIP, a smaller cycle is started: One or more projects execute the proposed new process and changes. Project results and behavior is measured. Feedback is attached to the process for each project. That feedback is the basis for QIP step 5, in which all project results, measurements, and experiences are analyzed and compared. The overall insights are packaged and stored for future use. It will feed directly into the next improvement cycle. It can benefit from the insights gained and refocus on newly tuned goals for the next cycle.

Definition 6.4 (Quality improvement paradigm)

QIP is a measurement-based approach to process improvement. Defining goals in the beginning is the guiding concept, and measurement takes the place of "observations."

Some observations are not spectacular: They confirm the expectations. Others are surprising and may even trigger emotions. During the analysis, data must be interpreted. This corresponds with drawing a conclusion. All three components of an

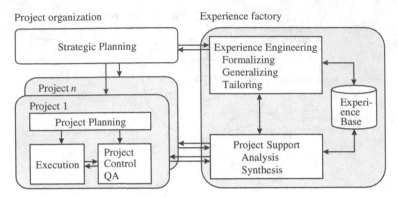

Fig. 6.12 The experience factory as a separate organizational unit for experience engineering and management according to Basili [11]

experience are involved, although measurement is an observation that is structured *a priori* (before the measured event), whereas accidental "observations" in a project are identified *a posteriori* (after the event). When you are measuring the number of failures found per day, you have a reason to do so. If you happen to find a new type of error, this is an unplanned event that can later be described as an experience.

If QIP is working well, a growing number of packaged experiences will be created. They must be stored, compared, and maybe transformed into best practices. Basili invented the experience factory as an independent team or unit within an organization (NASA-SEL). The experience factory follows QIP, stores the resulting experience packages in an experience base, and refines them by engineering these findings (Fig. 6.12).

NASA-SEL had sufficient resources for a separate unit. The University of Maryland had experts to run the experience factory and to perform in-depth data comparison. It may be interesting to note that initially many "experience packages" were conventional paper reports with sophisticated measurement plans and data. The experience base was basically a wooden shelf.

Experience packages were sets of well-planned measurement results rather than occasional observations some software engineer happened to make. This first experience factory did not rely on those incidents. It was built on the concept of goal-driven measurement.

When the Internet took over, most organizations running an experience factory probably migrated the experience base to the Web. But the concept of an experience factory is about humans learning from experience – not about networking computers.

An experience factory requires an agreed-upon basis of understanding and of processes. It is difficult or impossible to compare data that comes from uncontrolled or different backgrounds [83]. Chances for reuse and benefit increase when there are many similar projects using similar processes.

Definition 6.5 (Experience factory)

An experience factory is a separate organizational unit dedicated to experience work.

Many knowledge management initiatives install a core group with similar jobs as the experience factory team. This type of EKM initiative requires substantial investments over an extended period of time and cannot be run "on the side" by fully booked software engineers. NASA-SEL was able to invest a lot over an extended period of time. In return, they received custom-made process improvement guidance. A number of other large companies have adopted the concept.

6.4.2 Experience Brokers at Ericsson

Many competitive advantages in mobile phones are implemented in software. Good software quality and efficient software development processes are essential for the success of a company. Fast release cycles put pressure on the software experts. In the late 1990s, Ericsson decided to create a learning software organization. Basili's experience factory concept was adopted as a model, but implementation would take an unusual form.

Like a classical experience factory, Ericsson created a group in charge of experience exchange within the development organization. There was also an experience base. An additional concept made the initiative unique: the roles of experience brokers and experience communicators.

The most visible role in the experience initiative was the *experience broker*. An experience broker would walk the aisles of the software development department. He would meet people at the coffee machine, talk to them in the cafeteria, or just say hello in the open office environment. He was invited to meetings, met people in their offices, and had a lot of coffee. His job was to match needs with existing expertise. An experience broker was a seasoned software engineer; he knew what he was listening to and talking about. However, as a broker he knew a number of experience communicators: experts in a specialized field, who also had the ability (and time assigned) to transfer their knowledge and experience. They would visit the project and simply help.

There is a paper [59] that describes this concept very well (Fig. 6.13).

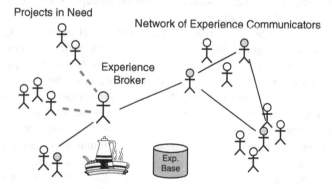

Fig. 6.13 Experience broker and communicators spread over projects

It is interesting to identify the elements and techniques in the Ericsson case:

- The *experience base* was small and mainly accessed by experience communicators or the experience broker. It was not considered a self-service device for software engineers.
- The *experience communicators* had a rich amount of well-organized knowledge and experience in their brains. They were a personalized variant of an experience base including engineered material. This base-in-a-brain would be filled in the traditional human way: by participating in projects, observing situations, and drawing conclusions.
- As professional *experience communicators* (a part-time job that consumed only a certain percentage of an expert's time), they were expected to reflect on their observations. Making experiences explicit was a job requirement. Effective reflection is a rare but valuable ability. Kolb [64] refers to reflection as a mandatory step for experiential learning (see Sect. 2.2).
- The *experience broker* used an expert network he knew very well: the profiles of the experience communicators. His main expertise as experience broker was metaknowledge: He knew *who knew what*.

This realization of the learning organization is fascinating. It is light-weight, relies on communication more than on documentation – which makes it different from the experience factory approach – but it is well-planned and provides active support for the entire experience life-cycle.

Example 6.4 (Two-level support in a hardware store)

A similar principle was studied by Reeves [87] in a different domain. He observed a hardware store in Boulder, Colorado: McGuckin's had a reputation of great customer service with remarkably knowledgeable staff. Fischer and his colleagues found a two-level human knowledge network that resembles the Ericsson setup. When customers had a question about a product or how to use it, they would easily find an employee in a McGuckin's shirt. This person had general knowledge of the store and its departments. He or she would point to the right department, where a specialized second-level "agent" would offer all the in-depth knowledge and experience a customer might appreciate.

Not every staff member can know all the details of all products. One solution is to use two types of agents: the router/broker and the communicator (as in the McGuckin case). A variant might be communicators *only* who are specialized in one field *and* know enough overview to send customers to the right department. However, it is easy to underestimate the difficulties and demands of a router/broker job. At Ericsson, it required a full-fledged software engineer with additional expertise in experience management and distribution. This is a rare and valuable profile.

There is a price for the speed and ease of communication-based experience transfer: When an experience broker leaves the company, a backbone of the initiative disappears. This risk could be mitigated by a little more written experience documentation or by several part-time brokers. The Ericsson approach was charming in its radical design.

6.4.3 DaimlerChrysler: Electronic Books of Knowledge and the Software Experience Center

Daimler-Benz Corporate Research had started in the late 1990 s to explore the potentials of experience-based process improvement [96]. Building on Basili's concept of an experience factory [11], the software process research group developed a family of techniques and tools to support systematic learning from experience.

Many companies started to consider the CMM capability maturity model [83] or SPICE (ISO 15 504) for process improvement. Climbing from one level to the next turned out to be a difficult and time-consuming endeavor. At Daimler-Benz (and later at DaimlerChrysler), CMM and experience-based approaches were combined in several cases. CMM represented the experiences of a large community but was rather unfocused. Experiences could be used to focus and sort improvement activities [93].

Several generations of **experience bases** were developed to the prototype stage. Practical experience uncovered misconceptions (cf. Sect. 5.5) and helped researchers to derive improved approaches. Those cycles of double-loop learning led to updated experience bases that were effectively used in practice.

Building experience bases was only a small fraction of supporting systematic learning from experience. In cooperation with the business units, all aspects were studied. Dedicated techniques like LIDs were developed and applied in the business units.

In 1998, Daimler-Benz started the **Software Experience Center (SEC)** initiative. It intensified earlier work in experience-based process improvement. Corporate research collaborated with three participating business units. Experience activation, elicitation, storage, engineering, and dissemination were supported in close collaboration with projects and teams.

SEC was embedded in the international Software Experience Center consortium. Five global companies scheduled regular experience exchange meetings on software engineering issues. On this level, strategic issues were emphasized. On the project level, operational support by experience reuse was the focus. And in between, SEC contributed to learning across business units [55] (Fig. 6.14).

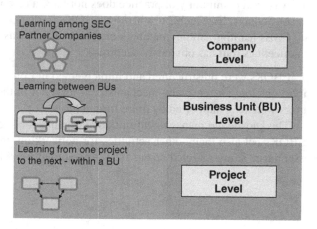

Fig. 6.14 Three levels of the SEC experiential learning initiative

As described in Ref. [92], experience exchange worked best on the company and the project levels. According to its design, SEC directly supported participating business units in a highly individual way. Findings can be generalized and applied in other environments. They substantiate many chapters of this book. This initiative gathered many insights and turned them into techniques [91], tools [94], and strategies [120].

When Daimler-Benz merged with Chrysler, a corporate-wide knowledge management initiative started. There was an exchange of ideas between SEC and that initiative, but the latter focused far more on operational goals. The knowledge management initiative was an important element in merging the company knowledge and making it available to knowledge workers. This was considered an important contribution to exploiting synergies. Merging key knowledge was considered a prerequisite to a successful merger of ideas and products.

6.4.3.1 Knowledge Management with Electronic Books of Knowledge and TechClubs

All elements of a large knowledge management initiative were installed. Two of them were highly visible within the company:

Electronic books of knowledge (EBOKs): EBOKs played the role of predefined, prestructured knowledge bases. They were defined for all important products and several further aspects. In our terminology, DaimlerChrysler experts outlined the EBOKs with respect to anticipated needs in the business units. Specialists had to fill the EBOKs, which were accessible over the intranet. However, an EBOK was not an unofficial write-up by a group of volunteers. Contents were solicited, and a lot of effort was put into defining and filling that part of the corporate knowledge base.

TechClubs were the teams assigned to chapters of an EBOK. High-level managers in a construction unit would be selected together with technical experts to identify and document relevant knowledge. Although TechClubs looked similar to communities of practice, they were different in a number of aspects:

- Membership was not voluntary; members were assigned. This was considered an honor and a job responsibility for company integration, not an informal add-on.
- A typical community of practice does not have a responsibility for documenting its findings, like TechClubs had for EBOKs.
- Cross-learning among members of the TechClub was not a primary goal of the meetings (but has obviously occurred).

EBOKs were prestructured and implemented in Lotus Notes. There was no (visible) ontology or reasoning mechanism, at least not in the beginning. Maybe some tasks were later supported by more formal tools.

The knowledge management initiative organized not only TechClubs with their EBOKs but also many other activities for networking, integration, and knowledge exchange. Some targeted social ties: An internal knowledge management award was co-celebrated via video link in Germany and in the United States. This activity incurred attention as a nonmonetary incentive. It also raised awareness for knowledge management.

DaimlerChrysler had more than one initiative running at a time. They had different goals and different target groups. Nevertheless, the concepts presented in this book can be identified – in different ways – in both initiatives. When you join or even direct a similar initiative, you will be able to map your individual situation to the concepts, concerns, advice, and tools you have seen in this book.

6.5 Internet and Web 2.0

During the past decade, the Internet has changed the world. Information that used to be spread over the world is now within the reach of our fingertips. Search machines provide access to electronic libraries, personal homepages, and company Web sites. Through blogs, Wikis, and social networks, the Internet turned millions of readers into authors. It blurs the distinction between the two groups. Such a revolution should have an impact on the management of experience and knowledge.

In a way, it has. It is no longer necessary to wait for information once you know where it is or who might have it. In former times (that is, more than 15 years ago), documents were usually printed on physical paper and shipped around the world. Books and scientific publications could be ordered from a library, which would send it via mail. Even with the most elaborate and fast logistics involved, response time was measured in days rather than minutes. Today, Internet and e-mail reach almost everyone in the professional world of software engineering. Because of fast and inexpensive Internet connections, most software engineers are no longer concerned about speed or cost of transfer. If there is an electronic document you want to share, there is no technical reason why the other party should not receive it within half an hour.

6.5.1 Impact of Internet Technologies on EKM Initiatives

But how do you know what document to share with whom? And how do you find a document or a person you want to interact with? When we put those questions back in context, Fig. 1.8 serves as a map and overview one more time.

We will now walk through Fig. 6.15 and discuss differences to the generic situation depicted in Fig. 1.8. The influences of new Internet technologies on experience and knowledge management can be discussed in this context.

Access to more bases and more people. There are more information bases and resources available over the Internet. As described above, access to those bases is much faster and cheaper. Most of those bases are not specific to software engineering or to any company. They reach from personal homepages of high school students

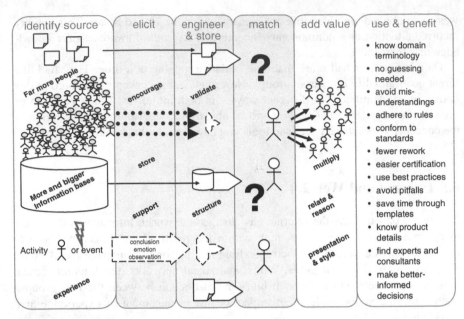

Fig. 6.15 The impact of Internet technologies on experience and knowledge management. This figure was derived from Fig. 1.8 but shows more sources and better dissemination. Central activities (shaded) are affected in both positive and negative ways

to sophisticated information bases like Wikipedia. But also within a company, the new technology provides faster and easier access to more internal bases. To indicate that change from Fig. 1.8 to Fig. 6.15, the information base symbol has been enlarged.

The widespread use of e-mail and other collaboration media on the Internet has made far more people accessible as potential sources of knowledge and experience. Because we are only interested in knowledgeable or experienced software engineers and their partners in this book, only a small subset of all Internet users are relevant for our consideration. Nevertheless, almost every software engineer and many domain experts are now in better reach of an EKM initiative. This has been symbolized by the much higher number of people drawn in Fig. 6.15 than in Fig. 1.8.

There is a downside of this opportunity: It is no less difficult to identify who can provide reliable and competent information for any given software engineering problem. When there are only a hundred employees, identifying the most knowledgeable or experienced source may seem doable. When there are hundreds of thousands of presumed software experts out on the Web, identification becomes an even bigger challenge. The risk of "identifying" a less competent source is growing.

Identification, encouragement, and elicitation. When it comes to experiences, the interactive and collaborative nature of "Web 2.0," such as blogs and Wikis, enables everyone to share their observations and experiences with everyone else. Contributions can simply be typed via a normal Internet browser. There is no need for expensive software that needs to be bought and installed. Many people around the world feel encouraged to share their adventures and opinions.

Software engineers and domain experts may feel encouraged to work on a Wiki in a distributed environment. This is indicated in Fig. 6.15 by the stronger arrows in the elicitation column. However, it is unlikely they will provide highly reflected experiences indicating observations, emotions, and conclusions. Although there is certainly more data and information on all kinds of raw experiences, the amount of useful and reusable software engineering experience is hard to estimate. When a company sets up its own experience exchange tool on top of an existing Internet technology, there should obviously be additional guidelines on how to use the new opportunity. Because resources and information are available outside the company, only very small portions need to be replicated and stored within the EKM initiative. Therefore, the other arrows in the elicitation column are not stronger.

Validation, structuring, and engineering. The middle column ("engineer and store") of Fig. 6.15 has changed in a surprising way. Whereas the necessity for validation and engineering of all the additional sources and their contributions has grown dramatically, most knowledge management initiatives cannot cope with that challenge. Instead, most symbols in that column shrank instead of growing: Many knowledge engineers do not even attempt to validate or engineer external sources. Unstructured and invalid sources offered by a knowledge and experience management initiative, however, will decrease its credibility and value. It may be smarter to ignore many supposed opportunities and focus on those parts of Fig. 1.8 where the smaller but better-controlled range of the initiative can be brought to bear.

Matching. The growing amount of potential sources provides more choices for those who seek support. However, decreasing rates of validation and engineering tend to put more of that burden on the shoulders of intended users. Although knowledge management needs to provide more and bigger stores of information, it also needs to maintain quality and reliability of those common assets. This is equally true for stored information and for links to people as sources.

Adding value. The first step of adding value through knowledge and experience is dissemination. This is again much easier, faster, and quicker than it used to be without new Internet technologies. Filtered dissemination of material, mailing lists, special interest groups, and newsletters provide improved opportunity for sharing. This can be used within companies for disciplined dissemination of information. Again, using those technical options without discipline and consideration will lead to a flood of messages. It will be considered spam and ruin the reputation of a knowledge management initiative. Being technically able to send more should by no means encourage the initiative to do so without consideration.

6.5.2 Using the New Internet in an Innovative Way

The discussion in the previous section has brought up a number of challenges and risks that come with the obvious opportunities of new collaboration mechanisms on the Internet. Although some of the core tasks of an initiative have become much easier, the sheer amount of information and the "availability" of so many sources can overwhelm knowledge engineers. By offering more input, the selection, engineering, and matching tasks have grown in difficulty – and in importance.

In principle, all chapters of this book apply to Internet-based EKM initiatives. They need to be applied to those tools just the same way they were supported by phone lists, physical newsletters, and traditional meetings. The distribution of stakeholders in a current project calls for a technological complement, which can be provided by phone or video conferences or by Internet tools. It is beyond the scope of this book to discuss remote collaboration in detail; success criteria and possible misunderstandings must be considered just as in traditional settings.

A new branch of promising approaches in many companies tries to merge the general opportunities of emerging Internet technologies with the demands of a specific EKM initiative. Important examples are Wiki systems that are tailored to software engineering purposes [106]. A Wiki offers the general features for reading and editing a Web page through an Internet browser. Texts can be written, formatted, and modified. Hyperlinks to other pages or other parts of the same page can be embedded as well as figures and tables. Depending on the particular Wiki framework, more or less features are available. Wikipedia (www.wikipedia.org) is a well-known Wiki system. It is a generic encyclopedia. Other Wikis exist for organizing a meeting, writing a publication with distributed authors, or collecting experiences.

This is a great technological basis for many of the concepts presented above. To make it useful, however, there must be appropriate structure and seeding, as has been pointed out above. In the case of a software engineering project Wiki, there should be a guiding structure to the Wiki when it is first published. For example, milestones, tasks, and deliverables should be defined as sections. Maybe, templates or examples can be provided for documents, and milestone criteria should be given. If a Wiki is prepared for its future use including guidelines and best practices that were turned into templates, structures, and recommendations, the best of two worlds can come together: experience, knowledge, and advanced technology. Nevertheless, all hints and warnings provided throughout the book still need to be considered! If a well-prepared Wiki is not used, or not used in the intended way, it quickly degrades and loses its power. Therefore, processes and conventions around a Wiki make the difference between a nice technological attempt and a serious contribution to experience and knowledge management.

Among the most interesting aspects of a shared Wiki is the potential of integrating dedicated tools (e.g., for project management or for working with ontologies). Challenges of making tacit knowledge explicit and of formalizing it for an ontology remain the same. But it is very likely that the future will bring well-seeded Wikis with integrated ontologies fit for company use. As with most technologies, it will take several years before visions turn into company solutions.

6.5.3 Integrating Technology and Workplace Learning

A recurring theme of this book is the necessity to integrate technical solutions with methodologies and techniques that take human participants seriously. Cognitive limitations must be taken into account. The issue of workplace learning (including but not limited to software engineering) was investigated in the APOSDLE project at the Know-Center in Graz, Austria. Many publications and resources can be found at www.aposdle.org. In particular, a background study was presented by Kooken et al. [66]. Lindstaedt et al. [70] discuss the technical implementation of related concepts.

Software engineers are exposed to high workloads and enormous time pressure in many projects. If they are supposed to use experience and knowledge, inventing additional tasks with additional effort is almost a guarantee for failure.

Kelloway and Barling [62] claim knowledge-workers need to be able to carry out knowledge work and learning. Technical support can help in this area. They also need to have an opportunity for learning and applying knowledge in the workplace. This criterion is only fulfilled if projects are planned to allow learning and participating in experience-sharing or communities of practice. Motivation is also important. In a workplace environment, many professionals are initially self-motivated. Management and an EKM initiative must take extreme care not to demotivate those knowledge workers.

Communities of practice serve for exchanging knowledge and experience. At the same time, they serve a social purpose and may even work as an incentive for its participants. They offer social recognition in a peer group, which is one precondition for volunteer contributions. Usable and modern tools, such as a tailored Wiki with useful seed and examples, can be yet another positive motivation factor. Whatever makes software engineering work easier and shows respect and appreciation for the additional work on knowledge and experience are good steps toward successful workplace learning.

6.6 Where We Stand Today

Software engineering is a field in flux, and so is knowledge management. Agile methods and model-based code generation, model-checking, and organic computing are just a few examples of the trends that come and go. However, there are challenges and opportunities in software engineering that remain the same beyond many trends. Making good use of one's own knowledge and experience is one of them.

6.6.1 The Age of Software

Software drives our companies and factories; it has reached our homes, our hospitals, and our schools. Developing useful software in a predictable and systematic way has become a pure necessity. However, keeping software projects on track and in sync with customer demands is not an easy task. It requires a sound background in computer science and continuous learning to stay up-to-date with emerging technologies. Processes are among the knowledge areas most essential for disciplined software engineering. They require management commitment, technical skills, and organizational learning. Agile approaches have emphasized the importance of human-to-human communication in software projects.

6.6.2 Experts in Structuring, Modeling – and Learning

In such an environment, the ability to handle knowledge and experience professionally often makes the difference between failure and success. There are many facts to know in software projects. The Software Engineering Body of Knowledge (SWEBOK) provides a good overview, but there are even more knowledge areas a professional software engineer has to handle.

This does not mean – and cannot mean – that a software engineer needs to be an expert in all areas his or her project touches on. Instead, it is a characteristic of software engineering that its experts need to be able to learn quickly and acquire a sufficient level of understanding in a short period of time. They need to be able to communicate effectively with different domain experts. Software is concerned with structure, patterns, and models. Knowledge management attempts to structure and model knowledge and experience. Therefore, software engineers should make good knowledge workers, with a deep understanding for some of its techniques.

Many problems and many opportunities in software projects are not technical in nature. It is the team or the department with its people that needs to be managed, as well as the knowledge that is spread over so many eager co-workers. At some point, knowledge management needs to provide opportunities for knowledgeable and experienced people to effectively exchange what they have. This will only work when the environment provides motivation and support for those who need or want to improve knowledge exploitation – if management allows and encourages opportunities for learning; and if individual software engineers have the ability to contribute and benefit. This book addresses all issues but emphasizes the last one.

A practitioner or student of software engineering needs to have a solid overview of and some insight into the mechanisms and techniques of organizational learning, knowledge management – and experience sharing.

We stress the importance and particularities of experience since we need to use it despite its vague and fluid nature. This is an important step in software engineering. Experience is important in all aspects of software engineering, but it is indispensable in ill-defined and evolutionary tasks, such as design, software quality, or requirements elicitation. There is no objective way to construct an ideal solution. Based on experience, a good solution must be developed, discussed, and improved.

6.6.3 A Tool Is Not Enough

There are software tools for many tasks in software engineering, and there are numerous tools on the market to support knowledge management. In large software projects, certain tools are indispensable, such as a configuration management tool and a modern integrated development environment.

For the challenge of organizational learning and knowledge management, tools come in handy, too. However, they will not do the job alone. Unlike configuration management, many issues in knowledge sharing and management are not fully understood. Human interaction is required, and human experts need to exchange experience and knowledge. For that reason, the mere technical ability to interact through a tool or the Internet is just one precondition for effective knowledge management. If knowledge workers (software engineers) are limited in their opportunities of applying interesting techniques, they will not do it. For example, a quality engineer will not invest time and effort in a "Company Quality Blog" if management criticizes doing it during working hours or demonstrates lack of support. The lack of motivation or of opportunities are frequent show-stoppers for organizational learning in the workplace.

The Internet and social networks provide a higher-level infrastructure that can be adopted, specialized, and used within a company initiative. They target various modes of communication, collaboration, and information exchange. Even a newsgroup can be a useful addition to a community of practice. However, a newsgroup alone will not make information and knowledge flow in a smooth and elegant way. There are so many assumptions and theories, as well as techniques required to consider the highly specific situation of workplace learning.

Hopefully, this book has contributed to your understanding of the interactions between "normal software engineering work" and the concepts and goals of knowledge management. Experience was added and emphasized as a subtype of knowledge that deserves special attention, as it offers special opportunities. Not many people have an interest in and some expertise with software engineering *and* knowledge management. Those who have can make valuable contributions to their companies – and to their own careers.

Use what you **know**!

6.7 Problems for Chapter 6

Problem 6.7.1: Life cycle

A friend tells you they are using a newsgroup as experience base. Which of the typical tasks of an experience base can be performed by a newsgroup, and which cannot? Provide arguments for all examples.

Problem 6.7.2: Risk of experience brokers

A situation like the one at Ericsson is risky: An experience broker may leave the company and disrupt the exchange of knowledge and experience. What could be done to mitigate that risk? That means: If a broker actually leaves, how will your suggestion improve the situation?

Problem 6.7.3: Risk mitigation

Name three important differences between a community of practice (CoP) and an expert network. What do they have in common?

Problem 6.7.4: Compare

The LIDs technique is optimized for "cognitive aspects." Explain what that means and provide two concrete examples within LIDs.

Problem 6.7.5: Cognitive aspects

Many knowledge management visions include the role of a knowledge manager. In the case of a software engineering knowledge base: What background should a knowledge manager have, and what existing role in a project (see Fig. 4.3) might be a good choice?

Problem 6.7.6: Seeding

You have designed a knowledge and experience base about test strategies and their effectiveness. What could you seed this knowledge base with, and where do you get that knowledge from?

Chapter 7
Solutions of Problems

7.1 Chapter 1

Problem 1.6.1: Data, information, and knowledge

A customer calls the requirements engineer and tells her about a feature they forgot to put into the specification. Where are data, information, and knowledge in this example?

The missing characters in the specification constitute "data." There is also "audio data" of the customer's voice. "Information" implies meaning. Interpretation of characters or spoken words as describing a feature of the product turns the data into "information." Both requirements engineer and customer have additional "knowledge" about the system before they start the conversation. This context turns the information about a new feature into "knowledge" that is related to other knowledge in their minds.

Problem 1.6.2: Missing the expert

Explain what could happen if a customer cannot reach the requirements engineer, but reaches a sales person instead. Assume the requirements engineer knows the project very well.

Data in terms of spoken words is transmitted just as in the previous problem. However, because of a lack of background knowledge, the sales person may be unable to interpret those words: Information about the missing feature could be lost when the sales person misinterprets what is being said. By all means, the sales person is missing contextual *knowledge*, so the *information* about the missing feature cannot be contextualized within preexisting *knowledge*. In this example, *data* has been transferred, *information* may be partially transmitted, but *knowledge* has not been successfully transferred.

Problem 1.6.3: Exact meaning

Your company has a cooperation project with an offshore development organization. You are not sure whether they use the same version of UML as you do. How do you make sure to transfer not just data but also the information implied in your UML 2.0 diagrams? Discuss your attempt using the terminology introduced in Chap. 1.

K. Schneider, *Experience and Knowledge Management in Software Engineering*,
DOI 10.1007/978-3-540-95880-2_7, © Springer-Verlag Berlin Heidelberg 2009

UML 2.0 is formally defined. When a UML 2.0 diagram is used to represent information, it is important to let the receiver know about this formal definition. For that purpose, a piece of metadata must be conveyed together with the operational data (the UML diagram itself). This metadata must at least tell the receiver that you used UML 2.0. Maybe, there should be additional metadata on the implications of that fact. After reading the metadata, receivers can interpret the diagram as UML 2.0 formally defined data. This helps them in assigning semantics (the implied meaning) to the UML syntax. In summary, the operational data (the diagram) is transferred together with metadata pointing out the version of UML and the formal meaning of the symbols. As a consequence, semantics is received together with syntax, thus conveying all information expressed in the details of a UML 2.0 diagram. With a knowledgeable receiver, this information can be reconstructed into the knowledge the sender intended to express in the UML diagram. Without that metadata, a receiver might have treated the diagram as a less formally defined sketch and missed part of the meaning (i.e., information and knowledge).

Problem 1.6.4: Experience in a review
During a review of a design document, the team finds out that there was a misunderstanding among customer representatives: They did not really need a distributed system. As a consequence, most of the design effort invested was wasted. Two of the authors participate in the review, and one will be told about it later. What will be the experiences of the authors and reviewers? Describe their observations, their emotions, and possible conclusions they may draw. Emphasize differences between different authors and between authors and reviewers.

Participating authors: They have observed the review and the finding. They "observed" the conversation that uncovered the misunderstanding. As they have invested so much effort into a document by mistake, they will be frustrated or angry – a strong negative emotion. They might draw very different conclusions from this observation and emotion: Either they might conclude that "it is not worth putting that much effort into a document, as it might be wasted effort" or they might conclude to "never start writing the full-fledged document without checking basic assumptions." It is important to note that there is no single, objective, or obvious conclusion in an observation – but any conclusion drawn will have an impact on future actions and performance.

The author who did not participate in the review does not share the same observation and, hence, misses the first-hand emotion. When the other authors tell him what happened, their own conclusions will influence their report. The listening author will "observe" this report, which will cause a second-hand emotion and – probably – a similar conclusion.

Reviewers participated in the same situation but see it from a different perspective. Their observation will include the success of finding a severe misunderstanding. Although this will cause extra effort for the designers, the reviewers will feel good about having detected the problem. Implementation effort was not wasted. Reviewers' emotions could be positive; at worst, they might feel bad for the authors. The resulting conclusion will look very different from the authors'. "A review is always worth the time, as you may find hidden misunderstandings" is one, but the author conclusion "never start writing the full-fledged document without checking basic assumptions" may also be concluded by the reviewers. This exercise highlights the importance of experiences – even though they may be highly individual, different, and unpredictable.

Problem 1.6.5: Experience capture form

Sketch a one-page form for capturing experiences when they occur. Explain your design and discuss how you will be able to effectively and efficiently collect what you need for your form and how you will use the collected information later. Did your first sketch cover all relevant information for successful reuse?

A predefined experience report form should help people to remember what needs to be recorded about a memorizable observation. It should solicit experiences and support people in documenting them – but it should not restrict their desire to express themselves. Therefore, experience collection mechanisms need to offer guidance without limiting expressiveness.

The sketch below is just one example. It contains only the essential fields (guidance) but allows people to add more or different information on the back. Note the "return to . . ." tag. Each report form should show where it needs to be sent when completed: by fax, e-mail, or company mail.

Experience Report Form		
Who reports?	Observation date	Place/context

Return to (put recipient here). Feel free to use back side of page

Observation: What happened?

Emotion: How did you feel?

Conclusions: What do you conclude?

The small fields collect essential metadata:
– Who made the observation?
– When was it observed (not documented!)?
– In which context was it collected?

Most space is reserved for operational data about the three key components of an experience:

– What was observed?
– What was the emotion it provoked?
– What is the conclusion or hypothesis derived from that?

The page should allow ample room for the operational data and allow people to document the experience with the lowest effort possible. It is rarely advisable to ask for more details or aspects. People who want to tell more can do so on the reverse side. People in a hurry will be turned off by more questions.

7.2 Chapter 2

Problem 2.7.1: Single- and double-loop learning
What is the difference between single-loop and double-loop learning? Explain both modes and give a short example from software engineering for each of the two.

In single-loop learning, a given goal is to be reached. Learning leads to reaching the goal faster or better. For example, a skilled software designer will become faster in drawing UML diagrams through single-loop learning. In double-loop learning, however, setting, reflecting, and adjusting goals are included in the learning process. In the software engineering example, software engineers will learn to use UML diagrams in only those situations in which they are advantageous. They may use Petrinets in other situations (e.g., for specifying process synchronization).

Problem 2.7.2: Framework XY learning scenario
A software company has used a certain framework XY for building business applications. Problems using that framework are reported to a hotline. The hotline releases a new version of its newsletter "XY Procedures." New projects are supposed to follow those procedures. This is supposed to spread learning across all projects. What kind of learning is this? How could this type of learning turn out to be counterproductive? Refer to the XY example. What concrete activities could help to prevent that negative effect?

The newsletter promotes single-loop learning: Existing procedures are presented and are supposed to be followed without criticizing them. However, if the XY framework turns out to be inadequate for a project, following the procedures might add to the problem: A better framework should be proposed instead, thus adjusting the goal. Promoted procedures could also be modified in order to circumvent the disadvantages of framework XY in the given project. In all cases, single-loop learning of using XY in the standard way is not helpful but counterproductive.

Problem 2.7.3: Formal reasoning patterns
You are working as a test engineer. Over the years, you have noticed that many tests fail due to the incomplete initialization of variables. Describe the three formal reasoning patterns (abduction, deduction, induction) and label the following statements with the corresponding reasoning pattern name:

Induction: A general rule is derived from one or more observations. This reasoning may be flawed.

Deduction: A special case is derived by applying a general rule.

Abduction: From an observation in a special case, a hypothesis is derived (what led to the observed situation?) as well as a general principle that supports the hypothesis.

Answers to the examples:

- "...there are often errors in initialization."

    Induction: Some errors were observed, the general rule ("are often") is derived.

- "Initialization looks so trivial, so many people are not very careful about it."

    Abduction: Provides an explanation for a specific observation (people forget initializations). Hypothesis leads to general rule ("people are not careful when they consider something trivial" and: "initialization looks trivial").

- "Programmers make more and more mistakes."

    Induction: General rule derived from several observations.

- "Setting a counter to 0 or 1 is often forgotten."

    Deduction from the general rule derived above ("there are often errors in initialization"). This is a special case of an initialization: setting a counter to 0 or 1.

- "Flawed initialization is easy to find by testing; that is why we find so much, because we test more systematically."

    Abduction: An observation is explained by a hypothesis about a generally applicable principle. Like induction, a principle is derived from a few (or a single) observations.

- "Programs have errors."

    Induction: The programs we have seen had errors, so we derive a general rule: (all) programs (seem to) have errors.

Problem 2.7.4: Schools and approaches of knowledge management
A company wants to encourage the exchange of knowledge among their software engineers. For each of the following suggestions, identify the respective school (according to Earl) and approach (product- or process-centric) it belongs to:

- "We develop a knowledge database and send an e-mail to all software engineers to enter their knowledge."

    Technocratic/Systems, product-centric: Infrastructure perspective.

- "Let's put an info terminal in the main lobby; every time you enter the building, you will see a new 'knowledge item of the day'."

    Behavioral/Space. Process-centric: The daily learning impulse.

- "We could use a Wiki to record everything we think others might need."

    Technocratic/Systems. Product-centric: A mechanism for exchanging knowledge chunks.

- "Okay, but there needs to be a moderator; plus, we should have monthly meetings of the Wiki User Group."

    Behavioral/Organizational. Process-centric: The learning aspect in several facets is being addressed.

- "Let's put up a coffee machine and two sofas."

    Behavioral/Spatial. Process-centric: Psychological and social aspects are highlighted, logistics of knowledge are not addressed.

- "There are powerful networks now, so we can even send movies. Everybody gets a camera on their desk, and when they want or have something interesting, they record a movie."

    Technocratic/Engineering. Product-centric: Movies are chunks of "knowledge" or "question," and this statement is concerned with the logistics of those movies.

- "Great idea! We hire a person who can index all incoming movies according to their SWEBOK category, and a few other attributes. We build a resolution machine that helps to match new entries with stored ones."

    Technocratic/Cartographic. Product-centric: Even more obvious focus on storing and managing chunks of "knowledge."

Problem 2.7.5: Knowledge management life-cycle

Draw Nonaka and Takeuchi's knowledge management life-cycle. Explain it by applying the concepts to the example of a group of software project leaders who meet in a community of practice in order to learn about cost estimation.

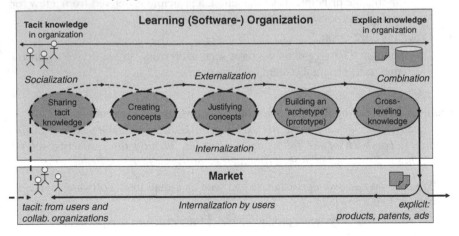

The CoP meets to exchange experience and knowledge. During the first meetings, most knowledge is implicit and often tacit. Participants will learn by socializing and talking about their projects. Some may not even be able to externalize their (tacit!) knowledge on cost estimation; they simply "do it." The CoP encourages its members to enter into the next phase of the life cycle: Those who listen might be able to derive concepts (by induction or abduction). Those concepts need to be tested, so later meetings can be used to collect additional reports in order to validate the concepts. During this phase, the more experienced participants externalize what they know (adding to the concepts, and finally, a constructive prototype of a cost estimation model). Others learn by internalizing the stories they hear: Applying models helps them to deeply understand (and internalize) what they hear. The final product of the cycle will be an externalized, documented package including the elicited and externalized knowledge that has been combined into a prototype, and finally a model with variants. This model is disseminated in the organization (in the CoP, to start with). When new needs arise to update or correct the model, the CoP may enter into a new iteration of the cycle.

7.3 Chapter 3

Problem 3.8.1: Pattern

What is a "pattern" with respect to knowledge and experience management? What are the core elements of a pattern and what are they used for when describing and reusing software engineering knowledge? Give an example from software testing.

A pattern is defined as a situation and a consequence or a problem (situation) and a solution (consequence). Core elements are the application condition, the situation or problem that is characteristic of the pattern, and the consequence. The consequence is usually the solution proposed by the pattern. Experience and knowledge can be represented in patterns. By making the application condition (including situation and context) explicit, this knowledge can be used more easily.

Example: A testing expert has seen many cases in which only very few errors were found during the first 3 days of testing. According to his experience, this is not an indication of supreme software quality but rather points to a poor testing strategy. This experience can be represented as:

- Problem/situation: Very few errors found during first 3 days of testing.
- Solution: Review testing strategy.

Although those two aspects make a pattern, it will be advantageous to document the rationale for the solution. This will often point to observations and experiences, like the concrete observations made in this example. Whenever the situation occurs in a project, the pattern should be used, and poor testing strategies will be detected. Applying the pattern is simple, and the benefit may be significant: No project will be deceived by the low number of findings. Even if the pattern should be wrong every now and then, this is not a major problem.

Note that the "problem" does not look like a problem at first. Therefore, it is more appropriate to call the triggering condition the "application situation."

Problem 3.8.2: Defining quality aspects
Finding a common language with the customer is important in software engineering. Assume you are defining quality attributes for a new piece of software with a customer from a medical background. Why is it important to define key terms like "reliability" or "ease of use" explicitly?

Customers and other project participants may use the same terms in different contexts and with different meanings (homonyms). In most cases, meanings will be similar but differ in important details. Quality attributes are part of quality requirements. Meeting the (quality) requirements is an important goal of a project, so it should be clear what they really mean. A misunderstanding could turn into a major problem: A medical customer may associate the reliability of a device with its availability during surgeries. A computer person may think about correctness of operation. Both associations of reliability are not precisely conformant to quality standards, but both "definitions" of reliability can be found in real projects. The common language needs to bridge the gap between participants.

Assume you are developing a banking system for teenagers on the Internet. This program is supposed to target young, inexperienced banking customers. They should be offered basic and additional information on the banking products, and each of their interactions should be explained in detail if they wish. Also, teenage customers should not be allowed to overdraw their account. This example is used for the following problems.

Problem 3.8.3: Mind map
In the process of developing the system, innovative ideas and important reminders are collected in a mind map. The intention is to gain an overview of important and "cool and catchy" concepts that should be taken into account to make the teenage bank account system a success. Draw a mind map of a teenage bank account with at least four directly related concepts and about two to four comments each. Comments should explain the innovation or importance of each concept.

(See the accompanying mind map.)

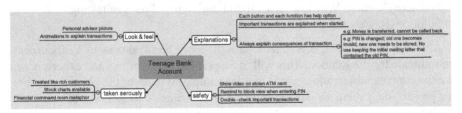

Problem 3.8.4: Brainstorming versus mind map

When you drew the mind map, you were not performing brainstorming, although some people might call it so. What are the main differences between drawing your mind map and "real" brainstorming?

Here are some important deviations. Not all of them may apply in your situation:

- Drawing the map alone. Brainstorming is supposed to be carried out in a group; participants should base their contributions on what they hear and see from others.
- In particular, a moderator is missing who would observe the brainstorming rules. In many cases, the moderator will also write down the contributions.
- Associations and relationships in a mind map were drawn while the mind map was generated. In brainstorming, the moderator should not influence the process, and there should be no online structuring (such as relationships, labeling, etc.).

Problem 3.8.5: Glossary entries

Provide glossary entries for "graphical user interface," "bank account," and "ATM card" (no debt allowed for teenagers) with respect to the teenage bank account.

- **Graphical user interface**: The screen of the banking application consists of different graphical elements for input and output. Young customers interact with the banking application by interacting with those elements, similar to a computer game. For example, screens contain symbols that represent functions. They can be clicked to trigger the respective function. Dragging and dropping banknote symbols with the mouse indicates money transfer (and so on: it is important to refer to specific aspects of graphical user interfaces in this application).
- **Bank account**: The amount of money put into the bank is stored individually for each customer. Administrative information (such as name, age, address, etc.) is stored together with the monetary information. When managed by the bank, the set of personal and monetary information is called an "account." It is identified by an eight-digit "account number," which is also part of the account. One customer may have multiple accounts, which will have different account numbers. (It is important to explain the term so that young customers will understand it. Most of them are computer-literate but not used to banks and financial operations.)
- **ATM card**: Personal card that enables a customer to carry out banking operations at a banking machine (called ATM; Automated Teller Machine). Customers receive ATM cards at their request. They cannot withdraw more money than they have in the bank. (This entry could have more or less detail on how to use the ATM card. In principle, a short definition might be enough. It is not recommended to explain the rules of usage within a glossary entry.)

Problem 3.8.6: Typos

Typos (incorrectly spelled words) are more common in mind maps than in glossaries. Why is that so and why is it usually not a problem for mind maps?

- Mind maps are mostly drawn using a computerized tool. The person drawing and writing tries to capture contributions of the entire group and write them down fast. This process requires drawing lines and links, rephrasing what people say, and typing fast. A typo will mostly not endanger meaning, so little care will be taken in deleting small mistakes.
- Glossaries will be used as a reference in a project. They should not have obvious mistakes, as those might put their credibility at stake. For that reason, a glossary will be checked before it is used in a project. In extreme cases, a typo or mistake may ripple through many documents that use the flawed glossary entry.

Problem 3.8.7: Domain model

What happens when a teenage customer turns legally adult? How can you find out what is supposed to happen then? Write a use case for this operation and highlight two pieces of "domain knowledge" it contains.

From the above-mentioned description, it is not clear what will happen. This situation of a customer turning adult may have been forgotten.

In that case, the customer (i.e., the bank building the young customer portal) will need to decide. A use case can help to facilitate precise communication between developing organization and bank. The following example shows a process that may be carried out automatically or manually. The two pieces highlighted describe simple but important pieces of domain knowledge that have been made explicit using the use case.

(See Use Case 42, "Adopting customer status to adult," below.)

Use Case 42	Adapting customer status to adult
Environment	Regular batch account processing
Level	Main level
Primary Actor	Bank
Stakeholders and their interests	Stakeholders Interests Customer: wants to be treated as a serious customer, no extra info needed Bank: wants to change account conditions, including user interface (and price)
Precondition	Customer has been a teenage customer for at least half a year
Guarantee	Basic account information remains the same (name, balance)
Success case	Customer receives a letter informing him or her about the new status. Status is set to adult, leading to higher prices and simplified "expert-mode" user interface
Trigger	Batch routine identifies a Young Customer turned legally adult
Sequence of Steps	Step Actor Activity 1 Bank Sends information letter to customer 2 Bank Modifies account status 3 Customer Uses ATM the next time 4 ATM Uses Adult dialogue and interaction
Extensions	1a If Customer has not been teenage customer for at least half a year, postpone status change for 1 month. 3a If customer does not use ATM for 60 days, send another letter inviting him to a visit.
Technology	If there is electronic contact information for the customer (SMS, email), send information to those in parallel.

Problem 3.8.8: Use case

Describe the use case of "changing the PIN" using the use-case template shown in Fig. 3.8. Make sure to address the characteristic need of young customers to learn about permitted PIN formats and the implications of changing a PIN (and maybe forgetting it). What happens when they enter incorrect input?

When they enter incorrect input, additional information is displayed – in contrast with normal ATM software that simply requests the correct PIN again.
(See Use Case 12, "ChangingPIN," below.)

Use Case 12	Changing PIN
Environment	ATM on a wall inside or outside bank building
Level	Main level
Primary Actor	Young customer (customer, for short)
Stakeholders and their interests	**Stakeholders** **Interests** Customer: wants to change PIN (to memorize it better, or to ensure higher security level) Bank: wants to avoid fraud (foreign interference, unauthorized modification of PINs) and forgotten PINs (=effort)
Precondition	Customer has a valid Young Customer account Customer has identified and authentified (PIN) him/herself
Guarantee	PIN is not changed without old PIN being entered correctly. Not changed without the new PIN being entered identically two times immediately after each other.
Success case	PIN is changed to the new PIN given by the customer. The customer has effectively been informed about all consequences of that change. The customer has demonstrated he or she remembers the new PIN.
Trigger	Customer inserts ATM card
Sequence of Steps	**Step** **Actor** **Activity** 1 Customer selects „change PIN" option 2 System asks for old PIN 3 Customer enters old PIN 4 System explains (a) old PIN will be invalid (b) no need looking up old PIN (c) new PIN needs to be memorized. Announce that this will be tested through a little game.. 5 System asks for new PIN 6 Customer enters new PIN 7 System asks for PIN in a modified way (e.g., "in reverse order", "typed as words") 8 Customer enters modified PIN 9 System acknowledges change, reminds Customer to memorize new PIN
Extensions	3a If customer cannot provide PIN, explain the security impact of changing PIN, ask to come back later. 6a If customer does not want to change PIN any more, provide option to cancel with no change made. 6b If customer enters the old PIN again, do not accept, but assume misunderstanding and go to 4. 8a If customer enters wrong modified PIN, explain game again, go to 7 – offer cancellation.
Technology	Do not speak text, even when speakers are available (can be overheard).

Problem 3.8.9: Writing a pattern

Let us assume the company developing the teenage banking system has gathered experience with many other systems for young people. During those projects, there was a recurring misunderstanding: When young customers were interviewed for requirements, they rarely checked "intuitive interface" as a high priority. Nevertheless, customer satisfaction seemed to depend on ease of use. Structure this observation as a pattern, and describe how the teenage banking project can make use of it.

Observation as a pattern:

- Situation/Problem: A young customer project.
- Solution: Ease of use is an important quality aspect. This is true no matter what teenage customers say in interviews.

Different possibility: We conclude from the observation that young customers either did not understand the term "intuitive interface" or they did not consider it important. This conclusion would lead to a different pattern:

- Situation: Interviewing teenage customers about software quality requirements.
- Solution: Ask about the importance of intuitive interface by using examples and concrete prototypes.
- Rationale: Teenagers seem to be unable or unwilling to associate with the abstract term of "intuitive interface." The question must be asked in a way teenagers can relate to.

The teenage banking project can benefit from either of the two patterns: When they find the situation matches their own situation, the solution part can be treated as advice. In the two examples: (1) ease of use will be treated as important, no matter what the interviewees say, and (2) the interviews will consider the teenagers' tendency to ignore or underestimate interface issues. Examples and concrete scenarios will help.

7.4 Chapter 4

Problem 4.9.1: Definition and purpose
What is the definition and the purpose of an ontology?

> An ontology is a data model that represents a set of concepts within a domain and the relationships between those concepts. It is used to reason about the objects within that domain (Wikipedia, August 30, 2007).

An ontology provides a clear reference for a certain domain. Knowledge workers, tools, and projects can refer to it. By introducing formally defined concepts, relationships, and properties, those elements can be used in searches, reasoning, and for computer-supported tasks.

Problem 4.9.2: RDF graph
Use the ontology sketched in Fig. 4.1: Describe a situation as an RDF graph in which Dr. Dieter Drew prescribes "weight lifting" as a physical therapy to patient Peter Painful. Nathalia Newton is a nurse who assists Peter in doing the weight lifting in a health-stimulating way. Treat names as string attributes defined in that same ontology.

Use http://ontoMed.schema/ as the name for the ontology shown in Fig. 4.1. The hospital maintains a list on the intranet. Employees, patients, and treatments offered are listed in http://hospital.mainList, with the subcategories /doctors, /nurses, /patients, and /treatments. A specific entry (e.g., XY) is accessible at #XY.

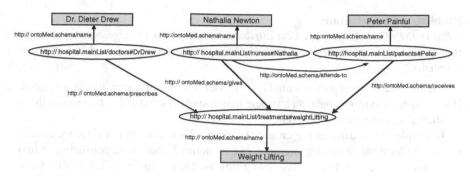

Problem 4.9.3: Inheritance

Explain what happened to the inheritance relationships in Fig. 4.1 when you drew the RDF graph, and why.

Inheritance relationships are not visible in the RDF graph. The RDF graph shows instances and refers back to where they are defined. For example, gray ovals point to the mainList for each instance. Predicates (arcs) point to the schema (Fig. 4.1) in which the respective relationship was defined. Literals like names were not defined anywhere, so they stand for themselves.

The name-relationship needs to be defined somewhere, and the problem description said you should assume they were defined in the ontoMed.schema ontology.

Inheritance is a relationship between classes (or types), but not instances. Each instance belongs to one type or class. The most specific class is referenced in the RDF graph. For "Weight Lifting," this is Physical Therapy as opposed to Treatment.

Problem 4.9.4: Multiple roles

Looking at the RDF graph above: Can an individual or instance have multiple roles (subject, predicate, object)? Substantiate your answer with an example.

Yes, this occurred to Peter Painful. He is the subject of the triple: Peter–receives–Weight Lifting, and at the same time, he is the object in the triple Nathalia–attends-to–Peter (this short notation for triples is not officially defined, as you know, but you should understand what it means).

Problem 4.9.5: xmlns

What does the statement (xmlns:medSchema= "http://ontoMed.schema/") mean and how can that be used in subsequent statements?

A shortcut (medSchema) is defined. The given prefix of URIs is the "path" to that schema. After opening that schema as a namespace, subsequent statements can use it instead of the lengthy prefix (e.g., medSchema:prescribes instead of http://ontoMed.schema/prescribes).

This makes the XML code more readable and avoids inconsistencies or typos.

Problem 4.9.6: Attributes
What is the difference between an attribute "name" in a Protégé ontology versus that in an object-oriented class model? How are attributes assigned in both environments?

An attribute in an object-oriented class model is a part of a specific class symbol. If several class symbols have an attribute that is spelled identically, like name, those attributes are nevertheless different.

In ontologies, attributes are entities by themselves and are not dependent on a class. The attribute name, for example, can be defined once (e.g., consisting of first name and last name). Every class using this attribute actually refers to that same entity, not just different entities with the same identifier.

In class models, the attribute is written in the second part of a class symbol. An attribute in an ontology is created in a separate editor before it can be assigned to none, one, or many classes.

Problem 4.9.7: OWL-DL
OWL-DL is often used as the variant for ontologies applied in practice. Name the two other variants available and provide reasons that make OWL-DL preferable.

OWL-Full is powerful but not decidable. This makes it inadequate for formal operations.

OWL-Light is very lean but not powerful enough for many applications.

OWL-DL is decidable and powerful enough. This makes it the best candidate.

Problem 4.9.8: Test ontology
Construct a simple ontology in Protégé with six classes. Sketch the ontology first using the bubble notation of Fig. 4.1 or Fig. 4.3. The purpose is to collect knowledge on test strategies. A test strategy determines what test cases look like. A test case is characterized by the provided input values (parameter values) and by the expected outcome or reaction. A test strategy is considered successful if it helps to find many errors. The test cases used as a reference are combined in a test suite. After this sequence of test cases has been performed, the number of errors detected is recorded.

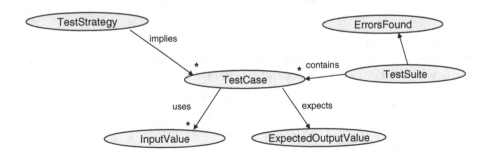

Problem 4.9.9: Knowledge acquisition

Who could provide what part of the knowledge you need to populate the above-mentioned knowledge base? Outline a plan for how you could get all required data into the knowledge base with the lowest possible effort.

Testers will be able to provide all data needed. They develop or use test strategies, derive test cases, and carry them out. When they analyze the results, they are able to count the number of errors detected.

Asking the testers looks straightforward. However, most of the data needed will probably be available anyway. In a mature software organization, test cases will be stored in a database, and so will test protocols. They contain errors and test cases performed (test suites, if you will).

It should, therefore, be possible to get that data from the test databases using an automated routine. Remember to save everybody's time – except for the knowledge management professionals, who should invest a little of their time to save a lot of the software engineer's effort.

From a knowledge management perspective, knowledge acquisition will often mean asking people for their knowledge or data. However, as this problem shows, sometimes a little tool can free human actors from unnecessary work.

7.5 Chapter 5

Problem 5.6.1: Life cycle

Draw the experience life-cycle and briefly explain each activity.

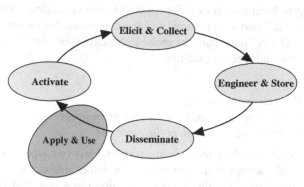

The life cycle may start in any state/activity, depending on existing material at a particular point in time. Usually, doing something (Apply & Use oval) is the first activity. In terms of the experience life-cycle, activation comes first: After having done something relevant, the interesting insights, experiences, and knowledge need to be made conscious.

Activated experience, knowledge, and insights need to be assembled. Elicitation refers to the activity of actively asking and digging for those materials, whereas collection emphasizes the administrative or technical part of actually getting all the provided data together in an organized way.

Engineering and storage means adding value to knowledge and experience by relating it to other material and by modifying its style. While an experience is about an observation made in the past, engineered experiences are often turned into recommendations or best practices: guidelines on what to do in a similar future situation.

Dissemination goes beyond making something available: It refers to an activity of delivering material in a specific format to people at the time they need it. Under these circumstances, recommendations can be used when performing a project duty. At that time, new observations are made, and the circle may start again.

Problem 5.6.2: Experience engineering
Assume your team is using a new framework for software development. Programmers report problems they have had. If possible, they also report how they solved them in the end. What should experience engineering do with those reports, and what roles can patterns play?

Experience engineering is the activity performed after collecting material. Once material has been elicited or collected in another way (e.g., measurement), it needs to be related to other observations. Statements and conclusions in similar situations should be compared and combined into a more believable (or more differentiated) view. If all conclusions agree, this strengthens the conclusion. If there is a different view on a similar situation, differentiating factors and preconditions need to be investigated (either by reading the submitted material or by performing additional interviews). Contents are derived by interpretation and comparison.

After that, the result of this analysis needs to be "turned around" from stories of what happened into recommendations of what should be done (best practices). Patterns can help to format both experiences and recommendations. The situation is described as an "IF" part of a pattern, and the conclusion (or recommendation) is written as the "THEN" part. Patterns make reuse easier, because they explicitly factor out conditions and recommendations.

Problem 5.6.3: Experience three-tuple
Describe one of your own experiences in software engineering as an experience three-tuple. Make sure you do not neglect the emotion!

Observation: We changed an interface in a project. Only one type was "relaxed," so an operation could accept more instances than before. However, it turned out that two groups had used the initial interface definition in a way that later caused problems during integration. It took some time to understand how "relaxation" could cause problems.

Emotion: We were stunned and felt bad, because we knew very well about the importance of interfaces. All three groups had to make changes and corrections, which took some of their time. It was an embarrassing situation for those who had decided the interface change was "neglectable."

Conclusion: Never ever change an interface without informing all affected groups. Let them consider implications before you take the freedom to change what you have agreed upon. Only during experience engineering will the experience be turned into a practice recommendation.

Problem 5.6.4: Best practice

All projects in a business unit need to follow a new process. The first project using it reports some experiences. Why can experience engineering usually not be shortcut by asking the projects to provide best practices right away?

A single experience is usually not sufficient for generalizing from it. Like a theory, a conclusion needs to be confirmed to be believable. Only when it is a pure technical problem that was solved and only if there is little doubt about the proposed solution could this one conclusion be presented as a recommendation.

It is better to have one experience than none. However, there is little use in reversing it into a practice – and the label "best practice" is not appropriate if there is no comparison with any other practice at all.

Problem 5.6.5: Contradictory experiences

Two testers report experiences on a test tool. Tester A is happy, because the tool helped him to create far more test cases than usual. A larger number of errors were found early in the testing process, and late testing phases were far more relaxed. Tester B, however, was disappointed because the tool provided only "trivial test cases," as he puts it. Assume you are an experience engineer and need to make sense of those contradictory experiences. Give at least two potential explanations for the different experiences! If both testers A and B are equally competent, what could experience engineering ideally try to derive from their experiences?

Given both partners are competent, the different situation and context should be the source of the different experiences. An experience engineer will, therefore, analyze those differences carefully. Maybe one of the two people had different expectations or was in a different situation.

For example, code in example A may contain more errors, so the tool can be used more effectively for finding them. Tester B might already have worked with code B for a longer time and have better preexisting test cases. In that situation, the tool has more problems exceeding the present state. Present state, quality of the code, and many other properties can be differentiating factors.

The IF-part of a pattern will have to reflect that differentiation. Future projects will need to classify themselves, so that the best-matching patterns are found. They should contain recommendations best suited for the particular context and situation at hand.

Problem 5.6.6: Delicate experience

Why is experience an even more delicate matter than factual knowledge? Describe two different kinds of experience: (1) one highly critical kind of concrete experience that would be very helpful to reuse, but that will be very hard to elicit; (2) one kind of knowledge that should be easy to get (and useful to reuse). As an experience engineer, what kind of experience would you focus on first?

Experience is always subjective. Because of a certain perspective, details or aspects of the situation may have been missed during the observation. Conclusions may be faulty, and the emotional aspect is deeply subjective. A raw experience is difficult to validate, and the subjective elements are difficult to preserve during the experience life-cycle.

1. There are experiences that either remain unconscious or that are embarrassing for somebody. Those experiences are hard to elicit ("get out of somebody to"). For example, a project manager may find that she is weak in planning and did not know how to use the planning tools correctly. Although conscious, this experience will hardly be made explicit by that project manager – but others on the team may have made the same observation. If a person has been doing something for a very long time, there is little chance it will be considered an experience. The challenge for experience elicitation lies in helping this person: Seeing the value and the details in daily (implicit, tacit) knowledge is difficult. A highly "experienced" project manager may master his planning tools without giving it a thought. It takes some questioning to find out more about those procedures.
2. Easy-to-get experiences are about events and things that people were very aware of (trying something new, having a success or problem).

It is advantageous to take the easier material first. Use the experience management effort wisely! When the easy material takes only a short time for elicitation, the experience that is more difficult to elicit will still be rather fresh afterward. Because there is only limited time available for total elicitation, as many useful experiences as possible should be collected – not starting with one that will use up all the time assigned.

Problem 5.6.7: Argue well
How do you react if your boss asks you to start developing a knowledge-building strategy for your team of eight people – with the option of spreading it across the entire business unit if it really provides substantial benefits. Once you reach that level, he promises to provide additional resources and promote you to "knowledge expert." Sketch your argumentation!

Starting at the point where you are is a good idea. However, a company-wide knowledge management initiative can hardly grow from bottom-up alone. It has been reported many times how important management commitment is for knowledge management. Starting with a small team may lead to effective support for that team (e.g., resulting in a team glossary and a simple repository of experiences). Larger teams or entire business units call for additional and different mechanisms. The same strategy will not work (i.e., everyone who made an important observation fills in a form and puts it into the paper folder). Knowledge management practices do not scale up easily.

Therefore, you should take the chance to build something for your team but point out the above-mentioned argumentation. It is derived from experience in several companies. Ask for more commitment upfront or recommend setting more modest goals.

7.6   Chapter 6

Problem 6.7.1: Life cycle

A friend tells you they are using a newsgroup as experience base. Which of the typical tasks of an experience base can be performed by a newsgroup, and which cannot? Provide arguments for all examples.

- Activation: When a problem is discussed in a newsgroup, this may show some participants how relevant their experiences are.
- Collecting: Because communication in a newsgroup works through writing, nothing is lost and everything is collected.
- Engineering: A moderated newsgroup may contain elements that resemble engineering. However, most newsgroups offer the stored material more or less in the way it is typed in. There is no major reformatting or rephrasing.
- Dissemination: When the newsgroup offers mechanisms for distinguishing threads or sub-newsgroups, a reader has a better chance of finding relevant entries. However, there is usually no sophisticated mechanism for dissemination.

Problem 6.7.2: Risk of experience brokers

A situation like the one at Ericsson is risky: An experience broker may leave the company and disrupt the exchange of knowledge and experience. What could be done to mitigate that risk? That means: If a broker actually leaves, how will your suggestion improve the situation?

Let two or more brokers work together. That way, a lot of implicit knowledge can be exchanged without the need to document it. When one of the brokers leaves, the other one can take over.

Documenting everything is not such a good idea. A core concept is the fast and unbureaucratic response to a demand. Documentation would slow down and disrupt the reaction chain.

Problem 6.7.3: Risk mitigation

Name three important differences between a community of practice (CoP) and an expert network. What do they have in common?

- A CoP is a volunteer organization; an expert network is organized and supported by the organization.

- Entering and leaving a CoP is up to the participants. The members of an expert network are usually nominated by the company.
- A CoP is a network of people who work in the same domain. An expert network connects people whose expertise may complement each other.
- Participants benefit from a CoP by learning about other experiences. In the best case, some of those experiences are documented and made available to other projects. Members of an expert network are often supposed to provide advice or guidance to a new project. There is more direct support.

In both forms, there is a group of people defined by their knowledge. Connecting those people is considered a way to sustain implicit and tacit knowledge.

Problem 6.7.4: Compare

The LIDs technique is optimized for "cognitive aspects." Explain what that means and provide two concrete examples within LIDs.

Cognitive aspects refer to the human abilities (and disabilities) during the task of providing or reusing experience. Considering cognitive aspects should help to avoid unrealistic expectations and demands that cannot be met by most people.

For example, people cannot distinguish the crucial from the irrelevant aspects of an extended task. Without support (by an agenda or a table of contents), they may get lost.

People are not willing to spend long hours on capturing experience; they prefer to continue with the next assignment. Therefore, minimizing the LIDs session duration is a contribution to a cognitive aspect.

Problem 6.7.5: Cognitive aspects

Many knowledge management visions include the role of a knowledge manager. In the case of a software engineering knowledge base: What background should a knowledge manager have, and what existing role in a project (see Fig. 4.3) might be a good choice?

A knowledge manager should have an EKM background, as presented in this book. There should be a good overview of the techniques relevant for structuring knowledge and the ability to describe knowledge and experience in patterns and maybe ontologies.

In most cases, it is more important to have experience in setting up learning initiatives than to know all details of a formalism. The latter can be acquired faster than can good judgment about EKM options.

Quality people are often a good choice. They have a cross-cutting concern for quality. Many of them are organized in CoPs or other networks. And they should be organized in the quality hierarchy, which helps them to consider other project experiences.

Problem 6.7.6: Seeding

You have designed a knowledge and experience base about test strategies and their effectiveness. What could you seed this knowledge base with, and where do you get that knowledge from?

Seeding could start with a book or with single experiences that someone tells you in a meeting. With book material, make sure to keep advice concrete. With experiences, try to generalize them toward reusable information. The combination of both book (general) and specific aspects helps to make a good seed. Do not try to cover too many aspects, but rather to reach a certain depth.

References

Web Sites for More Ideas and Visions

A software engineering ontology based on SWEBOK : http://www.seontology.org (2009-04-18).

AIFB, U.o.K. *OntoEdit, http://www.ontoknowledge.org/tools/ontoedit.shtml* (2007-07-09).

Gesellschaft für Informatik e.V. *http://www.gi-ev.de/english/* (2007-07-09).

IEEE. SWEBOK: Software Engineering Body of Knowledge, *www.SWEBOK.org* (2007-03-09).

Initiative, D.C.M. *Dublin Core, http://dublincore.org/* (2007-08-30).

OpenGALEN Foundation. OpenGALEN, http://www.opengalen.org/

Protégé. *http://protege.stanford.edu/* (2007-07-09).

SchemaWeb. A collection of many different Ontologies: http://www.schemaweb.info/ (2009-04-18).

Smith, M.K. *Chris Argyris: Theories of action, double-loop learning and organizational learning, www.infed.org/thinkers/argyris.htm* (2007-03-09).

The Association for Computing Machinery. *http://www.acm.org/* (2007-07-09).

W3C. *OWL Language Guide, http://www.w3.org/TR/owl-guide/* (2007-08-30).

W3C. *OWL Web Ontology Language Semantics and Abstract Syntax, http://www.w3.org/TR/owl-semantics/* (2007-08-30).

W3C. *RDF Primer, http://www.w3.org/TR/rdf-primer/* (2007-08-30).

W3C. *Resource Description Framework (RDF): Concepts and Abstract Syntax, http://www.w3.org/TR/rdf-concepts/* (2007-08-30).

W3C. SPARQL Query Language for RDF, *http://www.w3.org/TR/rdf-sparql-query/* (2007-08-30).

Citations

1. Ahern DM, Clouse A, Turner R, *CMMI® Distilled: A Practical Introduction to Integrated Process Improvement*, 2001, Reading, MA: Addison-Wesley.
2. AIFB U o K, *OntoEdit, http://www.ontoknowledge.org/tools/ontoedit.shtml* (2007-07-09).
3. Alexander I, *Initial industrial experience of misuse cases.* in *IEEE Joint International Requirements Engineering Conference, 9–13 September 2002.* 2002. Essen.
4. Alexander I, Maiden N, eds. *Scenarios, a Stories, Use Cases: Through the Systems Development Life-Cycle: Through the Systems Development Life-cycle.* 2004, New York: John Wiley & Sons.
5. Althoff K-D, Nick M, Tautz C, *Improving organizational memories through user feedback.* in *Workshop on Learning Software Organizations.* 1999. Kaiserslautern, Germany.
6. Aonix – Software through Pictures. *A graphical modeling tool with a powerful transformation engine, http://www.aonix.com/stp_se.html* (2008-11-25).
7. Argyris C, Schön D, *Organizational Learning: A Theory of Action Perspective.* 1978, Reading, MA: Addison-Wesley.
8. Argyris C, Schön DA, *Organizational Learning II: Theory, Method and Practice.* 1996, Reading, MA: Addison-Wesley.
9. Bartsch-Spörl B, *Transfer of experience – issues beyond tool building.* in *Workshop on Learning Software Organizations.* 1999. Kaiserslautern, Germany.
10. Basili V, Rombach HD, *The TAME project: Towards improvement-oriented software environments.* IEEE Transactions on Software Engineering, 1988. 14(6): 758–773.
11. Basili V, Caldiera G, Rombach DH, *Experience factory*, in *Encyclopedia of Software Engineering*, Marciniak JJ, Editor. 1994, New York: John Wiley & Sons. pp. 469–476.
12. Basili V, Caldiera G, *Improve software quality by using knowledge and experience.* Sloan Management Review, 1995. Fall: 55–64.
13. Basili V, *Evolving and Packaging Reading Technologies <publications/journals/J68.pdf>*, Journal of Systems and Software, July 1997. 38(1): 3–12.
14. Basili VR, Caldiera G, McGarry F, Pajersky R, Page G, and Waligora S, *The software engineering laboratory – An operational software experience factory.* in *14th International Conference on Software Engineering (ICSE'92).* 1992, New York: ACM Press.
15. Beck K, *Extreme Programming Explained.* 2000, Reading, MA: Addison-Wesley.
16. Beedle M, Schwaber K, *Agile Software Development with Scrum.* 2001, Englewood Cliffs, NJ: Prentice Hall.
17. Berners-Lee T, Fischetti M, *Weaving the Web.* 1999, San Francisco, CA: Harper.
18. Birk A, Kröschel F, *A Knowledge management lifecycle for experience packages on software engineering technologies.* in *Workshop on Learning Software Organizations.* 1999. Kaiserslautern, Germany.
19. Birk A, Dingsoyr T, Stfilhane T, *Postmortem: Never leave a project without it.* IEEE Software, special issue on knowledge management in software engineering, 2002. 19(3): 43–45.
20. Birk A, Dingsøyr T, Lindstaedt S, Schneider K, eds. *Learning Software Organisation and Requirements Engineering: The First International Workshop.* Special Issue of the J. UKM Electronic Journal of Universal Knowledge Management. 2006.
21. Boehm B, Turner R, *Balancing Agility and Discipline – A Guide for the Perplexed.* 2003, Reading, MA: Addison-Wesley.
22. Buchloh T, *Erstellung eines Baukastens für Experience Bases*, in *Fachgebiet Software Engineering.* 2005, Hannover: Universität Hannover.
23. Calero C, Ruiz F, Piattini M, *Ontologies for Software Engineering and Software Technology.* 2006, Berlin: Springer.
24. Cockburn A, *Writing Effective Use Cases.* 14th Printing. 2005, Reading, MA: Addison-Wesley.
25. Cypser RJ, *Communications for Cooperating Systems – OSI, SNA, and TCP/IP.* 1991, Reading, MA: Addison-Wesley.

26. Davenport TGP, *Knowledge Management Case Book – Best Practices*. 2000, München, Germany: Publicis MCD, John Wiley & Sons.

27. Davies C, *Kolb Learning Cycle Tutorial – Static Version, http://www.ldu.leeds.ac.uk /ldu/sddu_multimedia/kolb/static_version.php* (2008-02-23).

28. DeMarco T, *Structured Analysis and System Specification*. 1979, Englewood Cliffs, NJ: Prentice Hall.

29. Dennis M, Ahern AC, Richard Turner, *CMMI® Distilled: A Practical Introduction to Integrated Process Improvement*, 2001, Reading, MA: Addison-Wesley.

30. Diegel D, *Konzept zur Verknüpfung von Use Cases mit ereignisgesteuerten Prozessketten*, in *Fachgebiet Software Engineering*. 2006, Hannover: Gottfried Wilhelm Leibniz Universität Hannover.

31. Dingsoyr T, *An evaluation of research on experience factory*. in *Workshop on Learning Software Organizations*. 2000. Oulu, Finland.

32. Dodgson M, *Organizational learning: A review of some literatures*. Organizational Studies, 1993. 3(14): 375–394.

33. Dreyfus HL, Dreyfus SE, *Mind over Machine: The Power of Human Intuition and Expertise in the Era of the Computer*. 1986, Oxford: Basil Blackwell.

34. Drucker PF, *Post-Capitalist Society*. 1993, Oxford: Butterworth Heinemann.

35. Earl M, *Knowledge management strategies: Towards a taxonomy*. Journal of Management Information Systems, 2001. 18(1): 215–233.

36. Eraut M, *Non-formal learning and tacit knowledge in professional work*. British Journal of Educational Psychology, 2000. 70: 113–136.

37. Eraut M, Hirsh W, *The significance of workplace learning for individuals, groups and organisations, http://www.skope.ox.ac.uk/WorkingPapers/Eraut-Hirshmonograph.pdf* (2008-11-18).

38. Fagan ME, *Design and code inspections to reduce errors in program development*. IBM Systems Journal, 1976. 15(3): 182–211.

39. Feldmann RL, Nick M, Frey M, *Towards industrial-strength measurement programs for reuse and experience repository systems*. in *Workshop on Learning Software Organizations*. 2000. Oulu, Finland.

40. Fischer G, *Turning breakdowns into opportunities for creativity*. Knowledge-Based Systems, 1994. 7(4): 221–232.

41. Fischer G, Nakakoji K, Ostwald J, Stahl G, Sumner T, *Embedding critics in design environments*, in *Readings in Intelligent User Interfaces*, Maybury M, Wahlster W, Editors. 1998, San Francisco, CA: Morgan Kaufmann, pp. 537–561.

42. Fischer G, *Social Creativity, Symmetry of ignorance and meta-design*. Knowledge-Based Systems Journal, 2000 13(7–8): 527–537.

43. Floridi L, *Is semantic information meaningful data?* Philosophy and Phenomenological Research, 2005. LXX(2).

44. Floridi L, *Semantic conceptions of information*. The Stanford Encyclopedia of Philosophy (Summer 2006 Edition), 2006.

45. Fowler M, Rice D, Foemmel M, *Patterns of Enterprise Application Architecture*. 2002, Amsterdam: Addison-Wesley Longman.

46. Gamma E, Helm R, Johnson R, Vlissides J, *Design Patterns – Elements of Reusable Object-Oriented Software*. 1995, Reading, MA: Addison-Wesley Publishing Company. 395.

47. Gesellschaft für Informatik e.V. *http://www.gi-ev.de/english/* (2007-07-09).

48. Gilb T, Graham D, Finzi S, *Software Inspection*. 1993, Amsterdam: Addison-Wesley Longman.

49. Gruber T, *Ontology*, in *Encyclopedia of Database Systems*, Özsu MT, Liu L, eds. to appear in June 2009, Berlin: Springer-Verlag.

50. Grudin J, *Social evaluation of the user interface: Who does the work and who gets the benefit*. in *INTERACT'87. IFIP Conference on Human Computer Interaction*. 1987. Stuttgart, Germany.

51. Happel H-J, Seedorf S, *Applications of ontologies in software engineering.* in *2nd International Workshop on Semantic Web Enabled Software Engineering (SWESE 2006).* 2006. Athens, GA, USA.
52. Hartshorne C, Weiss P, eds. *Collected Papers of Charles Sanders Peirce, Vol. I–VI.* 1958, Cambridge, MA: Harvard University Press.
53. Hindel B, Hörmann K, Müller M, Schmied J, *Basiswissen Software-Projektmanagement.* 2004, Heidelberg: dpunkt-Verlag.
54. Houdek F, Kempter H, *Quality patterns – An approach to packaging software engineering experience.* in *Symposium of Software Reusability* (SSR' 97). 1997.
55. Houdek F, Schneider K, *Software experience center. The evolution of the experience factory concept,* in *International NASA-SEL Workshop.* 1999.
56. IEEE, *SWEBOK: Software Engineering Body of Knowledge, www.SWEBOK.org* (2008-11-07).
57. Initiative DCM, *Dublin Core, http://dublincore.org/* (2007-08-30).
58. Jäntti M, Miettinen A, Pylkkänen N, Kainulainen T. *Improving the problem management process from knowledge management perspective.* in *Conference on Product-Focused Software Process Improvement (Profes 2007).* 2007. Riga, Latvia: Springer.
59. Johannson C, Hall P, Coquard M, *Talk to Paula and Peter – They are experienced.* in *International Conference on Software Engineering and Knowledge Engineering (SEKE'99). Workshop on Learning Software Organizations.* 1999. Kaiserslautern, Germany: Springer.
60. Johnson-Laird PN, *Mental models: Toward a cognitive science of language, inference and consciousness.* 1983, Boston, MA: Harvard University Press.
61. Jona MY, Kolodner JL, *Case-based reasoning,* in *Encyclopedia of Artificial Intelligence,* Shapiro SC, Editor. 1987, New York: John Wiley & Sons, pp. 1265–1279.
62. Kelloway EK, Barling J, *Knowledge work as organizational behavior.* International Journal of Management Reviews, 2000. 2(3): 287–304.
63. Kerth NL, *Project Retrospectives: A Handbook for Team Reviews.* 2001, New York: Dorset House Publishing Company.
64. Kolb DA, *Experiential Learning Experience as a Source of Learning and Development.* 1984, Englewood Cliffs, NJ: Prentice Hall.
65. Kontio J, Getto G, Landes D, *Experiences in improving risk management processes using the concepts of the Riskit method.* in *Sixth International Symposium on the Foundations of Software Engineering (FSE-6).* 1998. Orlando, FL, USA.
66. Kooken J, Ley T, de Hoog R, *How do people learn at the workplace? Investigating four workplace learning assumptions.* in *First European Conference on Technology Enhanced Learning (EC-TEL 2007), Crete, Greece.* 2007.
67. Krebs W, *Turning the Knobs: A Coaching Pattern for XP through Agile Metrics.* in *XP/Agile Universe.* 2002, New York: Springer.
68. Kulak D, Guiney E, *Use Cases – Requirements in Context.* 2000, New York: ACM Press.
69. Larman C, *Applying UML and Patterns: An Introduction to Object-Oriented Analysis and Design and the Unified Process.* 2nd ed., 2002, Upper Saddle River, NJ: Prentice Hall.
70. Lindstaedt S, Scheir P, Ulbrich A, *Scruffy technologies to enable (work-integrated) learning.* in *First European Conference on Technology Enhanced Learning (EC-TEL 2007), Crete, Greece.* 2007.
71. Lübke D, *An Integrated Approach for Generation in SOA Projects.* 2008, Hamburg: Verlag Dr. Kovac.
72. Mellor SJ, Balcer M, *Executable UML. A Foundation for Model Driven Architecture.* 2002, Amsterdam: Addison-Wesley Longman.
73. Mentzas G, Apostolou D, Abecker A, Young R, *Knowledge Asset Management – Beyond the Process-centered and Product-centered Approaches.* 2003, London: Springer.
74. Mindjet, *MindManager, http://www.mindjet.com/us/index.php* (2007-07-09).
75. Myers GJ, *The Art of Software Testing.* 1st ed. 1979, New York: John Wiley & Sons.

76. NFS-CeBASE, *Center for Empirically Based Software Engineering, http://www.cebase.org/www/home/index.htm* (13.3.2007).
77. Nonaka I, Takeuchi H, *The Knowledge-Creating Company.* 17th ed. 1995, Oxford: Oxford University Press.
78. OMG, *Unified Modeling Language: Superstructure (version 2.0).* 2005, Object Management Group (OMG). p. 710.
79. Omondo. *http://www.omondo.de/* (2007-07-09).
80. OpenGALEN Foundation, *OpenGALEN, http://www.opengalen.org/* (2007-08-30).
81. Orasanu J, Connelly T, *The reinvention of decision-making*, in *Decision Making in Action: Models and Methods*, Klein GA, Orasanu J, Calderwood R, and Zsambok CE, Editors. 1993, Norwood, NJ: Ablex, pp. 3–20.
82. Ostwald J, *The Evolving Artifact Approach: Knowledge Construction in Collaborative Software Development*, 1995, Boulder, CO: Department of Computer Science, University of Colorado.
83. Paulk MC, Weber CV, Curtis B, Chrissis MB, Averill EL, Bamberger J, Bush M, Garcia SM, Humphrey WS, Kasse TC, Konrad M, Perdue JR, Wise CJ, and Withey JV, *The Capability Maturity Model: Guidelines for Improving the Software Process.* 1st ed. SEI Series in Software Engineering, ed. Paulk, Weber, Curtis, and Chrissis. Vol. 1. 1994, Reading, MA: Addison-Wesley Longman.
84. Polanyi M, *The Tacit Dimension.* 1966, Garden City, NY: Doubleday.
85. Popper K, *Conjectures and Refutations: The Growth of Scientific Knowledge.* 1963, London: Routledge.
86. Protégé. – *a free, open source ontology editor, http://protege.stanford.edu/* (2008-11-25).
87. Reeves BN, *Locating the Right Object in a Large Hardware Store: An Empirical Study of Cooperative Problem Solving among Humans.* 1991, Technical Report CU-CS-523-91. Boulder, CO: University of Colorado Department of Computer Science.
88. Schneider K, *Dynamic pattern knowledge in software engineering.* in *Proc. of the Software Engineering and Knowledge Engineering Conference* (SEKE'95). 1995. Rockville, MD.
89. Schneider K, Deininger M, *The adventure of software project management – Overview of the SESAM project*, in *Metrics in Software Evolution. GMD Bericht 254*, Müllerburg M, Abran A, Editors. 1995, Oldenbourg Verlag: München.
90. Schneider K, *LIDs: A light-weight approach to experience elicitation and reuse.* in *Product Focused Software Process Improvement (PROFES 2000).* 2000. Oulo, Finland: Springer.
91. Schneider K, *Active probes: Synergy in experience-based process improvement.* in *Product Focused Software Process Improvement (PROFES 2000).* 2000. Oulo, Finland: Springer.
92. Schneider K, *Realistic and unrealistic expectations about experience exploitation.* in *Conquest 2001.* 2001. Nürnberg, Germany: ASQF Erlangen.
93. Schneider K, *Experience-based training and learning as a basis for continuous SPI.* in *Conference proceedings of European SEPG.* 2001. Amsterdam.
94. Schneider K, Schwinn T, *Maturing Experience Base Concepts at DaimlerChrysler.* Software Process Improvement and Practice, 2001. 6: pp. 85–96.
95. Schneider K, *What to expect from software experience exploitation.* Journal of Universal Computer Science (J.UCS). www.jucs.org,, 2002. 8(6): pp. 44–54.
96. Schneider K, *Experience based process improvement.* in *European Conference on Software Quality (ECSQ 2002).* 2002. Helsinki, Finland: Springer.
97. Schneider K, Hunnius J v, *Effective Experience Repositories for Software Engineering.* in *International Conference on Software Engineering.* 2003. Portland, Oregon.
98. Schön DA, *The Reflective Practitioner: How Professionals Think in Action.* 1983, New York: Basic Books.
99. Senge P, *The Fifth Discipline – The Art & Practice of the Learning Organization.* 1990, London: Random House.
100. Shannon CE, *The Lattice Theory of Information.* IEEE Transactions on Information Theory, 1953. 1(1): 105–107.

101. Shull F, Rus I, Basili V, *How Perspective-Based Reading Can Improve Requirements Inspections.* IEEE Computer, 2000. 33(7).
102. Simon HA, *The Sciences of the Artificial.* 3rd ed. 1969, Cambridge, MA: MIT Press.
103. Smith MK, *Chris Argyris: Theories of action, double-loop learning and organizational learning, www.infed.org/thinkers/argyris.htm* (2007-03-09).
104. Sourceforge. *FreeMind, http://freemind.sourceforge.net/wiki/index.php/Main_Page* (2007-07-09).
105. Stapel K, *Informationsflussoptimierung eines Softwareentwicklungsprozesses aus der Bankenbranche,* in *FG Software Engineering.* 2006, Hannover: Leibniz Universität Hannover.
106. Stapel K, Knauss E, Allmann C, *Lightweight process documentation: Just enough structure in automotive pre-development.* in *EuroSPI* ^{2}. 2008. Dublin, Ireland.
107. StarUML, *The Open Source UML/MDA Platform, http://staruml.sourceforge.net/en/* (2008-11-18).
108. Sunassee NN, Sewry DA, *A theoretical framework for knowledge management implementation.* ACM International Conference Proceeding Series, 2002. 20.
109. Tautz C, Althoff, K.-D., Nick, M. *A case-based reasoning approach for managing qualitative experience.* in *17th National Conference on AI (AAAI-00). Workshop on Intelligent Lessons Learned Systems.* 2000.
110. The Association for Computing Machinery. *http://www.acm.org/* (2007-07-09).
111. Tigris.org. *Subversion (including online book), http://subversion.tigris.org/* (2008-02-22).
112. Volhard C, *Unterstützung von Use Cases und Oberflächenprototypen in Interviews zur Prozessmodellierung,* in *Fachgebiet Software Engineering.* 2006, Hannover: Gottfried Wilhelm Leibniz Universität Hannover.
113. Vries L d, *Konzept und Realisierung eiens Werkzeuges zur Unterstützung von Interviews in der Prozessmodellierung,* in *Fachgebiet Software Engineering.* 2006, Hannover: Gottfried Wilhelm Leibniz Universität Hannover.
114. W3C, *RDF Primer, http://www.w3.org/TR/rdf-primer/* (2007-08-30).
115. W3C, *OWL Language Guide, http://www.w3.org/TR/owl-guide/* (2007-08-30).
116. W3C, *Resource Description Framework (RDF): Concepts and Abstract Syntax, http://www.w3.org/TR/rdf-concepts/* (2007-08-30).
117. W3C, *OWL Web Ontology Language Semantics and Abstract Syntax, http://www.w3.org/TR/owl-semantics/* (2007-08-30).
118. W3C, *SPARQL Query Language for RDF, http://www.w3.org/TR/rdf-sparql-query/* (2007-08-30).
119. Wenger E, *Communities of Practice – Learning, Meaning, and Identity.* 1998, Cambridge, England: Cambridge University Press.
120. Wieser E, Houdek F, Schneider K, *Push or pull: Two cognitive modes of systematic experience transfer at DaimlerChrysler.* in *11th International Conference on Software Engineering and Knowledge Engineering (SEKE 99). Workshop on Learning Software Organizations.* 1999. Kaiserslautern, Germany: Springer.
121. XING, *http://www.xing.com/* (2007-07-09).

Glossary

ATM: automatic teller machine; a banking machine.

CASE: computer-aided software engineering.

CMM: capability maturity model.

CoP: community of practice; a group of knowledge workers who share experience and knowledge in a common field of practice (usually not in the same project).

Double-loop learning: Learning by comparing desired with actual consequences and adjusting both actions and goals or constraints that define success.

EDM: electronic data management.

EKM: experience and knowledge management.

Elicitation: Asking knowledgeable or experienced people for their knowledge or experience. There are sophisticated techniques designed to support the process of actively finding out about tacit and implicit knowledge (and experience).

EPC: event-driven process chain; a business process modeling formalism.

Epistemology: the science of learning and understanding.

IEEE: Institute of Electrical and Electronics Engineers. Professional association in the United States of America. Publishes standards that are widely used in software engineering.

ISO/OSI: International Organization of Standardization/Open Systems Interconnection Reference Model. Seven-layer architecture for system communication and interaction.

Knowledge workers: Members of an organization who contribute to company success mainly by gathering, organizing, and structuring knowledge.

LIDs: lightweight identification and documentation of experiences; a technique for experience elicitation.

Mental model: Model created in the minds of people to guide their activities. Conveys the schemas and frameworks for anticipating the outcome of actions.

Metadata: Refers to primary data by describing its format, version, status, etc. Metadata is data about data.

Organizational learning: Addresses the issue of organizations (such as software companies or business units) that learn and become smarter. They react in a more competent way to modified demands. Important aspects of organizational learning include learning individuals, common repositories, and infrastructure for learning.

OWL: Web Ontology Language.

PERT: Program Evaluation and Review Technique. A technique to plan interdependent networks of tasks with probabilistic distribution of effort or time.

PIN: personal identification number (for authentication at an ATM banking machine).

Protégé: open-source tool for building and using ontologies.

RDF: Resource Description Framework.

RDFS or RDF-Schema: Resource Description Framework Schema.

Risk management: Software engineering practice to handle project risks in a systematic and professional way. Risks are not necessarily avoided but controlled and mitigated if necessary.

SEC: Software Experience Center; large project for systematic learning from experience.

Single-loop learning: Learning by comparing desired with actual consequences and adjusting actions in order to reduce deviation.

SOA: service-oriented architecture.

Socialization: Learning from observing a person, without making knowledge explicit or documenting it.

SPARQL: a recursive acronym for SPARQL Protocol and RDF Query Language. SPARQL applies SQL query mechanisms to protocols and RDF.

SQL: Structured Query Language. A widely used and standardized language for database access.

SWEBOK: Software Engineering Body of Knowledge.

Tacit knowledge: People use this type of knowledge unconsciously. Often, they do not even realize that they have and apply knowledge at all. This knowledge is not made explicit and not usually talked about, hence the term "tacit" knowledge.

UML: Unified Modeling Language.

URI: Universal Resource Identifier.

Wiki Web: Interactive World Wide Web application that permits users to modify content and style of a Web page directly. Modifications are visible immediately; no Web language (like HTML) needs to be used.

XML: eXtensible Markup Language.

Index